HUMAN FERTILITY
WHERE FAITH AND SCIENCE MEET

HUMAN FERTILITY
WHERE FAITH AND SCIENCE MEET

PROCEEDINGS OF AN INTERDISCIPLINARY CONFERENCE
AUGUST 11 & 12, 2006
WASHINGTON, DC

RICHARD J. FEHRING &
THERESA NOTARE
EDITORS

MARQUETTE
UNIVERSITY
PRESS

MARQUETTE STUDIES IN THEOLOGY
NO. 55
ANDREW TALLON, SERIES EDITOR

LIBRARY OF CONGRESS CATALOGING-IN-PUBLICATION DATA

Human fertility : where faith and science meet : proceedings of an interdisciplinary conference, August 11 & 12, 2006, Washington, DC / Richard J. Fehring & Theresa Notare, editors.
    p. cm. — (Marquette studies theology ; no 55)
Includes bibliographical references and index.
ISBN-13: 978-0-87462-732-9 (pbk. : alk. paper)
ISBN-10: 0-87462-732-X (pbk. : alk. paper)
1. Birth control—Congresses. 2. Birth control—Religious aspects—Congresses. 3. Fertility, Human—Congresses. I. Fehring, Richard J., 1948- II. Notare, Theresa, 1957-
HQ766.H85 2007
261.8'36—dc22

                                                    2007050985

♾The paper used in this publication meets the minimum requirements of the American National Standard for Information Sciences— Permanence of Paper for Printed Library Materials, ANSI Z39.48-1992.

Association of American
University Presses

MARQUETTE UNIVERSITY PRESS
MILWAUKEE

The Association of Jesuit University Presses

CONFERENCE CO-SPONSORS

UNITED STATES CONFERENCE OF CATHOLIC BISHOPS,
DIOCESAN DEVELOPMENT PROGRAM
FOR NATURAL FAMILY PLANNING
Theresa Notare, MA, Assistant Director

THE CATHOLIC UNIVERSITY OF AMERICA,
SCHOOL OF PHILOSOPHY,
SCHOOL OF THEOLOGY & RELIGIOUS STUDIES
Rev. Kurt Pritzl, OP, PhD, Dean, School of Philosophy
Rev. Msgr. Kevin W. Irwin, PhD, Dean, School of Theology
& Religious Studies, assisted by John Grabowski, PhD, Associate
Dean, Graduate Studies, Associate Professor

MARQUETTE UNIVERSITY, COLLEGE OF NURSING,
INSTITUTE FOR NATURAL FAMILY PLANNING
Richard Fehring, PhD, RN, Director

CO-SPONSOR, SCIENCE SECTION

GEORGETOWN UNIVERSITY, SCHOOL OF MEDICINE,
INSTITUTE FOR REPRODUCTIVE HEALTH,
SCHOOL OF MEDICINE, GEORGETOWN UNIVERSITY
Victoria Jennings, PhD, Director

PROCEEDING EDITORS

Richard Fehring, PhD, RN
Theresa Notare, MA

CONTRIBUTORS

Marcos Arévalo MD, MPH, MA, Director, Biomedical Research, Institute for Reproductive Health, Assistant Professor, Department of Obstetrics and Gynecology, School of Medicine, Georgetown University

Richard Fehring, PhD, RN, Professor, College of Nursing, Marquette University

Rev. Msgr. Brian Ferme, D.Phil (Oxon), JCD, Dean, School of Canon Law, Catholic University of America

Petra Frank-Herrmann, MD, Research Fellow, Assistant Professor, Department of Gynaecological Endocrinology and Reproductive Medicine, University of Heidelberg, Germany

Rebecka Lundgren, MPH, Director of Operations and Behavioral Research, Institute for Reproductive Health, School of Medicine, Georgetown University

Eileen Groth Lyon, PhD, Associate Professor, Department of History, State University of New York at Fredonia

Angela McKay, PhD, Assistant Professor, School of Philosophy, Catholic University of America

Msgr. James P. Moroney, STL, Executive Director, Secretariat for the Liturgy, United States Conference of Catholic Bishops

Jennifer Roback Morse, PhD, Senior Research Fellow, Economics, Acton Institute for the Study of Religion and Liberty

Cecilia Pyper, MB, BS, MRCS, LRCP, DFFP, Senior Research Fellow, University of Oxford, England

Irit Sinai, PhD, Senior Research Officer, Institute for Reproductive Health, Assistant Professor, Department of Obstetrics and Gynecology, School of Medicine, Georgetown University

Joseph Stanford, MD, MPH, Associate Professor, Department of Family Medicine, University of Utah

Pillar Vigil, MD, PhD, Doctor Surgeon, Cs. Biological: Physiological Sciences, Pontifical Catholic University of Chile

Most Rev. Donald W. Wuerl, STD, Archbishop of Washington, DC

CONTENTS

FOREWORD

In 2002, Richard Fehring, PhD, RN, Director of the Natural Family Planning Institute of Marquette University College of Nursing invited the Diocesan Development Program for Natural Family Planning (DDP/NFP), United States Conference of Catholic Bishops, to co-sponsor an academic conference entitled *Integrating Faith and Science through Natural Family Planning.* Theresa Notare, MA, Assistant Director of the DDP/NFP, took this invitation to her supervisors for approval – at the time, the U.S. Bishops' Committee for Pro-Life Activities. The bishops approved the request and noted the appropriateness of the activity. It represented the realization of a long term goal of the DDP/NFP—to foster serious thinking on the science of Natural Family Planning (NFP) and Catholic teachings which support its use in marriage.

Since the publishing of the proceedings of the first conference in 2004 by Marquette University Press, plans had been underway for a second conference. It had been hoped that the second conference would occur within two-years after the first. The nature of scientific research however, required that time would be allowed for the development and completion of new studies. The second conference was therefore offered four years later on August 11 and 12, 2006.

Entitled, *Human Fertility—Where Faith and Science Meet,* the 2006 conference saw two more Catholic institutions join in the co-sponsorship: the Catholic University of America (CUA), Schools of Philosophy and Theology and Religious Studies, and Georgetown University (GU), Institute for Reproductive Health, School of Medicine. Rev. Kurt Pritzl, PhD, OP, Dean of the School of Philosophy (CUA), took an active role in setting the agenda for the day of theology and philosophy, while Victoria Jennings, PhD (GU), ensured that the Institute co-sponsored the day of science in accordance with its mandate to sponsor only NFP research.

As with the long term goal of the DDP/NFP, the purpose of these academic conferences is to foster scholarly thinking on the scientific, philosophical and theological foundations of the natural methods of family planning. In addition, by providing an academic platform, scholars will be encouraged to explore these topics and enhance the credibility of the methods of NFP while mining the depths of Catholic teachings on married love and life. It is the hope of the co-sponsors that a third conference will not be too far off in the future and that another Catholic university will join in the co-sponsorship of this important work.

INTRODUCTION

The interdisciplinary conference, *Human Fertility—Where Faith and Science Meet* was held at the Catholic University of America, Washington, DC, on August 11 & 12, 2006. The co-sponsors were the Diocesan Development Program for Natural Family Planning, United States Conference of Catholic Bishops, Catholic University of America, Schools of Philosophy, and Theology & Religious studies; Georgetown University, the Institute for Reproductive Health; and Marquette University, the Institute for Natural Family Planning. Participants came from across the United States and from Canada. They included: professors of philosophy, theology and history; diocesan Marriage and Family Life directors; diocesan NFP coordinators and teachers; seminarians; health care professionals and members of the Catholic Medical Association.

The conference took place over two days. Day one featured papers from a variety of disciplines, including the Catholic liturgical tradition, Canon Law, philosophy, history and contemporary sociological perspectives. Day two treated the scientific foundations of the natural methods of Natural Family Planning (NFP).

On Saturday, August 12, 2006, the topic of Natural Family Planning (NFP), its science and public health history was discussed by special guest Jeffrey Spieler, Chief of Research, Technology and Utilization Division, at the Office of Population and Reproductive Health in the Bureau for Global Health, Washington, DC. Most supporters of NFP are not aware of the role that public health officials have played in the study and promotion of the methods of NFP. Mr. Spieler, a long time public health official, was involved with research on NFP from the 1970s. He provided the participants with an eye-witness account of how public health officials became aware of NFP, studied and supported its development.

In summarizing the history of public health officials' involvement in NFP science, Spieler noted that an important year for the new methods of Natural Family was 1972. At that time the *Lancet* published research from the doctors Billings (along with Brown and

Burger). Entitled, "Symptoms and Hormonal Changes Accompanying Ovulation," the study demonstrated the scientific rationale for the Billings Method. In the same year, the Billings also published in the *Lancet* (along with Weissman), "A trial of the Ovulation Method of Family Planning in Tonga." This study was the first clinical trial to demonstrate the "perfect use rate" of the Billings Ovulation Method (BOM). Because the study did not analyze the "typical use rates" for the BOM, more research was needed.

During the 1970s Jeffrey Spieler joined the World Health Organization (WHO) in Geneva. The WHO was then planning to establish the Task Force on Ovulation Detection. Spieler, who earlier in his nascent career had published on reproductive issues, became involved in the design of the Task Force. In the first Annual Report of the Expanded Programme of Research, Development and Research Training in Human Reproduction under the planned but not yet established Task Force on Ovulation Detection, Spieler wrote that "undertaking a systematic approach to the review and study of the various parameters which are characteristic of ovulation and which would lend themselves to easy detection could be rewarding." Thus the following year, 1973, the WHO officially established the Task Force on Methods for the Prediction and Detection of Ovulation (recognizing that detection of ovulation was not enough). Stimulated by the Billings' Tonga study and having advisors with some knowledge of the Billings Method, the WHO Task Force on Methods for the Prediction and Detection of Ovulation (hereafter "Task Force") planned "to evaluate in controlled clinical trials under different ethnic and cultural conditions the value of detection of these changes" (in cervical mucus), as a family planning method and "to correlate these changes with endocrine parameters."

Nineteen-seventy-four was another important year for Natural Family Planning. The International Federation for Family Life Promotion (IFFLP) was created in Washington, DC under the leadership of Claude Lanctot, MD and its first President, William (Bill) Uricchio, MD. IFFLP began its membership with delegates from fourteen countries and in the next ten years became an international non-governmental organization (NGO) of 120 members in 60 countries.

In 1975 the WHO renamed its Task Force. Now, the Task Force on Methods for the Determination of the Fertile Period. The WHO recognized the "importance to develop techniques which will permit women to determine by themselves when they will ovulate, or have already done so." In addition, the Task Force was asked, by groups that were promoting NFP, to help "improve and standardize the educational techniques that form an even more integral part of this approach to fertility regulation than is the case with other methods." The Task Force agreed to aid the NFP groups and also decided to validate and improve then currently used techniques for determining the fertile period including the Basal-Body-Temperature Method (BBT), the Ovulation Method-Billings and the Sympto-Thermal Method (STM). By 1976, the Task Force initiated a prospective multi-center clinical trial of the Ovulation Method in Auckland, New Zealand, Bangalore, India, Dublin, Republic of Ireland, Manila, Philippines and San Miguel, El Salvador. The Task Force also initiated the comparative evaluation of the Billings and STM in Colombia.

The above work resulted in the publishing of two seminal studies in 1980 in the *American Journal of Obstetrics and Gynecology*. One study treated the temporal relationships between ovulation and defined changes in the concentration of plasma estradiol, luteinizing hormone, follicle stimulating hormone and progesterone (WHO 1980. I. Probit analysis. *American Journal of Obstetrics and Gynecology* 138(4):383-90) and the other, the "Comparative evaluation of two methods of natural family planning in Colombia" (1980 Medina, Cifuentes, Abernathy, Spieler and Wade, *American Journal of Obstetrics and Gynecology*, 138 (no. 8): 1142-1147).

A series of important NFP studies next occurred in 1981, 1983, 1984, and 1987. They focused on the: teaching phase; effectiveness; characteristics of the menstrual cycle and the fertile phase; outcome of pregnancy; and psychosexual aspects of the prospective multi-centered trial of the Ovulation Method (WHO. A prospective multicenter trial of the ovulation method of natural family planning. I. The teaching phase. *Fertility and Sterility* 36(2): 52-158. II. The effectiveness phase. *Fertility and Sterility* 36(5):591-598. III. Characteristics of the menstrual cycle and the fertile phase. *Fertility and Sterility* 40(6):773-778). IV. The outcome of pregnancy. *Fertility and Sterility* 41(4):593-

598. V. Psychological aspects. *Fertility and Sterility* 47:765-772). It should also be remembered that during the 1980s, the IFFLP held international meetings as well where information was shared and subject were identified for further research and work.

Between the years of 1983 and1987, the United States Agency for International Development (USAID), received political pressure from Congress to increase funding for NFP. USAID complied and began to support two NFP organizations. During 1983-1985, IFFLP received support though a cooperative agreement. And in 1984-1988, USAID supported the Family of the Americas Foundation (FAF) for the development of teaching and training materials in the Ovulation Method (which included a video on the Billings Method), and US-based training of 250 NFP teachers and trainers from developing countries. NFP work was beginning to overwhelm the assigned staff of USAID by the mid-1980s. Help was needed. Therefore, in 1985 USAID issued a "Request for Applications" to select an organization to implement and manage all centrally-funded NFP related activities. Georgetown University's School of Medicine, Department of Obstetrics and Gynecology, was awarded the contract. The new Institute for International Studies in Natural Family Planning was established (later, the name would be changed to the Institute for Reproductive Health).

A shift in policy occurred in 1986 that dismantled the financial support between USAID and most NFP organizations. USAID/ USG Policy Determination 3 (what is called PD3) Informed Consent legislation, was reauthorized to safeguard against potential abuse of sterilization and ensure that no incentive payments were made to accept, provide or refer clients for voluntary sterilization. That may seem compatible with NFP philosophy, but the legislation continued and went on to say that "informed consent in the selection of a contraceptive method" had to be ensured. Further legislative work which spanned 1985-1989, mixed language of tolerance for religious beliefs with an insistence on referral for contraceptives as seen in the following examples:

> . . . no applicant shall be discriminated against because of such applicant's religious or conscientious commitment to offer only natural family planning. (Section 104, Foreign Assistance Act)

> . . . none of the funds made available under this heading [Popula-
> tion, Development Assistance] may be used to pay for the perfor-
> mance of abortion as a method of family planning or to motivate
> or coerce any person to practice abortions; and that in order to
> reduce reliance on abortion in developing nations, funds shall be
> available only to voluntary family planning projects which offer,
> either directly or through referral to, or information about access
> to, *a broad range of family planning methods* [emphasis added]."
> (DeConcini amendment/ legislation under Title II of the Foreign
> Operations, Export Financing, and Related Programs Appropria-
> tions Act, 1989 (Public Law 100-461), "Population, Development
> Assistance": Revisions added by Rep. Livingston in 1987 and Rep.
> Obey in 1989.)

> . . . all such applicants shall comply with the requirements of the
> previous proviso...." (*Ibid.*)

The above last point meant that even NFP organizations had to provide information about where a client could get information about
other methods of family planning. Understandably, most NFP organizations could not comply and were defunded.

In reflecting on future trends for NFP, Spieler noted that many of
the issues which were relevant in the 1980s continue to have impact
for the 21st century. NFP providers and researchers continue to be almost "obsessed" with "failure" rates or "effectiveness" rates and there is
dispute about the relative importance of perfect use rates versus typical
use rates. Methodological issues and absence of high quality randomized control trials limit the evidence on the efficacy of NFP methods.
Questions still surround the methods of NFP and are important to
address for future research. They include: "How acceptable are NFP
methods to clients?"; "Who can use NFP methods?"; "How long is
the required period of abstinence for pregnancy avoidance?"; "How
well can couples comply with the periodic abstinence requirements?";
"What effect does the method have on the marriage relationship?"

Finally, Spieler maintained that among public health family planning policy makers and family planning program managers, a negative bias continues to exist. He said that they have been hesitant

to include NFP in national programs of family planning because there is controversy with regard to NFP's demand, use-effectiveness and cost-effectiveness. This continues despite NFP's main advantages of lack of side-effects, high effectiveness if used correctly, and educational value. Speiler urged that it is "up to the NFP community to provide data from their programs demonstrating that these are myths." Spieler suggested that unless NFP is mainstreamed with public and NGOs it will remain a "boutique method" for the very few at least as far as the secular world is concerned. Spieler pointed out that in the example of the research and program development that Georgetown's Institute for Reproductive Health has demonstrated, especially as seen in their main-streaming of the Standard-Days-Method, the NFP community has been given an example of how a natural method can be accepted on a large scale.

The importance of the history that Jeffrey Spieler provided cannot be overstated. It demonstrates the good will of a wide group of people who sought to understand human fertility without doing it harm. Although members of the Catholic Church have championed NFP research because of its compatibility with the faith of the Church, NFP is non-sectarian. Researchers, teachers and promoters of the natural methods understand the great value of NFP and should promote it to all people. Whereas contraception exists just for pregnancy avoidance, the methods of NFP can help couples to both avoid as well as achieve a pregnancy. In this sense, NFP is authentic family planning. As a natural, healthy approach to the management of human fertility, NFP methods have great educational value. These advantages move beyond biology and include enhancing the couple's relationship through greater communication and shared responsibility. Lastly, encouraging research that will strengthen the practice of NFP methods and move them from the "boutique" to the public square, is a worthy goal of the NFP community. This interdisciplinary conference is an attempt to facilitate this movement.

RECOMMENDED SOURCES

World Health Organization. 1980. Temporal relationships between ovulation and defined changes in the concentration of plasma estradiol-17 beta, luteinizing hormone, follicle-stimulating hormone, and progesterone. I. Probit analysis. *American Journal of Obstetrics and Gynecology* 138(4):383-90.

Medina, J.E., A. Cifuentes, J.R. Abernathy, J.M. Spieler, and M.E. Wade. 1980. Comparative evaluation of two methods of natural family planning in Columbia. *American Journal of Obstetrics and Gynecology* 138(8):1142-7.

World Health Organization. 1981. A prospective multicenter trial of the ovulation method of natural family planning. I. The teaching phase. *Fertility and Sterility* 36(2): 52-158.

_____. 1981. A prospective multicenter trial of the ovulation method of natural family planning. II. The effectiveness phase. *Fertility and Sterility* 36(5):591-598.

_____. 1983. A prospective multicenter trial of the ovulation method of natural family planning. III. Characteristics of the menstrual cycle and the fertile phase. *Fertility and Sterility* 40(6):773-778.

_____. 1984. A prospective multicenter study of the ovulation method of natural family planning. IV. The outcome of pregnancy. *Fertility and Sterility* 41(4):593-598.

_____. 1987. A prospective multicenter study of the ovulation method of natural family planning. V. Psychological aspects. *Fertility and Sterility* 47:765-772.

HUMAN FERTILITY
WHERE FAITH AND SCIENCE MEET

CATHOLIC UNIVERSITY OF AMERICA

WASHINGTON, DC

OPENING PRAYER & WELCOME
FRIDAY, AUGUST 11, 2006
THE MOST REVEREND DONALD W. WUERL, STD
ARCHBISHOP OF WASHINGTON

I am grateful for this opportunity in the context of this conference, entitled "Human Fertility—Where Faith and Science Meet," to say a word of welcome and to join you in the opening prayer.

One of the reasons we can be so confident about this conference, with its focus on both faith and science, is because we recognize that the more science studies the human condition and the more research is done, relative to such basic human institutions as marriage, human fertility and the family, the more we recognize the profound wisdom in God's word to us that sheds light—a profound, divine light—on the very topics of our concern. Human life and the understanding of its origin, integrity and purpose all emanate from the same divine source. Thus, we are not surprised to find in our understanding of marriage, in the beauty of the wedding liturgy, and in our theology of the human person a divinely inspired and necessary frame of reference for the scientific exploration of marriage.

A conference such as today's gives us an opportunity to do the one thing that is often missing from scientific elaboration and medical studies today. Technology and science must always be guided by ethical reflection and moral conviction. Too often with the advances made in science today given the extraordinary gift of technology, we run the risk of having our technology move so rapidly that it outpaces the faith context that provides for sustained ethical and moral reflection.

Over twenty years ago, Pope John Paul II during his general audiences from July 11 to November 28 in 1984 called the faithful to reflect on Pope Paul VI's letter *Humanae vitae* as an application of the catechesis he had been presenting on the theology of human love in God's plan. In these reflections on conjugal morality and spirituality, the Pope recalled for us the Christian vision of marriage, the family and conjugal love. He also highlighted the harm to such a vision that contraception and, particularly the justification of artificial contraception as a good in itself, was doing to families and, therefore, our society and culture.

One of the concerns that motivates the Church's constant proclamation of the integrity of the marital act is the recognition that, once we assume to ourselves the power to define in a way differently than creation has already designated some human actions, we open a door to a process that is practically without limits.

From contraception, it was a relatively easy move to abortion, and then to euthanasia, and now to genetic engineering, embryonic stem cell research, and ultimately the redefinition of marriage and even what constitutes human life.

In all of this, the Church remains a calm, clear voice of God's created plan, of the wisdom of God reflected in that plan, and of our capability of understanding that plan and articulating it in a moral law that reflects that natural moral order.

As you begin your work today, it is truly a joy to welcome you, to ask God's blessings on your efforts, and to thank God that you are a part of that continuing voice of faith and reason in our world.

Let us now pray.

Lord God,
 you created mankind in your image
 and made man and woman
 to be joined as husband and wife
 in union of body and heart,
 and so fulfilled their mission in the world.

Father,
 to reveal the plan of our love,
 you made the union of husband and wife
 an image of the covenant between
 you and your people.

In the fulfillment of this sacrament,
 the marriage of Christian man and woman
 is a sign of the union between
 Christ and His Church.

As we come together in study of
 the blessed reality of marriage and its
 true identity and purpose,
 we ask you to bless us with
 wisdom and understanding,
 also with courage and fortitude,
 so that we may both praise you for
 the gift of life, the blessings of marriage,
 and the joy of children,
 but we might also come to know more deeply
 the importance of your revelation
 as we reflect on it and
 the circumstances and challenges of our day.

Make this day be one of enlightenment,
 as we study more profoundly your wisdom,
 and of encouragement, as we attempt to share
 that wisdom in a culture that too often finds
 its inspiration elsewhere.

May all that we say and do today redound
 to the glory of your name
 and the good of your kingdom.

 This we ask, through Christ our Lord.

Amen.

RAISED TO A HIGHER DIGNITY: MARRIAGE, FAMILY AND THE ORDO CELEBRANDI MATRIMONIUM

JAMES P. MORONEY

The Roman Catholic document, Ordo Celebrandi Matrimonium (OCM) serves as the source for this reflection on marriage and the family. The OCM provides the prayers and sets the norms for celebrating marriages in the Roman Catholic Church. Since worship expresses the heart of the Church's beliefs, an examination of the rite is not only appropriate, but its themes concerning covenant, Christ and children are timeless in their relevance for shedding insight on the meaning of marriage.

INTRODUCTION

I have a friend, who in college majored in "soap operas" with a specialization in weddings. So intense is her obsession that she viewed the introduction of the Wedding Channel to her local cable system as a turning point in her life. When I recently told her that I was delivering a lecture on the meaning of marriage and family in the light of the *Ordo Celebrandi Matrimonium*, she was all ears. In fact, she offered a rather cogent observation, which I propose as a starting point for my reflections. "People know all about Catholic marriages," she suggested, "and they learn it all from the weddings on TV."

While I would expand my friend's observation to allow for the influence of actual participation in the ritual celebration of the sacrament of marriage, I would essentially agree with her suggestion, that the common Catholic belief in the meaning of marriage is formed not so much from catechisms or codes but from the rites themselves. This is the definition of the axiom: *lex orandi, lex credendi*. What's marriage all about? Go to the wedding scheduled for ten o'clock this Saturday in your local parish Church and see.

I am suggesting that such a mystagogical methodology, which derives its meaning from the very words and rites which the Church has preserved in the sacred liturgy, is at once timely and timeless. In an age in which legislators and newly empowered cultural groups find themselves unable to agree on a basic definition of marriage, we would do well to attend to these immemorial rites as a source of meaning. Through these rites, we hear the voice of the Church, conservator and guardian of truth. Rather than recreating the will of God in the image and desires of each new generation, the liturgical rites articulate for us, in an unambiguous manner, the very will of God and the truth manifested in his creation.

ORDO CELEBRANDI MATRIMONIUM

The source for this reflection on marriage and the family is the second typical edition of the *Ordo Celebrandi Matrimonium.*[1] The first typical edition of the rite was developed under the mandate of the Second Vatican Council, whose Constitution *Sacrosanctum Concilium* (December 4, 1963) directed, "The marriage rite now found in the *Roman Ritual* is to be revised and enriched so that it will more clearly signify the grace of the sacrament and will emphasize spouses' duties." (*Sacrosanctum Concilium*, no. 77, hereafter *SC*.) This resulted in the deliberations of study committee number 23 of the *concilium liturgicum* and the publication of the rite in Latin on the feast of Saint Joseph, March 19, 1969. The American vernacular edition of the *Rite of Marriage* was confirmed and published the following year.

Exactly twenty-one years later, the second typical edition of the *Ordo Celebrandi Matrimonium* was published by the Congregation for Divine Rites and the Discipline of the Sacraments. While the translation into English and the adaptation of this edition to usage in the United States of America must await the completion of more pressing projects, the Latin *editio typica altera* will serve as the basis for this lecture.

Like all liturgical books of the Roman Rite, the *Ordo Celebrandi Matrimonium* begins with a theological reflection on the sacrament. Based largely on the Second Vatican Council's *Pastoral Constitution On the Church in the Modern World* (*Gaudium et Spes*) chapter 48, it provides fundamental challenges to our notions of marriage and family life. I will focus on three challenges in particular, those concerning covenant, Christ and children.

COVENANT AND THE DEFINITION OF MARRIAGE

There are many definitions of marriage in use today. Some are technical, like the dictionary which suggests that marriage is a "socially approved and legally acknowledged emotional, sexual, and economic relationship between two or more individuals."[2] An anthropology instructor at the University of Minnesota is even more careful to include all variables when he defines marriage as "a *more or less* stable union, *usually* between two people, who are *like, but not necessarily*, to be co-resident, sexually involved with one another, and procreative with each other."[3]

Perhaps nowhere, however, is the changing definition of marriage more evident than on the website of the Federal Canadian Government, which defines marriage in the following way:

> Prior to 2003, marriage was defined as the legal conjugal union of two persons of the opposite sex. Since 2003, the definition of marriage has been changed in some provinces and territories to include the legal conjugal union of two persons of the same sex. Common-law relationships are excluded.[4]

Constantly changing civil definitions of marriage, each competing for the attention and loyalty of Catholics and non-Catholics alike, differ in three significant ways from the Catholic definition articulated by the *Ordo Celebrandi Matrimonium*. First, the popular definition of marriage views it as a social institution that is subject to the whims of every social convention rather than a divinely willed reality. Marriage, therefore, is thought to be an evolving reality whose very ambiguity of meaning is understood to be a sign of vitality and growth. Finally, marriage is defined primarily by those who choose to get married since their essential freedoms seem to include the right to redefine social realities as they see fit.

In the face of such a relativistic approach to marriage, the *Ordo Celebrandi Matrimonium* (hereafter, *OCM*), provides the definition of marriage which the Church has embraced throughout the centuries. On the natural level, marriage is a *foedus*, a covenant by which a man and a woman establish a *consortium*, an *indissolubilum vinculi*, an unbreakable bond of total fidelity by means of an irrevocable and free consent, a *consensus* (*OCM*, no. 2). But the real difference between this definition of marriage and those in the civic arena is its origin. The foundational meaning of marriage, the *OCM* tells us, is grounded in God's loving act of creation. God created marriage to be a covenant and a life-long bond between man and woman.

This is the conclusion of the theological praenotanda, but no one ever reads the praenotanda. The way the liturgy effectively expounds the "meaning and dignity" of marriage, moreover, is by its very celebration, both the source and the most effective expression of the sacrament.

COVENANT

What does it mean to say that marriage is a covenant between a man and a woman? The prayers of the *OCM* explain that, while the couple brings about the covenant by their exchange of binding consent, it is God who then acts through this *foedus nuptialis*. Thus, the preface for the wedding Mass prays, "In the covenant of marriage, you draw man and woman together in a life-long bond of harmony and peace." (*OCM*, Preface, no. 234) Once the couple has been made one, God draws together husband and wife, not only now, but for the rest of their lives in "a bond of harmony and peace." This is not to say that each day is replete with nothing but harmony and peace. But always, and really and truly from the first moment of their married life, the Spirit of God is at work deep within their hearts and their very beings, drawing them together and urging them to harmony and peace.

This covenant brings about a bond, which is both a *consortium*, a partnership in life, and an *indissolubilum vinculi*, an unbreakable bond. The nature of this bond is beautifully expressed in the first words with which the priest greets the bride and groom: "On this day, in the presence of God our Father, you will establish with each other a total partnership of life." (*OCM*, no. 53) This phrase, "a total partnership of life" (*totius vitae consortium*), is taken directly from the opening words of *Gaudium et Spes*, no. 48: *Intima communitas vitae et amoris coniugalis* ("The intimate partnership of married life and love has been established by the Creator and qualified by His laws."). It is reflected in the definition of marriage in the *Code of Canon Law* (Canon 1055 § 1), and in the opening words of the praenotanda to the present ordo: *Matrimoniale foedus, quo vir et mulier inter se totius vitae consortium constituent vim et robur a creatione sumit* ("The marriage covenant by which a man and a woman establish a life-long bond with each other, derives its force and strength from creation.").

Such an indissoluble bond (*indissolubilum vinculi*) is reflected in Sacred Scripture. The Vulgate uses *vinculum* in two of the marriage texts from the epistles. Both references are included in the lectionary for the marriage liturgy (see *OCM*, nos. 193, 196). They are *Colossians* 3:14, "and over all these put on love, the bond of perfection (*vinculum perfectionis*)," and *Ephesians* 4:3, "bearing with one another... striving to preserve the unity of the Spirit through the bond of peace (*in vinculo pacis*)."[5] Notice that the constant characteristic of this covenant bond is that it is indissoluble. This is brought about by the active presence of Christ in the lives of the persons who have celebrated the sacrament. The same Christ who changed simple water into wine at Cana in Galilee, now changes this man and woman into a sign and an instrument of his creative, redeeming, paschal love.

Among the sample intercessions of the rite we find the prayer "that the Lord, who graced the wedding at Cana with his presence, may keep this couple faithful to the covenant of marriage." (*OCM*, no. 251). *Fidelity* is the word most frequently associated with *covenant* in the Catholic wedding liturgy. In contrast to secular preconceptions, however, such fidelity is not seen as the result of self-control, good intentions, or psychotherapy. In the Church's prayers, life-long marital fidelity is not so much an act of man or woman, as an act of God. Thus, we repeatedly beg God to "keep them faithful throughout their lives to the covenant they have sealed in your presence," (Interpolation for Eucharistic Prayer III) and "with hearts infused with your love, may they remain faithful to the covenant they have made with each other" (Blessing B).

Perhaps this notion of God's perduring role in the marriage covenant is most clearly conveyed not so much by words, but by the very fact that couples come before the altar of God to be married. Every generation has included in its popular songbooks secular songs about a marriage, a large portion of which make reference to the presence of God in nurturing and preserving the marriage covenant in harmonious fidelity. Indeed, a Google search for the word 'altar' returns such popular responses as "Left at the Altar," "Gays Lead Charge Back to the Altar," and the ever popular wedding planner blog, "Five Smart Steps to the Altar." Recently NBC aired the finale of a reality series, the prize of which is described as "the wedding of a lifetime, provided by world-renowned event planner Coline Crowie." Its title was *Race to the Altar*.

So when my friend watches the wedding on *Days of Our Lives* this afternoon, the presence and action of God, even in a non-ecclesial setting, conveyed by the use of traditional Christian wedding symbolism and secular rites derived from sacred sources, will implicitly convey the notion that while this man and woman are beginning their marriage today, they are utterly incapable of bringing it to a successful conclusion without the perduring presence of God's gracious action.

CHRIST

Marriage, then, has a dignity all its own, God-given and God-willed, as a *foedus* and *consortium* brought about by the consent of the couple. But the rite does not allows us to stop there, for it tells us that marriage is given a higher dignity (*altiorem dignitatem*) because it has been numbered *inter novi foederis Sacramenta*, among the sacraments of the new dispensation (*OCM*, no. 5). The praenotanda to the *OCM* describes how Christ the bridegroom has identified the covenant of marriage with the paschal covenant, sealed with his own blood, between himself and the Church (*OCM*, no. 6). For every baptized person, therefore, incorporated into this covenant and assumed into Christ's love, marriage is always a sacrament (*OCM*, no. 7). By this sacrament a man and a woman participate in the love of Christ and the Church, following his example of undivided love, *indivisa dilectione* (*OCM*, no. 8). Conjugal love and family life are, therefore, a matter of striving for perfection in Christ and it is faith which gives meaning and growth to married life (*OCM*, no. 10).

If it is difficult for popular culture to apprehend the significance of the foundational definition of marriage established by God through creation (a *foedus, consortium, vinculi* nurtured by God), it is even more difficult for the world to comprehend this higher definition of marriage in terms of redemption and participation in the divine life.

For in this definition of marriage, Christ is the primary actor and the end of all marital action is participation in his divine life.

That Christ is the actor in all liturgical action is at the heart of Catholic sacramental theology. *Sacrosanctum Concilium* reminds us that "Christ is always present in his Church, especially in her liturgical celebrations. He is present in the sacrifice of the Mass, not only in the person of his minister, 'the same now offering, through the ministry of priests, who formerly offered himself on the cross,' but especially under the Eucharistic elements. By his power he is present in the sacraments, so that when a man baptizes it is really Christ himself who baptizes." (*SC*, no. 7) It is, therefore, Christ, who is always present and acting in the sacraments, and it is only by the power of his paschal presence that a man and a woman can pledge to love one another faithfully for as long as they both shall live.

Like all of creation, marriage is utterly transformed by the Paschal sacrifice of Christ. The second preface of the marriage rite recalls that by Christ's death and resurrection, God has forged a new covenant with his people, "making us partakers of the divine nature and joint heirs with him to eternal glory." The preface continues: "In the love that binds husband and wife, you have given us a sacrament that speaks of Christ's outpouring of grace and calls to mind the wonderful plan of your love." (*OCM*, no. 235) The sacrament of marriage is then, like all sacraments, a mystery of Christ's redeeming love. It is a paschal sacrament, not so much the story of a man and a woman and their love for each other, but rather a sign of the ways in which human love is utterly transformed and joined with the love which comes from God and flows from the side of the crucified Christ.

This is why we say that a couple is married "in Christ," and that "through the sacrament of Christ's body and blood, God will unite in love this couple now joined in the holy covenant of marriage." (*OCM*, no. 69) There is an identity between the kenotic self-giving of Christ upon the cross, which hangs above the altar, and the participation in that divine love by those who stand before it. But there is something more, rooted in Saint Paul's reflection that the love of husband and wife is a reflection of and participation in Christ's love for the Church (*Eph* 5:25-33). Thus, one of the prayers of blessing at the end of the marriage rite prays that this husband may worship his bride "with due honor and love her always with that love which Christ loves his bride, the Church." (*OCM*, no. 70) This "excellent mystery…the mystical union between Christ and the Church," lies at the heart of a Christian understanding of marriage.

The struggle to establish this Christo-centric notion of the sacrament of marriage and the wedding liturgy is a real challenge, not always met with great success. The popular wedding planning site mywedding.com describes its mission as "dedicated to helping you make *your special day* both perfect and stress-free." The site provides us with insights from brides after the day of their wedding, including this sage piece of advice: "My advice to all brides-to-be? Listen to your heart, do what *you* want and don't worry about hurt feelings. You'll regret not doing what you want more than you'll regret hurting feelings!"

Another newly married bride writes:

> The best thing I did at my wedding was having a simple, short, but sweet ceremony that lasted approximately thirty-five minutes in which I was able to spend less money on decorating the church .... The rest of my budget went to the reception where I knew people would probably stay the full five hours. It was beautiful. Family members later stated that my simple ceremony was much more enriching than the three hour ceremonies most people have to sit through. (mywedding.com)

What is this sacrament all about? It is participation in a divine love of which I will never be worthy, but which is an infinite source of fidelity and truth. Is it "a matter of striving for perfection in Christ…and faith which gives meaning and growth to married life?"(*OCM*, no. 10) Or is it about my fulfillment, my pleasure, and having my way?

Yet, lest you think that liturgical celebrations of the sacrament of marriage have utterly failed to infuse a Christo-centric dimension into the popular sacramental imagination, I remind that for more than twenty years, the most popular wedding song at weddings of every sort has been the omnipresent "Wedding Song" by Noel Paul Stooke. I daresay that little else of the music of Peter, Paul and Mary is still in active and popular use on this, the fiftieth anniversary of the foundation of that trio. Despite the many vulnerabilities of this song, it *is* Christo-centric, speaking of He who is now among you and "is acting on His part" (capital H in the original manuscript). It goes on: "whenever two or more of you are gathered in His name there is Love."

While the song may be something less than metrical setting of *Gaudium et Spes*, the very fact that the Wedding Song heard by my friend as she watches the wedding on "The Days of our Lives" this afternoon, will probably be about Christ, gives us some reason to hope.

CHILDREN

Only within this context, of man and woman sharing in divine creation and paschal redemption, can marriage be rightly understood as "ordained for the procreation and education of children" (*Gaudium et Spes*, no. 48, hereafter *GS*). This is why the praenotanda to the marriage rite reminds us that to understand marriage as an "intimate communion of life and love" (*GS*, no. 48) in fulfillment of God's own plan (*OCM*, nos. 3, 4) is to understand the gift of children as the "ultimate crown" of Christian marriage (*GS*, no. 48).

My earlier reflections focused on the action of God in drawing together a man and woman to live in "a life-long bond of harmony and peace." Recall that this line is taken from the first of the prefaces of the marriage rite and has been in use since the days of the *Gelasian Sacramentary* (hereafter, *GEL*) over a millennium ago.[6] This leads to the question, "*Why* does God bless this covenant and give this man and woman grace to live in 'a life-long bond of harmony and peace?'" Is it solely for their self-actualization or personal fulfillment, the experience of pleasure, or the well ordering of society? These are all good things, but none of them finds a place in this ancient prayer. No, God draws men and women together and strengthens their life-long bond in harmony and peace "so that their chaste and fruitful love may bring forth children whom God adopts as his own." (*OMC*, no. 17)

This central prayer of the marriage rite continues:

> For by your providence and grace
> you carry out this wonderful design;
> the birth of children brings beauty to the world
> and their rebirth in baptism enriches the Church.

This theme is echoed in another ancient prayer from the *Ordo Cel-ebrandi Matrimonium*, that is, in the fourth collect, which is based on an alternate prayer over the gifts from the tenth century *Fulda Sacramentary*.[7] The original tenth century text reads:

> ut quod generacio ab mundi aedidit ornatum,
>
> *regeneracio ad aeclesiae perducat augmentum.* (*GEL*, no. 1446)
>
> (What generation brings forth to enrich the world,
>
> Regeneration leads to the growth of the Church.)

This insistent theme is likewise heard in the first preface for marriage, originally from the *Gelesian Sacramentary* and the *Roman Missal* of 1570 (*OCM*, no. 354). The preface asks God that the "chaste and fruitful love" of the spouses might "bring forth children you adopt as your own," and insists that as "the birth of children brings beauty to the world, so their rebirth in baptism enriches the Church." (*OCM*, no. 354)

The gift of married love, then, comes from God, and the children, which are its crown, are returned to him in the sacrament of baptism. This is why the third question in the declaration of consent asks the couple, "Will you accept children lovingly *from God* and bring them up according to the law of Christ and his Church?" (*OCM*, no. 60)[8] The wording of this promise is taken directly from the Second Vati-can Council's *Dogmatic Constitution on the Church* (*Lumen Gentium*) no. 41, which declares that "Christian married couples, following their own way, should support one another in grace all through life with faithful love, and should train their children lovingly received from God [*amanter a Deo acceptam*] in Christian doctrine and evan-gelical virtues." (*LG*, no. 41)

Despite the sometimes successful technological attempts of our culture to divorce the procreation of children from marriage, I would suggest that the traditional connection between procreation of chil-dren and the sacrament of marriage is far more deeply rooted than popular culture may admit. By way of example, a recent survey of mothers, both single and married, reported that a vast majority of respondents listed the promoting of healthy marriages an as impor-tant priority. When asked why this was important, both married and single mothers "emphasized a strong relationship between mother and father as the foundation of a strong family and an important example for children."[9] The Church's teaching about children as the crown of married life has been heard, and is believed, even when other factors (far beyond the competence of this essay) intervene.

CONCLUSION

In these brief reflections, I have attempted to show how the Church's immemorial teaching on the meaning of marriage as covenant, marriage in Christ, and marriage as crowned with the joy of children is articulated by the *Ordo Celebrandi Matrimonium*. Down through the centuries, in words and rites, the Church has proclaimed her faith as she worships her Savior. Throughout the ages, and still today, that constant voice catechizes and forms a broken world, in a constant refrain of joyful truth.

It is the same song we will sing in heaven, one with the angels in one grand chorus of praise. It is the song for which we were made, and the duet to which married couples are called to dedicate their lives. It was this duet which Tertullian described almost two millennia ago and which the rites of the Catholic Church seek to foster for the millennia to come:

> [Christian marriage] is brought about by the Church, strengthened by the sacrifice (*oblatio*), sealed by blessing, witnessed by the angels, and ratified by the Father... How wonderful this bond of two faithful Christians! They are one in hope, one in the ordering of their lives, one in serving others! They are like brother and sister. They are fellow workers. There is not distinction between them, either in body or soul. Indeed they are two in one flesh; and where there is one flesh, there also is one spirit.[10]

NOTES

[1] *Ordo Celebrandi Matrimonium* (Typis Polyglottis Vaticanis, 1991).

[2] *"Elmer" Social Science Dictionary Online*, http://www.elissetche.org/dico/M.htm.

[3] Website of Instructor Brian Myhre, Department of Anthroplogy, University of Manitoba, http://www.geocities.com/brianmyhre/8Def.htm.

[4] Website of Canada's National Statistics Agency, www.statcan.ca/english/freepub/84F0212XIE/2002/definitions.htm.

[5] See Albert Blaise, *Le Vocabulaire latin des principiaux themes liturgiques* (Brepols: Turnohout, 1955). §476.

[6]*Gelesian Sacramentary*, no. 1446, in Leo Mohlberg, Petrus Siffrim, and Leo Eizenhöfer, *Liber Sacramentorum Romanae aeclesiae ordinis ann circuli*, Rerum eccesiasticarum documenta, Series major: Fonte, 4 (Rome: Herder, 1960), 102.

[7]Georg von Kopp, Gregor Richter, and Albert Schönfelder, *Sacramentarium Fuldense saeculi X* (Farnborough, England: St. Michael's Press, 1982),n. 2608; Text in Ritzer, p. 371 (no. 2608). Stevenson 158.

[8]Bugnini once noted that "Some, even within the Concilium, wanted the words 'from God' removed. They were kept, however, in order, as Bishop Colombo said, to bring out 'human and Christian responsibility and docile reverence for God' in the acceptance of children" Annibale Bugnini, "Marriage," in *The Reform of the Liturgy: 1948-1975*. (Collegeville, MN: The Liturgical Press, 1990) 702, note 17.

[9]Martha Farrell Erickson and Enolga G. Aird, *The Motherhood Study: Fresh Insights on Mothers' Attitudes and Concerns. A Report Commissioned by the Mothers' Council.* (New York: The Institute for American Values, 2005). http://www.motherhoodproject.org/wp-content/themes/ mothe2/pdfs/ themotherhoodstudy.pdf.

[10]The theological section of the *praenotanda* concludes by quoting Tertullian's fourth century treatise *ad uxorem*. Cf. R. Uglione, "Il matrimonio in Tertulliano tra esaltazione e disprezzo," *Ephermerides Liturgicae* 93 (1979) 479-94; H. Crouzel, "Deus texts de Tertullien concernent la procedure et les rites du marriage chrétien," in *Bulletin de literature ecclésiastique* 74 (1973) 3-13.

FROM CONTRACT TO COVENANT:
MARRIAGE IN CANON LAW

BRIAN FERME

In order to illustrate the development of the Catholic Church's understanding of marriage, select canons of the Church's 1983 *Code of Canon Law* are discussed. The analysis of these canons can help in gaining an understanding of the Church's beliefs about marriage and consequently, family life. The *Code* reflects and captures both conciliar and post-concilar teaching and the ongoing understanding of what it means for a baptized Catholic to be married and raise a family.

A little over thirty-eight years ago, on 25th July 1968, Pope Paul VI issued his encyclical *Humanae Vitae*. While it triggered much discussion and in far too many quarters much opposition, due as much to erroneous and misplaced concerning the role and meaning of the Church's Magisterium as to its specific teaching on human life, it was and remains one of that Pontiff's most important and courageous acts. Unfortunately its remarkable and sublime teaching on married life, within and upon which its teaching against artificial means of contraception was placed, has been far too often forgotten or effortlessly passed over as other issues drew greater attention.

The encyclical is also significant for another reason as it lies between two other critical events in the life of the Church and specifically its understanding of and approach to marriage: the completion of Vatican II and the promulgation of the new *Code of Canon Law* in 1983. At a practical level *Humanae Vitae* served as one of the key sources for the renewal of the Church's marriage law, along with the Second Vatican Council's *Gaudium et Spes* (7th December, 1965) and to a lesser extent the Apostolic Exhortation, *Familiaris Consortio*, issued by Pope John Paul II (22nd November, 1981).

I should begin by stating both what I would like to do and what I do not intend to do in this paper. My intention is not to offer a survey of the canons on marriage as they appear in the present *Code of Canon Law* (cc. 1055-1165). The canons deal with a wide array of questions as a cursory glance at the specific chapters in the *Code* illustrate: pastoral care and those things which must precede the celebration of marriage; matrimonial impediments; matrimonial consent; the form and celebration of marriage; mixed marriages; marriages celebrated secretly; the effects of marriage; the separation of the spouses; the convalidation of marriage. The presentation of these questions would require more time than I have at my disposal. Further, I will not treat of the question of marriage annulments. For many individuals, Catholic and non-Catholic alike, the terms 'marriage' and 'canon law' are inevitably associated with the process of marriage annulment, namely a legal judicial process conducted by ecclesiastical tribunals through which a marriage presumed to be valid is declared null, that is the marriage, despite appearances to the contrary, is declared as never having actually been contracted. A marriage declared null, which canonically speaking means that the juridical act called marriage never actually occurred, results, among other things, in the freedom of the parties to contract marriage anew, or properly speaking for the first time. The marriage annulment is declared on the basis of an established canonical procedure determined by the present *Code of Canon Law* (cc. 1671-1685). While vitally important to the lives of many and equally important to the life of the Church, my concern is not with this process.

Rather, my concern is somewhat more modest though, I believe, equally important. I should like to offer a study of a selected number of canons of the 1983 *Code* and in the process illustrate the development of the Church's understanding of marriage. This development necessarily involves a consideration of how the Church presented its teaching on marriage in the 1917 *Code* and how it was profoundly deepened and significantly redirected through the teaching in the documents I have just mentioned.

The canonical texts we have before us remain not only the universal and binding law of the Church, but also encapsulate, albeit in juridical terms, the Church's own understanding of and approach to marriage and consequently to family life. They reflect and capture both conciliar and post-concilar teaching and the ongoing understanding of what it means to be married and raise a family. They also reflect the title of this paper – 'From Contract to Covenant' – which remains a succinct means of capturing the Church's current teaching on marriage.

That the Church should be involved in deepening and developing its understanding of marriage should come as no surprise. *Gaudium et Spes*, in the first of six dense paragraphs devoted to marriage, stated: "It is for these reasons that the Council intends to present certain key points of the Church's teaching in a clearer light (*in clariorem lucem*)…" (*GS*, no. 47).[1]

Putting her teaching 'in a clearer light' has always been a solemn task of the Church, especially concerning those matters which touch in a unique fashion on the interplay of divine and human life. Marriage, in a particularly unique manner, is situated within this dynamic relationship between God and man. We read in *Humanae Vitae*: "Married love particularly reveals its true nature and nobility when we realize that it derives from God and finds its supreme origin in Him who 'is Love,' the Father 'from whom every family in heaven and on earth is named" (*HV*, no.8).[2] In other words, the gift of marriage, along with the gift of the other sacraments, has a quality of the infinite about it which necessarily challenges and stretches our minds to understand it 'in a clearer light.' In this sense, we might apply to the Church's constant reflection on matrimony what, centuries ago, was attributed to Bernard of Chartres by John of Salisbury concerning the intellectual enterprise in the Church: "We are like dwarfs sitting on the shoulders of giants; we see more things and more distant things than they did, not because our sight is keener nor because we are taller than they, but because they lift us up and add their giant stature to our height" (*Metalogicon*, III, 4).[3] Mention of Bernard suggests that something very briefly needs to be said about the historical context in which some of those giants worked when considering the question of marriage.[4]

We know that one particular concern of the Church was the determination of what was the efficient cause of marriage, or put in other terms, what made marriage, what was the absolutely essential requirement for a valid marriage. In the period after the fall of the Roman Empire in the West and especially under the influence of what in general can be termed 'Germanic law,' various marriage customs modified the central view of Roman Law that it was consent that made marriage.[5] For these peoples marriage was effected, not by consent, but by series of other acts which might include: *desponsatio* or betrothal through public pacts or agreement between the parties' respective families; *dotatio* or the consignment of the dowry; *traditio*, the actual handing over of the woman to the man; *consummatio*, the physical consummation of the union through sexual intercourse. Marriage was held to be validly effected only on the performance of some or all these acts. Medieval canonists devoted considerable ink to the consideration of these issues in light of the overall concern as to what precisely made marriage.

As the jurisdiction of the Church over marriage developed decisions on its validity would also influence questions of legitimacy which in turn would be central in the determination of inheritance. It therefore became critically important to determine what made marriage. We know that in the twelfth century, two schools of thought emerged in response to this question. One, generally centered on Paris, and represented in a singular fashion by Peter Lombard, argued that marriage was constituted by words of present consent alone. The other, centered on the School of Bologna, and represented by Gratian, the father of the science of canon law, took the view that while consent certainly initiated a marriage it was not fully constituted until consummation occurred. Perhaps it was no chance that a canonist Pope, Alexander III, cut what appeared to be this canonical Gordian knot: consent by the parties alone constituted marriage but that prior to consummation a valid marriage could be dissolved for a grave reason, as for example entry into religious life. The present *Code* still retains a procedure for the dissolution of a valid (*ratum*) but non-consummated marriage (cf. cc. 1697-1706).

My purpose in briefly describing the vital question of what constitutes marriage is certainly to point to the inescapable fact that an understanding of marriage has been the object of the Church's constant and ongoing reflection. On the other hand, given that marriage was essentially constituted by consent which inevitably gave rise to rights and obligations, it was a relatively easy step to perceive marriage as a contract which provided the classical legal paradigm for an agreement between individuals that also gave rise to specific rights and obligations. In many respects the understanding of marriage as a contract would dominate the Church's legal approach to marriage, and this view was especially evidenced in the 1917 *Code*.[6] It would undergo a significant change with Vatican II and the 1983 *Code*.

VATICAN II

Gaudium et Spes, devotes paragraphs 48-52 to marriage in which a significant new perspective is developed. This was provided in a singular fashion in paragraph 48:

> The intimate community (*communitas*) of life and conjugal love (*amoris coniugalis*), founded by the Creator and structured with proper laws, is established with the conjugal covenant (*foedere coniugii*), that is with irrevocable personal consent. And so, by the human act with which the spouses mutually give and accept each other (*sese mutuo tradunt atque accipiunt*) an institute is born which is stable by divine ordinance and also in the eyes of society. This sacred bond, ordained to the good of the spouses, offspring and society (*intuiti boni tum coniugum et prolis tum societatis*), does not depend on human decision. (*GS*, no. 48)

Even a cursory reading of this seminal text suggests a number of fundamental insights, especially in light of previous presentations of marriage, especially as found in the 1917 *Code*. The conciliar text speaks of a 'community of life,' 'conjugal love,' and instead of 'contract' adopts the term 'conjugal covenant.' Further, it describes marriage as an act in which spouses 'mutually give and accept each other' and finally determines that this covenant is ordained 'to the good of the spouses, offspring and society.' These relatively new concepts would be taken up in *Humanae Vitae* and *Familiaris Consortio* and be given juridical form in the renewed 1983 *Code of Canon Law*.

THE 1983 CODE OF CANON LAW

I should now like to flesh out a number of these ideas by reference to two canons in the 1983 *Code*.

THE DEFINITION-DESCRIPTION OF MARRIAGE

The matrimonial covenant, by which a man and a woman establish between themselves a partnership of the whole of life and which is ordered by its nature to the good of the spouses and the pro-creation and education of offspring, has been raised by Christ the Lord to the dignity of a sacrament between the baptized. (Canon 1055 §1)

While the 1917 *Code* as such offered no definition of marriage, though a definition or description could be gleaned by a consideration of various canons, the 1983 *Code* begins its treatment of marriage with a description-definition that is derived from the text just considered. The canon is divided into two clauses. The main clause ("The matrimonial covenant...has been raised by Christ the Lord to the dignity of a sacrament between the baptized") affirms the doctrine that Christ raised the marriages of the baptized to sacramental dignity. Behind this statement is a rich theology and a long history which was encapsulated in a precise form at the Council of Trent when it defined as a dogma of faith that marriage is one of the seven sacraments.[7] While marriage is a natural institution, with its own laws etched into the nature of man, the matrimonial consent of the baptized that gives rise to the partnership of the whole of life, has been raised by Christ to the sacramental dignity. In this fashion conjugal love is the means through which the faithful and irrevocable covenant love of God in Jesus Christ becomes visible and real. *Humanae Vitae* puts it in this way:

> In humble obedience then to her voice, let Christian husbands and wives be mindful of their vocation to the Christian life, a vocation which, deriving from their baptism, has been confirmed anew and made more explicit by the sacrament of matrimony. For by this sacrament they are *strengthened* and, one might almost say, *consecrated* to the faithful fulfillment of their duties, to realizing to the full their vocation, and to bearing witness, as becomes them, to Christ before the world. For the Lord has entrusted to them the task of making visible to men and women the holiness, and the joy too of the law which unites inseparably their love for one another and the co-operation they give to God's love, God who is the Author of human life. (*HV*, no. 25)

Spouses therefore participate in the Church's own mission of being "a sort of sacrament or sign of intimate union with God, and of the unity of all mankind…an instrument for the achievement of such union and unity" (*Lumen Gentium*, no.1). In this sense the family can rightly be understood as "the domestic church" (*LG*, no. 11).

On the other hand, the subordinate clause ("by which a man and a woman establish between themselves a partnership of the whole of life and which is ordered by its nature to the good of the spouses") describes the natural law aspect of marriage, namely the very core of marriage as established by the Creator and which must be present in any marriage. It is precisely these natural elements that form the essential foundation upon which marriage between the baptized has been raised to the dignity of a sacrament. Again, *Humanae Vitae* makes this same point:

> Marriage, then, is far from being the effect of chance or the result of the blind evolution of natural forces. It is in reality the wise and provident institution of God the Creator, whose purpose was to establish in man his loving design. As a consequence, husband and wife, through that mutual gift of themselves, which is specific and exclusive to them alone, seek to develop that kind of personal union in which they complement one another in order to co-operate with God in the generation and education of new lives. (*HV*, no. 8)

A number of key concepts found in the description of marriage as presented in canon 1055 §1 warrant closer attention as they mirror the new insights into the Church's understanding of marriage.

COVENANT-CONTRACT

The first concerns the use of the terms covenant and contract.

The description in can.1055 §1 sees marriage as a covenant rather than a contract, thereby following the teaching of Vatican II. While it is true that the *Code* refers to marriage as a covenant in only three canons (1055 §1; 1057 §2; 1063, 4) and uses contractual language in many other instances (paragraph 2 of can. 1055 reverts to the word contract), there is little doubt that the new emphasis on covenant was an important change. It reflected an understanding of marriage that in many respects was richer than that of contract.

Though a covenant was a term used in Roman law for pacts between peoples and pacts with a religious significance, it has a long
and important history in the Old Testament as designating the faithful and loving relationship between Yahweh and His chosen people,
Israel. We know that especially in the prophetic books, this unique
covenant was understood as a marriage between Yahweh and his
people, a union to which Yahweh was unfailingly faithful. In other
words, the use of the term *foedus* – covenant – underscored the particularly sacred dimension of marriage in analogy to the eminently
sacred dimension of God's relationship with his people:

> For this reason the central word of Revelation, 'God loves his peo-
> ple,' is likewise proclaimed through the living and concrete word
> whereby a man and a woman express their conjugal love. Their
> bond of love becomes the image and the symbol of the covenant
> which unites God and his people. (*FC*, no. 12)

Further, this covenant was transformed into the new covenant in
Christ and marriage is understood as exemplifying the union between Christ and his Church:

> The communion between God and his people finds its defini-
> tive fulfillment in Jesus Christ, the Bridegroom who loves and
> gives himself as the Savior of humanity, uniting it to himself as
> his body…the marriage of baptized persons thus becomes a real
> symbol of that new and eternal covenant sanctioned in the blood
> of Christ. The Spirit which the Lord pours forth gives a new heart,
> and renders man and woman capable of loving one another as
> Christ has loved us. (*FC*, no. 12)

The covenant analogy also helped to correct an approach to marriage
that was centered on the narrow, though important, focus on the
precise moment when marriage and its rights and obligations came
into being. Classically, canonists have distinguished *matrimonium in
fieri* – the act of consent that gives rise to marriage (efficient cause)
– from *matrimonium in facto esse* – the living out by the spouses of
their marital commitments. If a fundamental constitutive element
is missing in *matrimonium in fieri* there is no *matrimonium in facto
esse*. On the other hand, once valid consent has been placed, the marriage continues despite the actual difficulties a marriage may face.
An emphasis on this precise contractual moment had traditionally
meant that while much thought was dedicated to marriage prepara-

tion, considerably less was devoted to aiding couples in the living out of their marriage. The covenant approach emphasizes the ongoing personal aspects of marriage. In other words, marriage seen as covenant reflected the ongoing task of the spouses mutually giving and accepting one another on the model of God who continues to be faithful to his covenant.

As a matter of fact, this canon nicely balances and fuses the classic understanding of marriage *in fieri* – the element, consent, that brings marriage into being as its efficient cause (cf. can. 1057 §2), and marriage *in facto esse* – the actual living out of the reality that has been established, namely the permanent and exclusive community (cf. can. 1056) of the partnership of the whole of life between husband and wife ordained to the good of the spouses and the procreation and education of children

PARTNERSHIP – CONSORTIUM –
OF THE WHOLE OF LIFE

A second aspect of this definition turns on the description of the matrimonial covenant itself.

The canon describes marriage as a *consortium* or partnership of the whole of life, which reflects the classic Roman law definition of marriage of Modestinus (D. 23.2.1: "Marriage is the union of a man and a woman, and a lifelong fellowship, *consortium omnis vitae*, a sharing of sacred and human law"). The term *consortium* defies precise translation though it does connote a close association or community of persons who share their common lot. It is of course a unique type of *consortium*, namely one of the whole life and thereby underlines that the spouses' lives are inextricably intertwined.

THE ENDS OF MARRIAGE

A third point turns on an issue that had regularly caught the attention of canonists and continues to the object of ongoing canonical thinking and jurisprudence. I refer to the question of the 'ends' of marriage.

The 1917 *Code* in canon 1013 §1, established the ends of marriage in an hierarchical fashion: 'The primary end of marriage is the procreation and education of children; the secondary, the mutual assistance and the remedy of concupiscence."

While these ends of marriage are also considered in the revised *Code* (can. 1055 §1) it nevertheless did not adopt this hierarchical ordering but rather held that both the good of the spouses and the procreation and education of children are equally essential to and inseparable as ends of marriage. This was emphasized in *Gaudium et Spes* and reiterated by John Paul II in *Familiaris Consortio*:

> Conjugal love, while leading the spouses to the reciprocal 'knowledge' which makes them 'one flesh,' does not end with the couple, because it makes them capable of the greatest possible gift, the gift by which they become cooperators with God for giving life to a new human person. Thus, the couple, while giving themselves to one another, give not just themselves but also the reality of children. (*FC*, no. 14)

THE GOOD OF THE SPOUSES

The 'good of the spouses' has been the subject of considerable discussion given that it is now held to be an end of marriage. What precisely does it entail? What specific 'goods' are included? It clearly means more than the 1917 *Code's* "mutual assistance and the remedy of concupiscence," though it does include them. In addition, both the establishment of the *consortium* which is marriage and the understanding of the meaning of the 'good of the spouses' in that reality is linked to what various documents term 'conjugal love.' Thus in speaking of conjugal love, *Gaudium et Spes* remarked:

> Fully human as it is, in being willed by one person for another, such love embraces the good of the entire person (*totius personae bonum*) and is therefore capable of endowing human expressions with a particular dignity and of ennobling them as special features and manifestations of married friendship. (*GS*, no. 49)

Humanae Vitae devotes a paragraph (no. 9) to conjugal love underscoring certain of its key elements: fully human, total, faithful and exclusive and creative of life.

Canonical jurisprudence has devoted considerable energy in attempting to determine the precise juridical meaning of the 'good of the spouses,' if for no other reason than the fact that, as an end of marriage, the incapacity to will the good of the spouses or its exclusion by a positive act of the will, would formally invalidate the matrimonial act of consent. In general it is seen as a good distinct from the three traditional Augustininan *bona* of marriage: *bonum fidei* (fidelity), *bonum sacramenti* (permanence), *bonum prolis* (children).

Given that, it is not identified with the spouse's subjective happiness, sense of fulfillment or the achievement of personal ambitions, or even a lack of personal harmony between the married couple. Clearly a lack of harmony could result from many varied causes – character differences, competing ambitions, understandings of life, differing sensitivities or indeed any number of accidental qualities that might determine married life. On the other hand, while frequently having significant effects on the overall 'good of the spouses' they do not necessarily amount to a genuine incapacity to exclude the 'good of the spouses.'

Rotal[9] jurisprudence has seen it as something more than that simple though necessary mutual assistance. It has been considered as, "the sum of all the goods which flow from the interpersonal relationship of the spouses" which "bring about and promote the spiritual, intellectual, physical, moral and social good of the spouses." In order that it be realized the spouses must enjoy the minimum psychosexual integration, "without which the very communion of conjugal life would become impossible." A couple must have the capacity for and willingness to engage in genuine interpersonal communication and to establish a minimally tolerable personal relationship. The question remains the object of canonical jurisprudence both at the Rota and other tribunals.

PROCREATION AND EDUCATION OF CHILDREN

While the procreation and education of children is recognized as an end of marriage in both codes, we know that simple failure to produce children is not a basis for the nullity of the marriage. To a certain extent and in specific situations the procreation of children is not within the full control of the spouses. The law is quite clear that nullity of a marriage without children is based on two possibilities: the fact that one or both of the spouses were incapable of completing a sexual act at least potentially open to the conception of new life, namely impotence (can. 1084); or one of the spouses excluded, by a positive act of the will, the exercise of the right of the other spouse to those acts open to the generation of children (can. 1101), legally considered a form of partial simulation of marriage.

The latter situation occasionally generates a certain confusion. The law is nonetheless quite clear. The exclusion (simulation of marriage consent) of this end of marriage, namely the procreation and education of children, occurs when the spouse denies, with a positive act of the will, the right of the other spouse to those acts which are apt per se to the generation of children. In a very real sense the spouse arrogates to himself or herself the (absolute) right to determine the exercise of a right that belongs both to the very nature of marriage and in this context to the other spouse.

Canonical jurisprudence has long distinguished between the clear and absolute exclusion of the right to the *bonum prolis* from its non-exercise (or abuse). In other words, and especially in a society drenched with artificial means of contraception, the difficult legal question that frequently must be considered in cases of this type, is whether the spouses' decision to practice birth control actually constitutes a positive act of the will that excludes the right to the *bonum prolis*, hence invalidating the marriage, or rather a decision not to exercise the right, or rather to delay-postpone the exercise of the right, which does not invalidate the marriage. The difficulty as such is not with the law but rather with the application of the law to the facts of the case.

THE FORMAL OBJECT OF MARRIAGE

A second canon that follows logically from can. 1055 §1 refers to what concerns the formal object of matrimony, namely, what the spouses consent to:

> Matrimonial consent is an act of the will by which a man and a woman mutually give and accept each other through an irrevocable covenant in order to establish marriage. (Canon 1057 §2)

A comparison with the equivalent canon in the 1917 *Code* underlines two significant differences (Canon 1081 §2: "Matrimonial consent is an act of the will by which both parties give and accept the perpetual and exclusive right to the body ordered to acts per se apt to the generation of children").

Canon 1081 §2 of the 1917 *Code* used the phrase "both parties" which has been replaced by "a man and a woman" in the present legislation which reflects the aim of underlining the personal dimension of consent. In other words matrimonial consent can never be perceived as an impersonal contract but rather a profoundly personal act between a man and a woman whose purpose is clear, the establishment of an irrevocable covenant. While the adoption of the new phrase does not seem to have arisen due to the reality of 'same sex marriages,' there is no legal doubt whatsoever that so-called 'same sex marriages' are a complete misnomer, as marriage can only take place between a man and a woman.

Canon 1081 §2 of the 1917 *Code* also specified the formal object of matrimonial consent, namely what the parties mutually gave and accepted: "the perpetual and exclusive right to the body ordered to acts per se apt for the generation of offspring." While the phrasing of the former law contained a fundamental truth in terms of the formal object of marriage, it could be argued that it was somewhat too restrictive in terms of what the spouses mutually gave and accepted in marriage consent. *Gaudium et Spes* offered further insight into the formal object of matrimonial consent by describing it as "the human act whereby spouses mutually bestow and accept each other (*sese mutuo tradunt atque accipiunt*)." (*GS*, no. 48) This has been incorporated into the present legislation.

It must be admitted that this description is not particularly juridical in nature and that the mutual giving and acceptance by spouses cannot mean a total surrender of their human faculties which might destroy their sense of personal autonomy fundamental to human dignity. On the other hand, we know that the oblative self-donation of the spouses given in matrimonial consent was underlined in *Gaudium et Spes* as well as *Humanae Vitae* (no.8) and *Familiaris Consortio*:

> Consequently, sexuality, by means of which man and woman give themselves to one another through acts which are proper and exclusive to spouses, is by no means purely biological, but concerns the innermost being of the human person as such. It is realized in a truly human way only if it is an integral part of the love by which a man and a woman commit themselves totally to one another until death. (*FC*, no. 11)

Such self-donation cannot be reduced simply to the right to the body for acts per se apt for the generation of children, though it obviously also includes this essential aspect. As John Paul II stated in *Familiaris*

Consortio the right to the body is "a real symbol of the giving of the whole person" (*FC*, no. 80).

The spouses give and accept one another not in some unqualified manner but rather to establish the covenant of marriage, which is the formal object of matrimonial consent. As canon 1055 states, such consent to the formal object of marriage, involves a partnership of the whole of life ordered by its very nature to the good of the spouses and the procreation and education of children. It encompasses a complex of specifically marital rights and obligations that arise from this conjugal *consortium* and which is based on conjugal love, a point underscored in *Gaudium et Spes*, *Humanae Vitae* and *Familiaris Consortio*.

CONCLUSION

In the Apostolic Constitution, *Sacrae Disciplinae Leges*, with which John Paul II promulgated the present *Code*, the Pontiff underscored the essential link between the Church's new legislation and Vatican II:

> Indeed, in a certain sense this new *Code* could be understood as a great effort to translate this same conciliar doctrine and ecclesiology into *canonical* language. If, however, it is impossible to translate perfectly into *canonical* language the conciliar image of the Church, nevertheless the *Code* must always be referred to this image as the primary pattern whose outline the *Code* ought to express insofar as it can by its very nature...Hence it follows that what constitutes the substantial newness of the Second Vatican Council, in line with the legislative tradition of the Church, especially in regard to ecclesiology, constitutes likewise the newness of the new *Code*.

The *Code*'s presentation of marriage admirably reflects this insight of the former Pontiff. The realization, adopted from Vatican II and confirmed in *Humanae Vitae* and *Familiaris Consortio*, that marriage is more effectively understood as a covenant modeled on the life giving covenant between God and his people, was taken over and translated into juridical language. While the *Code*, except in a particular legal situation, does not directly concern itself with overall theological questions of human life, it does offer a sure foundation in support of the eminently personal exchange between the spouses that must characterize, not only their own *consortium* of married life, but in a unique fashion their openness to life. Such openness to life is radically thwarted by a contraceptive mentality. Tragically, such a mentality has the potential to strike at the very heart of the matrimonial covenant established according to God's plan. The present *Code's* description of marriage provides a fundamental legal foundation to secure and maintain the sacredness of that live-giving covenant.

NOTES

[1] All quotations from the documents of Vatican II are taken from A. Flannery (ed.), *Vatican Council II Constitutions Decrees Declarations* (New York: Costello, 1996).

[2] Paul VI, *Humanae Vitae* (*On the Regulation of Birth*), (Washington DC: United States Catholic Conference, 1968).

[3] John of Salisbury, *Metalogicon*, Daniel D. McGarry (ed.), *The Metalogicon, a twelfth century defense of the verbal and logical arts of the trivium* (Berkeley: University of California Press, 1962).

[4] The literature is immense but for excellent accounts, see James A. Brundage, *Law, Sex, and Christian Society in Medieval Europe* (Chicago: University of Chicago Press, 1987) and Christopher N.L. Brooke, *Marriage in Christian History: An Inaugural Lecture* (Cambridge: Cambridge University Press, 1978); *The Medieval Idea of Marriage* (Oxford: Oxford University Press, 1989).

[5] The classic Roman legal definition of marriage was formulated by Modestinus: "Marriage is the joining of a man and a woman and their union for life by divine and human law" (*Digest* 23.2.1). This formulation implied that the mutual consent of the parties was fundamental to the bilateral contract called marriage. See P. Krueger, Theodor Mommsen, Rudolf Schoell &Wilhelm Kroll, 3 vols., (Berlin: Weidmann, 1872-1895).

[6] The first canon on marriage in the 1917 *Code* underlines this point: can. 1012 §1 *Christus Dominus ad sacramenti dignitatem evexit ipsum contractum matrimonialem inter baptizatos. §2 Quare inter baptizatos nequit matrimonialis contractus validus consistere, quin sit eo ipso sacramentum. 1917 Code of Canon Law* (Vatican City: Typis Polyglottis Vaticanis, 1933).

[7] Session XXIV, *De Doctrina*, c. 1: *Si quis dixerit, matrimonium non esse vere et proprie unum ex septem legis evangelicae sacramentis, a Christo domino institutus, se dab hominibus in ecclesias inventum, neque gratiam conferre,* a.s. H. Denzinger (ed.), *Enchiridion symbolorum* (Fribourg: Herder & Co., 1937).

[8] For an excellent overview of the significance of covenant language, see John P. Beal, "Marriage," in *New Commentary on the Code of Canon Law*, (New York: Canon Law Society of America, 2000):1240-1246.

[9] A tribunal of the Holy See that treats appeals of marriage cases in the Catholic Church.

SUMMARY OF RELEVANT CHURCH TEACHINGS AND CANONS
TREATING THE NATURE OF CHRISTIAN MARRIAGE

DEFINITION OF MARRIAGE

THE SECOND VATICAN COUNCIL, GAUDIUM ET SPES (1965)

The intimate community (*communitas*) of life and conjugal love (*amoris coniugalis*), founded by the Creator and structured with proper laws, is established with the conjugal covenant (*foedere coniugii*), that is with irrevocable personal consent. And so, by the human act with which the spouses mutually give and accept each other (*sese mutuo tradunt atque accipiunt*) an institute is born which is stable by divine ordinance and also in the eyes of society. This sacred bond, ordained to the good of the spouses, offspring and society (*intuitu boni tum coniugum et prolis tum societatis*), does not depend on human decision. (*GS*, no. 48)

CODEX IURIS CANONICI (1983)

Can. 1055 §1. The matrimonial covenant, by which a man and a woman establish between themselves a partnership of the whole of life and which is ordered by its nature to the good of the spouses and the procreation and education of offspring, has been raised by Christ the Lord to the dignity of a sacrament between the baptized.

[*Matrimoniale foedus, quo vir et mulier inter se totius vitae consortium constituent, indole sua naturali ad bonum coniugum atque ad prolis generationem et educationem ordinatum, a Christo Domino ad sacramenti dignitatem inter baptizatos evectum est.*]

CODEX IURIS CANONICI (1917), "ENDS OF MARRIAGE"

Can. 1013 §1. The primary end of marriage is the procreation and education of children; the secondary, mutual assistance and the remedy of concupiscence.

[*Matrimonii finis primarius est procreatio atque educatio prolis; secundarius mutuum adiutorium et remedium concupiscentiae.*]

OBJECT OF MATRIMONIAL CONSENT

CODEX IURIS CANONICI (1983

Can. 1057 §2. Matrimonial consent is an act of the will by which a man and a woman mutually give and accept each other through an irrevocable covenant in order to establish marriage.

[*Consensus matrimonialis est actus voluntatis, quo vir et mulier foedere irrevocabili sese mutuo tradunt et accipiunt ad constituendum matrimonium.*]

CODEX IURIS CANONICI (1917)

Can. 1081 §2. Matrimonial consent is an act of the will by which both parties give and accept the perpetual and exclusive right to the body ordered to acts per se apt to the generation of children.

[*Consensus matrimonialis est actus voluntatis quo utraque pars tradit et acceptat ius in corpus, perpetuum et exclusivum, in ordine ad actus per se aptos ad prolis generationem.*]

AQUINAS ON THE END OF MARRIAGE

ANGELA MCKAY

This paper examines the question of whether and to what extent the Medieval philosopher and theologian, Thomas Aquinas is attentive to "personalist" considerations in his treatment of marriage. This discussion argues that although Aquinas appears unconcerned with the interpersonal character of marriage in his early *Commentary on the Sentences*, he is markedly more attentive to the married relationship in his later *Summa Contra Gentiles*.

In his seminal work, *Love and Responsibility*, Karol Wojtyla argues that love plays a pivotal role in sexual ethics in general and marriage in particular. To the extent that men and women love each other in the appropriate way, their relationship is well ordered, and to the extent they fail to do so, their relationship is disordered. All the requirements associated with sexual ethics and marriage, Wojtyla argues, can be derived from considerations about the things that are necessary for or prohibitive of the cultivation of the appropriate sort of love between a man and woman. Even more importantly, Wojtyla argues that while adherence to the Church's teachings on sexual ethics is necessary for a well-ordered relationship, it is not sufficient: which is to say, adherence to the Church's teachings on sexual ethics provides the foundation on which a well-ordered marriage can be built. Obedience to the letter of the Church's sexual teachings is only the first step of a far more difficult undertaking.

At a first glance, a similar emphasis on the relationship between man and wife seems markedly absent from Aquinas' writings on the purpose of marriage. For while Wojtyla claims that "the inner and essential *raison d'etre* of marriage is not simply eventual transformation into a family but above all the creation of a lasting personal union between a man and woman based on love," (Woytjla 1981,

218) Aquinas remarks that man is naturally ordered to marriage for two reasons: first, because man is naturally inclined to beget and raise children, and secondly, because "among those works that are necessary to human life some are becoming to men, others to women. Wherefore nature inculcates that society of man and woman which consists in matrimony." While Aquinas does make some remarks about the proper character of the relationship between men and women in later texts, it is not immediately clear why he makes those remarks, and given the absence of any claim that love is a central purpose of marriage, these remarks often seem to play a rather *ad hoc* role in his arguments.

Scholars have attempted to explain Aquinas' apparent lack of concern for the interpersonal character of marriage in a variety of ways. Rita Ranke-Heinemann, calling Aquinas a "pleasure-hating cleric" (Ranke-Heinemann 1990, 156), charges that Aquinas simply despised women, believing them to be accidents of nature whose capacity for child-bearing "exhausted their usefulness" (Ranke-Heinemann 1990, 188). If a woman is no more than, to use Ranke-Heinemann's phrase, "a kind of flower pot for the male semen" (Ranke-Heinemann 1990, 187), then Aquinas' lack of attention to the interpersonal aspects of marriage would be easily explained: for on such an analysis it would seem that – contrary to Wojtyla's claim – the woman simply *is* an object to be used; in this case, for the production of children. The more charitable John Noonan, who correctly notes that Aquinas displays at least some concern for the character of the married relationship, hypothesizes that the lack of emphasis on married love on the part of medieval theologians in general (and Aquinas in particular) had to do not with a failure on the part of the clerics, but with medieval culture itself:

> ... the theologians of the great theological age were, I would suggest, somewhat in advance of their society in their declarations on the ideal of married love. If they generally phrased their arguments against sexual sins not in terms of this ideal but in terms of an offense to nature or to life, an unarticulated reason for their approach must have been the social acceptance of their arguments. (Noonan 1965, 256)

In this paper, I wish to examine the question of whether and to what extent Aquinas recognized the "personalist" concerns so central to

Wojtyla's account. The key to answering this question, I will argue, lies in Aristotle's account of friendship. The differences between the ways that Aquinas appropriates Aristotle's remarks on friendship into his early derivations of the requirement that marriage be monogamous and indissoluble, and the way he incorporates them into his later derivations of the same requirements, demonstrate an increasing attentiveness to the character of the relationship that should exist between a man and wife.

THE ARISTOTELIAN BACKGROUND

Aquinas' account of marriage, especially his arguments for the necessity of monogamous, indissoluble marriage, is heavily indebted to Aristotle. In both his earlier treatise on marriage in the *Commentary on the Sentences* and his later account of marriage in the *Summa Contra Gentiles*, Aquinas draws heavily on Aristotle's account of the natural friendship that exists between men and women in order to argue first that marriage is in keeping with the natural law and second that the natural law requires that marriage be monogamous and indissoluble. The differences in the portions of Aristotle's discussion of friendship that Aquinas relies on in order to make his case, however, indicate an important shift in Aquinas' thinking. In order to see this, it will be necessary to examine the Aristotelian background that Aquinas assumes.

Aristotle's account of the friendship that naturally exists between men and women occurs after a more general account of friendship. In his broader discussion of friendship, Aristotle has already explained the difference between "true" or complete friendships and friendships of pleasure or utility, which are incomplete and called friendships only by similarity. All friendships, however, consist in some sort of shared activity, and it is the assertion that there are activities that men and women naturally share that forms the basis of Aristotle's claim that there is a "natural" friendship between men and women.

For Aristotle any friendship – be it a true friendship or merely a friendship of pleasure or utility – consists in a shared activity. Friends, Aristotle says, desire to live together, and not merely to live together but to share in the same activities:

> Whatever someone regards as his being, or the end for which he chooses to be alive, that is the activity he wishes to pursue in his

friend's company....They spend their days together on whichever pursuit in life they like most; for since they want to live with their friends, they share the actions in which they find their common life. (Aristotle 1999, 153)

This feature of friendship – shared activity – is a feature of complete and incomplete friendships alike, and this is why friendships with good people make one better, while friendships with vicious people make one worse (Aristotle 1999, 153).

It is the activities that men and women naturally share that form the basis of Aristotle's claim that there is a natural friendship between men and women. Men and women naturally share two of the most basic activities in life. First, they naturally come together for child-bearing – which, says Aristotle, "produces a certain gentle association even among beasts" (Aristotle 1999, 134). Secondly, while animals only come together for procreation, men and women

...share a household not only for childbearing, but also for the benefits in their life. For the difference between them implies that their functions are divided, with different ones for the man and woman; hence each supplies the other's needs by contributing a special function to the common good. (Aristotle 1999, 134)

Because men and women naturally share the basic activities of life, Aristotle argues that friendship between them is not only natural, but even more natural than man's inclination to live in society (Aristotle 1999, 133).

Aristotle's argument that there is a "natural" friendship between men and women, however, only establishes that men and women naturally associate with each other. His argument in this text does not address the character that this association should take. In fact, Aristotle notes that this natural association can take the form of either complete or incomplete friendship. Since men and women share in the basic activities of life, there is at the very least some form of incomplete friendship between them, for they at the very least come together for the advantages that each gains from the other (Aristotle 1999, 134). However, Aristotle also notes that there can also be true friendship between them: "...their friendship seems to include both utility and pleasure. And it may also be a friendship for virtue, if they are decent" (Aristotle 1999, 134).

While the existence of at least some sort of friendship between men and women is established by the fact of shared activity, the *kind* of friendship that exists between them has to do not with the activities they share but they way they share those activities, something Aristotle has already addressed earlier in book eight. Although Aristotle defines friendship in its most general sense as "reciprocated goodwill," with the added stipulation that the parties involved must be aware of the goodwill they bear each other, he distinguishes between different types of "reciprocated goodwill" and hence between different types of friendship. Some friendships, says Aristotle, are based on either the pleasure or the utility that the parties involved derive from the relationship. To the extent that a friendship is based solely on the pleasure or utility that each derives from the other, it lacks something of the character of true friendship. This is the case because the friendship is based not on the love the friends feel for each other, but on the benefits that each derives from the other. The other person is, as it were, coincidental to the relationship: it is not the *person* that is loved but the benefits that the person provides:

> Those who love each other for utility love the other not in his own right, but insofar as they gain some good for themselves from him. The same is true of those who love for pleasure; for they like a witty person not because of his character, but because he is pleasant to them. Those who love for utility or pleasure, then, are fond of a friend because of what is good or pleasant for themselves, not insofar as the beloved is who he is, but insofar as he is useful or pleasant. Hence these friendships as well as the friends are coincidental, since the beloved is loved not insofar as he is who he is, but insofar as he provides some good or pleasure (Aristotle 1999, 121).

Such friendships, moreover, are fragile and easily dissolved: the friendship ceases as soon as one or both parties cease to provide either pleasure or usefulness (Aristotle 1999, 121).

In true friendship, on the other hand, the parties involved do not love each other merely for the sake of personal benefit. Although true friendships may involve both pleasure and utility, it is neither pleasure nor utility that forms the basis of the friendship. Rather, in true friendship, the love is directed at the person rather than the benefits that derive from the relationship. This is the sort of friendship that virtuous people have for each other:

> But complete friendship is the friendship of good people similar in virtue; for they wish good in the same way to each other insofar as they are good, and they are good in their own right. Hence they wish goods to each other for each other's own sake. Now those who wish goods to their friends for the friend's own sake are friends most of all; for they have this attitude because of the friend himself, not coincidentally (Aristotle 1999, 121).

Unlike friendships of pleasure and utility, these friendships are enduring and difficult to dissolve. Only good people, moreover, are capable of forming such friendships, because vicious people are incapable of loving any but their own advantage: "only good people can be friends to each other because of the other person himself; for bad people find no enjoyment in one another if they get no benefit" (Aristotle 1999, 123).

While friendships of pleasure and utility arise quickly, dissolve easily, and can be had with many different people, complete friendships are rare, and enduring. They must be cultivated over a long period of time, and can be had with very few people. The scarcity of true friendship is due not merely to the fact that the virtuous people needed to sustain such a relationship are rare, but to the fact that such friendships must be cultivated over a long period of time:

> These kinds of friendships [i.e. true friendships] are likely to be rare, since such people are few. Further, they need time as well, to grow accustomed to each other; for as the proverb says, they cannot know each other before they have shared their salt as often as it says, and they cannot accept each other or be friends until each appears lovable to the other and gains the other's confidence (Aristotle 1999, 123).

Although complete friendships are rare and must be cultivated over a long period of time, once such a friendship is formed, it endures, for it is based on the other person's character, something that is far less changeable than the incidental goods the other provides.

Although both complete and incomplete friendships involve some sort of equality, Aristotle argues that complete friendships are the most equal of all forms of friendship. Friendships of pleasure and utility involve a sort of equality, because each party receives something from the other in exchange for what they themselves provide (Aristotle 1999, 126). Complete friendships, however, are the most equal of all friendships because each loves the same thing:

> . . . in loving their friend they love what is good for themselves; for when a good person becomes a friend he becomes a good for his friend. Each of them loves what is good for himself, and repays in equal measure the wish and pleasantness of his friend; for friendship is said to be equality. And this is true above all in the friendship of good people (Aristotle 1999, 125).

Applying the distinction between complete and incomplete friendship to the friendship that naturally exists between men and women, we can see why the mere fact of shared activity is an insufficient determinant of the kind of friendship that exists between them. To the extent that a man and woman associate with each other *only* for the benefits that each receives from the other – because one, perhaps, desires children, or because the other desires the benefits the other provides – they do not love the other person, but only the things that the other person provides. Hence the other person is coincidental to the relationship, and the friendship is incomplete. If, however, the man and woman love each other "in their own right" and not merely for the goods that each provides, they will have a true friendship.

Aristotle's explanation of the differences between true and incomplete friendships also illustrates the difficulty that would be entailed in an attempt to make shared activities alone the basis for arguments that marriage should be monogamous and indissoluble. For if the man and woman share in those activities merely for the sake of pleasure or utility, then at least on Aristotle's account, the relationship will be by its very nature prone to dissolution, and also one which could be shared with many people rather than one alone.

This last point sets the stage for the remainder of our discussion. For, as I will show in what follows, although Aquinas consistently constructs his natural law arguments for the necessity of monogamous, indissoluble marriage on an Aristotelian framework, in his early writings he attempts to derive these arguments entirely from the activities that men and women naturally share. In his later writings, by contrast, he is demonstrably attentive not merely to the shared activity, but to the *way* men and women should engage in that shared activity.

II. AQUINAS ON MARRIAGE

CHRONOLOGY

Although Aquinas offers isolated discussions of topics connected with marriage in other texts, his most extensive treatments of marriage occur in his *Commentary on the Sentences* and in his *Summa Contra Gentiles*. Aquinas wrote his *Commentary on the Sentences* between 1252 and 1256, while his *Summa Contra Gentiles* appeared between 1259 and 1265 (Torrell 1996, 328). In both texts, Aquinas addresses the question of the "naturalness" of marriage – which is to say, in both texts Aquinas argues that human beings are naturally ordered not only towards marriage, but towards monogamous, indissoluble marriage. In both cases, it is clear that Aquinas draws heavily from Aristotle's account of friendship in constructing his arguments. Thus, it is clear that at the very least, Aquinas understands marriage as a kind of friendship. Only in the later text, however, does it become clear that Aquinas recognizes that marriage should be a complete friendship, rather than merely one of pleasure or utility.

MARRIAGE IN THE COMMENTARY ON THE SENTENCES

Aquinas' treatment of marriage in the *Commentary on the Sentences* is a lengthy one, and much of it is concerned with theological topics outside the scope of this paper. Because my primary concern in this paper is to compare the natural law arguments that Aquinas makes in the earlier text with those he offers in his later *Summa Contra Gentiles*, I will examine Aquinas' arguments that (a) the natural law requires marriage and (b) the natural law requires that marriage be monogamous and indissoluble. It is worth noting, however, that the lack of interest in the character of the relationship between man and wife that pervades Aquinas' natural law arguments also seems characteristic of the theological arguments that appear in this text.

Aquinas' derivation of the requirements associated with marriage in the *Commentary on the Sentences* is clearly indebted to Aristotle's account of the "natural" friendship that exists between man and woman. However, as I shall show in what follows, his arguments in this earlier text are concerned exclusively with the activities that men and women naturally share.

In the *Commentary on the Sentences* Aquinas argues that marriage falls under the natural law. Aquinas offers two reasons in support of this claim, both of which look to Aristotle's account of the activities that men and women naturally share. First, man is naturally inclined towards the begetting and rearing of children. However, although man can beget children outside of marriage, the proper education of children requires the institution of marriage:

> . . . nature intends not only the begetting of offspring, but also its education and development... Now a child can not be brought up and instructed unless it have certain and definite parents, and this would not be the case unless there were a tie between the man and a definite woman, and it is in this that matrimony consists (Aquinas 1981, 2699).

Marriage, then, is required because the rearing of children requires "certain and definite" parents. In response to the objection that some animals do not remain together after procreation, Aquinas explains that the education of human children requires more time and hence requires that the man and the woman remain together (Aquinas 1981, 2670). The second reason Aquinas offers for the "naturalness" of marriage has to do with the natural division of labor. Since men are naturally suited for some activities and women for others, they naturally come together for the "benefits of life":

> . . . just as natural reason dictates that men should live together, since one is not self sufficient in all things concerning life, for which reason man is described as being naturally inclined to political society, so too among those works that are necessary for human life some are becoming to men, others to women. Wherefore nature inculcates that society of man and woman which consists in matrimony (Aquinas 1981, 2670).

These two activities – the begetting and rearing of children and the "benefits of life" – are, Aquinas argues, the primary and secondary "ends" of matrimony. Man is naturally inclined towards both ends; matrimony provides the context in which those ends can be realized.

As Aquinas himself notes, the argument that matrimony is in keeping with the natural law is a relatively straightforward appropriation of Aristotle's description of the two activities that men and women naturally share. Aquinas has simply added the further claim that these two activities cannot be properly carried out unless there be "a lasting association with some definite woman." After stipulating that this "lasting association with a definite woman" is matrimony, Aquinas argues that even the requirements that marriage be indissoluble and monogamous derive from the two activities that men and woman naturally share.

Just as the proper education of children requires that man "form a lasting association with some definite woman," so, Aquinas argues, does the proper education of children require that the association so formed be indissoluble. Aquinas argues against divorce on the grounds that the rearing of children, which as we saw above requires that the man remain with the woman, is an occupation which extends over the course of a lifetime: it is never finished, and hence never appropriate for the man to leave the woman. Divorce is thus incompatible with man's natural ordering to the begetting and rearing of children:

> By the intention of nature marriage is directed to the rearing of the offspring, not merely for a time, but throughout its whole life. Hence it is of natural law that parents should lay up for their children, and that children should be their parents' heirs. Therefore, since the offspring is the common good of husband and wife, the dictate of natural law requires the latter to live together for ever inseparably: and so the indissolubility of marriage is of natural law (Aquinas 1981, 2806).

Just as the man needs to remain with the woman after procreation for the sake of the offspring so created, then, so does he need to remain with her for his entire life. Men and women ought to remain married, Aquinas seems to be arguing, for the children's sake.

Aquinas attempts to apply the two activities naturally shared by men and women in a similar way to the question of whether it is licit to have more than one wife and to the question of whether it is allowable to have a concubine. Although many wives would not hinder either the begetting or the rearing of children (Aquinas will contradict himself on this point in the *Summa Contra Gentiles*), it might hinder the second end of marriage, namely the cooperation of man and woman in the works necessary for life, because the presence of many wives can cause strife in the household:

> . . . plurality of wives neither wholly destroys nor in any way hinders the first end of marriage, since one man is sufficient to get children of several wives, and to rear the children born of them. But though it does not wholly destroy the second end, it hinders it considerably, for there cannot easily be peace in a family where several wives are joined to one husband, since one husband cannot suffice to satisfy the requisitions of several wives, and again because the sharing of several in one occupation is a cause of strife: thus *potters quarrel with one another*, and in like manner the several wives of one husband" (Aquinas 1981, 2794).

Even the "strife" that Aquinas is concerned with here, we should note, is not that which might arise between man and wife, but between the wives themselves: and this strife, it seems, is objectionable primarily because it hinders the completion of household tasks. Aquinas gives roughly the same analysis of concubines: taking a concubine is directly contrary to the natural law insofar as it is opposed to the begetting and rearing of children, though only indirectly opposed if the man intends to have children with the concubine and sees to their education (Aquinas 1981, 2801). It would be directly contrary to the natural law, on the other hand, for a woman to have many husbands, because the male would not know which offspring were his, and hence would not be able to rear them (Aquinas 1981, 2797).

What we see in Aquinas' early arguments, not only for the necessity of marriage but also for the requirements that marriage be monogamous and indissoluble, is an attempt to derive these requirements strictly from the two activities that men and women naturally share. We see no mention on Aquinas' part regarding the character of the relationship that ought to exist between men and woman. It is the absence of this, I think, that causes the arguments themselves to be deeply unsatisfying. It is certainly true that the task of raising children occupies a long period of time, and it is also certainly true that the possession of many wives is hardly conducive to harmony within the household. But surely this is not *all* there is to be said about the matter? If divorce, for instance, is unlawful only because of the time that the upbringing of children requires, then why should it not be licit for those spouses who are infertile or whose children have died to divorce? Or, on the other hand, suppose that by some lucky accident one managed to find women who didn't mind sharing a husband. Would it then be licit to have several wives? In his derivation of the indissoluble and monogamous character of marriage Aquinas is certainly rigorously attentive to the two "ends" of marriage he specified earlier in his discussion of marriage – i.e., to the two activities that men and women naturally share – but this might lead us if anything to think that there must be more to marriage than he says, for the arguments that he provides aren't very convincing.

When we consider the above derivations against the background of Aristotle's account of friendship, it is easy to see where Aquinas' early arguments fall short. In this early text, Aquinas attempts to derive the requirements that marriage be monogamous and indissoluble solely from the activities that men and women naturally share. Yet, as Aristotle notes, men and women can share in these activities in different ways: the friendship that consists in these shared activities is not necessarily complete friendship, but might merely be a friendship of pleasure and utility. Without further specifying what sort of friendship ought to exist, it is difficult to see how Aquinas could argue that the union should be indissoluble and monogamous, especially since relationships predicated solely on pleasure and utility are by definition both easily dissolved and capable of being shared with many different people.

Given Aquinas' silence regarding the character of the friendship that ought to exist between a man and wife, moreover, it is easy to see why so many find Aquinas' treatment of marriage unsatisfactory. For Aquinas' lack of attention to the character of the relationship, together with his assertion that the two "ends" of matrimony are the begetting of children and the necessities of life, almost seems to imply that marriage is a rather utilitarian arrangement. One who reads the text from the *Commentary on the Sentences* in isolation might well think that Aquinas believed that marriage could be justified *only* by procreation and the other necessities of life.

Aquinas may well have found his own arguments insufficient, for in his later *Summa Contra Gentiles* he offers rather different arguments for the indissoluble and monogamous character of marriage. In order to do so, however, he is also forced to move beyond the "ends" of marriage he offered in the sentences and to introduce more "personalistic" considerations – namely considerations having to do with the relationship that ought to exist between the man and the woman.

MARRIAGE IN THE SUMMA CONTRA GENTILES

In his later *Summa Contra Gentiles* Aquinas again argues that man is naturally ordered towards marriage, and that, moreover, marriage should be monogamous and indissoluble. The arguments he offers in this text, however, are markedly different than his earlier arguments, for rather than attempting to derive all the requirements of marriage from the shared activities that constitute it, Aquinas argues on the basis of both the activities and the character of the friendship that ought to exist between a man and a woman. The new emphasis on the kind of friendship that ought to exist between a man and woman, I will argue, indicates a recognition on Aquinas' part that monogamous, indissoluble marriage can only be defended if the friendship that ought to exist between a man and wife is a complete friendship.

Although Aquinas offers a more detailed explanation in the *Summa Contra Gentiles*, his argument for the naturalness of marriage is for the most part identical to the argument he gives in the earlier text. Marriage falls under the natural law, Aquinas argues, because man is by nature ordered towards the begetting and rearing of children, and although children can be begotten without marriage, they cannot be properly reared without it (Aquinas 1975, 144). In this text, however, Aquinas offers a more detailed explanation of this claim. Women are insufficient for the upbringing of children, not only because they cannot adequately provide for them, but because they lack the strength required to punish them and the intelligence needed to educate them. Thus while it is not necessary for the male of other species to remain with the female after procreation, it is necessary for the man to remain with the woman in order to see to the children's education (Aquinas 1975, 145). Aquinas' argument against promiscuity, then, remains more or less unchanged, or if anything becomes even less palatable. For those looking for a defense of married love will hardly be heartened to find that the man must remain in order to compensate for the female's intellectual and physical insufficiency.

A marked change occurs, however, when Aquinas considers the question of whether marriage should be monogamous and indissoluble.

Although Aquinas initially offers the same reason for the indissolubility of marriage that he offered in his *Commentary on the Sentences*, namely that it takes a lifetime to raise children, he no longer seems to believe that this argument is sufficient, for he supplements it with a number of other points. After offering relatively the same argument found in his earlier account, Aquinas offers a string of further arguments based on the proper character of the relationship that should exist between a man and woman – namely the importance of equality in the relationship between the man and the woman, and even more tellingly, the friendship that ought to exist between a man and his wife. It is clear from Aquinas' remarks that he believes that a man and wife ought to have a complete friendship, and that it is the need for complete friendship that now grounds his assertion that marriage should be indissoluble.

After remarking that it requires a lifetime to raise one's children, Aquinas offers a markedly different argument for the indissolubility of marriage, one that focuses on the equality that ought to exist between a man and woman. If a man were to take a woman when she was young and fertile and then send her away when she had reached advanced years and was incapable of associating with anyone else, Aquinas argues, he would damage the woman "contrary to natural equity" (Aquinas 1975, 148). Moreover, since women are not allowed to send away their husbands, if the man were allowed to send away his wife the relationship between a man and his wife "would not be an association of equals, but instead, a sort of slavery on the part of the wife" (Aquinas 1975, 148). Aquinas' attention to the equality that should exist between man and wife is a marked change from his earlier statements, particularly because as evidence for this assertion Aquinas references Aristotle's assertion that equality is above all a condition of complete friendship (Aquinas 1975, 148). Allowing divorce would not preclude the sort of equality that exists in friendships of pleasure and utility, for equality in such friendships exists only so long as there continues to be an exchange of services. It would, however, preclude the kind of equality that exists in complete friendship.

In the immediately following remarks, Aquinas offers a reason for the indissolubility of marriage that goes beyond even the assertion that the relationship between a man and his wife should be a relationship of equals. In the earlier text, recall, Aquinas based his argument for the indissolubility of marriage on the claim that childrearing is an occupation that occupies an entire lifetime. Although Aquinas reiterates this argument in the *Summa Contra Gentiles*, he then offers a second argument, one that has to do with the relationship that ought to exist between a man and woman. The sort of friendship that exists between a man and woman, Aquinas argues, requires that marriage be indissoluble:

> . . . the greater friendship is, the more solid and long lasting it will be. Now, there seems to be the greatest friendship between husband and wife, for they are united not only in the act of fleshly union, which produces a certain gentle association even among beasts, but also in the partnership of the whole range of domestic activity. Consequently, as an indication of this, man must "leave his father and mother" for the sake of his wife, as is said in Genesis. Therefore, it is fitting for matrimony to be completely indissoluble (Aquinas 1975, 148).

This is a pivotal text, not only because it goes far beyond Aquinas' earlier account of the requirement of indissolubility, but because for the first time Aquinas mentions friendship between the man and wife as a component of marriage.

It is clear from Aquinas' description of the friendship, moreover, that he is deriving his remarks about the character that the friendship between man and wife should have from Aristotle's description of complete friendship, and not a friendship of pleasure or utility. Aristotle certainly does say that the greatest friendships are solid and long lasting, but what makes a friendship solid and long-lasting has to do not only with the activities that are shared but with the kind of friendship that exists: friendships are solid and long-lasting when the parties involved love each other rather than the goods they derive from the relationship.

A similar shift is evident in the explanation Aquinas offers in the *Summa Contra Gentiles* regarding the need for marriage to be between one man and one woman. As in his earlier account, Aquinas notes that the possession of many wives by one husband or many husbands by one wife would be a cause of discord, and that "certainty as to offspring" would be precluded if one woman were allowed to have many husbands (Aquinas 1975, 151). He also adds here what he appears to deny in the earlier text, namely that it would be difficult for one man to raise the offspring of many wives (Aquinas 1975, 151). Having offered these reasons, however, Aquinas again appeals to the considerations about the equality and friendship that should exist between a husband and wife in order to explain why it would be wrong for one man to have many wives and vice versa. As with the dissolution of marriage, Aquinas points out that since a woman cannot have several husbands (certainty as to offspring would be precluded) it would be contrary to natural equity and hence create a servile relationship between the man and his wife:

> Besides, friendship consists in an equality. So, if it is not lawful for the wife to have several husbands, since this is contrary to certainty as to offspring, it would not be lawful, on the other hand, for a man to have several wives, for the friendship of the husband and wife would not be free but somewhat servile. And this argument is corroborated by experience, for among husbands having plural wives the wives have a status like that of servants (Aquinas 1975, 152).

Strong friendships, moreover, can not be had among many people:

> Furthermore, strong friendship is not possible in regard to many people, as is evident from the Philosopher in Ethics VIII. Therefore, if a wife has but one husband but the husband has several wives, the friendship will not be equal on both sides. So, the friendship will not be free, but servile in some way (Aquinas 1975, 152).

In direct contrast to Aquinas' earlier version of the same argument, then, we find a distinct concern not merely for equality, but for the type of friendship that ought to exist between a man and his wife, a concern that is strikingly absent from his earlier remarks. Aquinas' reference to Aristotle's stipulation that "strong friendship is not possible between many people," moreover, is clearly a reference to true friendship. For Aristotle contrasts complete and incomplete friendships precisely on these grounds: friendships based on pleasure and utility can be shared with many people, while true friendships cannot.

CONCLUSION

The comparison between the arguments for the necessity of monoga-mous, indissoluble marriage that Aquinas offers in his early *Commentary on the Sentences* with those that he offers in his later *Summa Contra Gentiles*, reveals that Aquinas is progressively more aware of the importance of the character of the married relationship. Marriage, Aquinas increasingly seems to recognize, is a friendship that consists in the sharing of a certain kind of activity. The norms associated with marriage, however, cannot be derived entirely from these activities alone. For what Aquinas' remarks seems to demonstrate is an increasing awareness that marriage consists not merely in sharing activities, but also about sharing those activities in a highly specific context, namely in the context of complete friendship.

The progression of Aquinas' natural law arguments is of more than historical interest, particularly for those of us interested in formulating philosophical defenses of the Church's position on contraception. For the differences between Aquinas' early arguments in the *Commentary on the Sentences* and those he offers in his later *Summa Contra Gentiles* should serve to remind us of Wojtyla's foundational point: the Church's teachings about the morality and immorality of individual sexual acts can only truly be understood in the context of the Church's deeper teachings about the proper character of married love. To the extent that we attempt to defend the Church's stance *only* via philosophical analysis of the isolated actions involved in the sexual act, we run the risk of obscuring the true depth of Church's sexual ethics.

SOURCES CONSULTED

Aquinas, Thomas. *Summa Contra Gentiles*. Translated by V. Bourke. South Bend, IN: University of Notre Dame Press, 1975.

_____. *Summa Theologica*. Vol. 5. Translated by the Fathers of the English Dominican Province. New York: Benziger Bros, 1948; reprint, Allen, TX: Christian Classics, 1981.

Aristotle. *Nicomachean Ethics*. Translated by T. Irwin. 2nd edition. Indianapolis: Hackett, 1999.

Noonan, John. *Contraception*. Massachusetts: Harvard University Press, 1965.

Ranke-Heinemann, U. *Eunuchs for the Kingdom of Heaven*. Translated by P. Heinegg. New York: Doubleday, 1990.

Torrell, J. *Saint Thomas Aquinas.* Translated by R. Royal. Washington, DC: Catholic University Press, 1996.

Wojtyla, K. *Love and Responsibility.* Translated by H. Willetts. San Francisco: Ignatius Press,1981.

CATHOLIC ACTIVISM IN THE CAMPAIGNS AGAINST ARTIFICIAL CONTRACEPTION & THE STERILIZATION OF THE "UNFIT" IN INTER-WAR BRITAIN

EILEEN GROTH LYON

This paper examines the movements for the wider distribution of contraceptive devices among the poor and the sterilization of the unfit in inter-war Britain. In particular, the Catholic response to these developments, which sought to employ new strategies in the political arena, is examined. Catholic physicians such as Halliday Sutherland and Letitia Fairfield presented a powerful scientific case against eugenics. The Guild of SS. Luke, Cosmas and Damian and the League of National Life vigorously pressured the government to prevent the wider distribution of information about artificial contraceptives and the implementation of schemes for the sterilization of the unfit. Despite their minority status, Catholic opponents proved so successful that eugenic legislation was ultimately abandoned.

The use of artificial contraception and of abortifacient drugs ("regulating pills") increased dramatically in Britain in the late nineteenth and early twentieth centuries. The impact of such practices was evident in the steep and continued decline in the fertility rate by the early twentieth century, especially among the middle and upper classes. These individuals were able to afford contraceptive devices and the services of physicians who might be required to fit them. The National Birth-Rate Commission found that the fertility rate among unskilled workers was approaching one and a half times that of the upper and middle classes, a trend that greatly alarmed many observers who spoke of a "dysgenic" birth rate.[1] Such findings became central in the national debate and parliamentary enquiry about unemployment, poverty and "racial degeneration." W. R. Inge, Dean of St. Paul's Cathedral (Anglican), said, "I plead for the preservation of those stocks to which the country has owed the greater part of its glory. It is here that eugenics may find in religion a potent ally."[2] How potent an ally was religion in this period? Christian churches with their hitherto unequivocal rejection of artificial contraception were brought into the service of "positive' eugenics which sought to promote reproduction among the "better stocks." In an effort to increase the number of "desireable stocks," contraceptive use among the middle and upper classes was strongly condemned. Clergy also were amongst those who urged greater restraint and responsibility on the part of the poor in their denunciations of reckless breeding. It must be noted that at least into the early 1920s, this call to greater responsibility on the part of the poor was not generally coupled with the promotion of artificial means of contraception. However, "positive" eugenics and exhortations to greater responsibility would soon give way to a more aggressive program of "negative" eugenics which sought to check the fertility of the "lesser stocks." This trend was accelerated in the early 1930s when the Church of England, soon to be followed by other Protestant groups, gave qualified approval to artificial contraception.

It is the campaigns that sought to employ "negative eugenics" that are my concern in this paper. I will begin with some brief remarks on the connections between eugenics, contraception and the sterilization of the "unfit" which provide an important backdrop to the story I will tell. Then, the paper will examine the movements for the wider distribution of contraceptive devices among the poor and the sterilization of the "unfit." In particular, I will examine the Catholic response to these developments and the new strategies they employed. Catholic physicians such as Halliday Sutherland and Letitia Fairfield presented a powerful scientific case against eugenics. The Guild of SS. Luke, Cosmas and Damian and the League of National Life vigorously pressured the government to prevent the wider distribution of information about artificial contraceptives and the implementation of sterilization schemes. Despite their minority status, Catholic opponents proved so successful that eugenic legislation was ultimately abandoned.

CONNECTIONS BETWEEN EUGENICS, CONTRACEPTION & STERILIZATION OF THE "UNFIT"

The connections between contraception and eugenics are integral to an understanding of the early birth control movement. It must be remembered that nearly all advocates of contraception in early-twentieth-century Britain argued for its use principally on eugenicist grounds. Concerns about racial degeneration led many to consider ways of limiting what they termed the "lesser stocks." Birth control was, in the words of one Anglican priest, a "truly great humanitarian movement and one which alone can solve the problem of a nation burdened with an extraordinarily large percentage of unwanted and defective babies."[3] Economic and sociological considerations began to drive the whole question of the morality of contraception in Anglican discussions. Some clergy had no qualms about articulating extreme positions on the question of the disadvantaged. One Anglican priest, writing from his parish in Surrey, lamented the burdens placed on the "professional and cultured classes." He wrote:

> ...the old live too long ∞ I am speaking economically, and I think the time is not far distant when we shall have to consider seriously what we are to do with the insane, the hopeless invalid, and all irredeemably degraded in mind and body. They are a burden such as the community can scarcely bear; and a painless extinction seems to me the only remedy.[4]

Another urged "having lunatics and weakminded castrated before leaving the asylum."[5] While it is unlikely that most clergy, even those sympathetic to eugenics, would have gone as far as these two, it is clear that encouragement of contraceptive use among the poor was desirable to many as one possible solution. Arguments about overburdened mothers and feminist considerations were very much secondary. This early context is often lost on modern audiences. Eugenics was in large part discredited in the aftermath of the Nazi atrocities. As the use of artificial contraceptives for "temporary" sterilization won wider acceptance, efforts to legalize "permanent" sterilization of the "unfit" came to the fore.

MARIE STOPES AND THE ADVOCACY OF
ARTIFICIAL CONTRACEPTION

In the immediate post-war years, Marie Stopes, a paleobotanist, emerged as the key figure in the advocacy of artificial contraception. She claimed that her interest in sexual relations and birth control grew out of the unhappiness of her first marriage which was eventually dissolved on the grounds of non-consummation. She said that she sought to spare others the pain of sexual ignorance and wished to enhance the pleasure of sexual relations for women by taking away the fear of pregnancy. To this end Stopes published a number of books providing romantic discussion of marriage and practical advice about contraception. Of course, this is only part of the story. She was a member of the Eugenics Society almost from its inception and it is likely that her advocacy of the provision of birth control to poor women was more related to her eugenic concerns than to any romantic notions about marriage. In 1921, she founded the Society for Constructive Birth Control and Racial Progress, which sought to pressure the government to join in the work of providing information and services relating to contraception.[6] In explaining the aims of her new society in a meeting at the Queen's Hall, she proclaimed that "constructive birth control is the key of all racial progress."[7] In further describing the higher ideal she had in mind, she was concerned not only with the romantic aspects of married love but also with a very specific view of procreation. In a widely applauded statement, she said that "married lovers should play the part of parents *only* when they can add individuals of value to the race."[8] She decried the amount of money spent to keep "wastrels in institutions and prisons" and "on schools for detention and institutes for wastrel children." The only solution, in her view, "to get rid of wastrels in a Christian way" was to "see that they are not born."[9] James Barr, Vice-President of the British Medical Association, wrote to Stopes, "you and your husband have inaugurated a great movement which I hope will eventually get rid of our C3 population and exterminate poverty."[10] The precise means by which the physically inferior or C3s would be eliminated was the careful use of a cervical cap which she called the "Pro-Race Cap." In an effort to communicate her message to poor women more effectively, she opened the first birth control clinic to provide both information and services on Holloway Road in London. Similar services soon became available in many other English cities.

EARLY EFFORTS OF CATHOLICS IN OPPOSING ARTIFICIAL CONTRACEPTION

C. V. Drysdale, president of the Malthusian League, indicated in 1922 that all organized opposition to birth control was dead except for that of the Roman Catholic Church.[11] Yet, these efforts of Catholics remained somewhat diffuse and ineffectual in the early 1920s. Vincent McNabb, O.P. was among a small group of Catholic protestors outside the Queen's Hall when Marie Stopes launched her Society. He lamented that "the Catholic protest, coming from only two or three Catholics scattered here and there amidst a great crowd could but accentuate our weakness. Yet the protest arose from a sense of duty that called for a symbolical and official act which would at once register and strengthen the official position of the Church."[12] As the birth control movement moved more toward the mainstream of British society, Catholics became much more organized in their opposition. Stopes came to believe that they were her principal adversaries.[13]

CATHOLIC VIEWS ON EUGENICS

Catholic moralists restated the Church's condemnation of artificial methods of birth control[14] and began to pursue a more vigorous campaign of promoting these teachings. Part of the process of becoming more politically engaged entailed grappling with contemporary discourse concerning eugenics. Eugenicists argued that they had a moral duty to posterity and as such were obliged to work toward "race improvement." W. R. Inge went so far as to say that "no moral duties are more imperative or more important than our duties toward posterity."[15] He said that "'sanctity of human life' must give way to the obvious truth that a good garden needs weeding."[16] Harold Cox also drew upon garden imagery in asserting that "every gardener knows that if seeds are sown too thick, the resulting plants will be poor in quality." He believed the same was true of the "production of human beings."[17] Clearly, such assertions which spoke of the "production of human beings" would have been hard for many

Catholic moralists to take seriously. Some refused to enter the debate. One Jesuit, writing in *The Month* rejected the whole idea of eugenics by attacking its fundamental premise. He wrote, "strictly speaking, since duty is a relation between existing personalities, we have no duty to posterity, posterity being a non-entity."[18] This approach won few supporters[19] and the debates surrounding eugenics could not be so easily dispatched. Other Catholic writers were more eager to engage with these debates in an effort to bring the fullness of Catholic moral and intellectual traditions into contemporary discourse. Of eugenics, Henry Davis, S. J., Professor of Moral Theology at Heythrop College, said "Catholics need not condemn the laudable aim of the science, though they rightly condemn some of the methods advocated by those who are, as it were intoxicated with the new wine of the science."[20] Rev. Thomas J. Gerrard said that "Catholicism, far from seeking to hinder eugenic reforms, seeks rather to promote it by setting it on a lasting basis, the basis of the spirit." Gerrard argued that "God is taken as the beginning and end of all racial improvement. He improves the race and He improves it for the manifestation of His own glory. We co-operate with him."[21] Such a conceptualization would allow

> . . . eugenics to take its place as a servant, not as a master. In thus co-operating with the Divine process it will derive from it the highest good. The supreme mistake of the eugenist in dealing with the religious factor is in making religion the handmaid of eugenics, instead of eugenics the handmaid of religion.[22]

He concluded that it would be futile to manipulate nature for "mere love of the race will not sustain our efforts." Instead, "we must love the power that controls the race."[23]

CONNECTIONS BETWEEN OPPOSITION TO BIRTH CONTROL & OTHER ASPECTS OF CATHOLIC SOCIAL TEACHING

Catholic writers, while seeking to place eugenics on what they deemed to be a proper footing, were not oblivious to the deplorable social conditions which made many sympathetic to birth control. One reformer declared that "Christian principles are the last bulwark of the poor and helpless against the insolent projects of those false humanitarians, who make no effort to remove slums and sweating and destitution, but are content to tinker with their effects."[24] In this period, the opposition to birth control was inextricably tied to Catholic social teachings on the rights of labor and other aspects of social justice. The Catholic Social Guild decried the fact that Labour Party leaders had cast their lot with the supporters of birth control: "There will be no need for remedying the intolerable social conditions of the slum dwellers, if the latter are to be eliminated by birth prevention."[25] In his discourse on the Catholic ideal for the continuance of the race, Lewis Watt, a Jesuit, spoke of "increase in accordance with the natural laws of fecundity working within the institution of holy matrimony."[26] He insisted that such an ideal "implies the possibility of securing to all men, women and children at least a decent sufficiency of this world's goods."[27] In a similar vein, Letitia Fairfield, a prominent Catholic physician and barrister-at-law, asked, "How is the working man ever going to obtain for himself Pope Leo's ideal of a living wage 'sufficient to maintain himself and his family in reasonable comfort' if it is an accepted thing (perhaps a compulsory thing) that in times of stress he is always to keep down the number of his family."[28] Here, Fairfield is making reference to Leo XIII's *Rerum Novarum* which had a profound impact on many of those engaged in the fight against artificial birth control.

Increasingly, Catholic writers coupled their rejection of birth control and broader campaign for social justice with a rallying cry to political action. Catholics, particularly women, were urged to "utilize every opportunity for action to remedy the social and economic evils which have created the demand for birth control."[29] These efforts might include using their vote to press for the continued work of the infant welfare centers which had been so instrumental in reducing the infant mortality rate, secure an adequate number of nursery schools, maintain the provision of free meals for needy children, greater tax benefits for large families and above all, the provision of adequate and healthful housing.[30]

MOBILIZATION & ACTIVISM OF CATHOLIC PHYSICIANS

The Archbishops and Bishops were integrally involved in the efforts to curb the use of artificial contraception. While they consistently put forth the moral arguments in pamphlets, homilies and pastoral letters, they also tried some new strategies.[31] One of these urged by the English and Scottish hierarchies was to mobilize Catholic *physi-*

cians to "attack the birth control problem from the pathological side or from its harmful effects on the human organism."[32] This is an interesting response because it contains an implicit recognition that the argument was not going to be won on moral grounds or that it wasn't politically astute to try to do so. It also paralleled a tactic employed by Anglicans and other Protestants who sought to promote birth control. They moved the issue to the political mainstream by framing it as a medical and social question rather than a religious and moral one. Lord Dawson of Penn, one of Britain's leading physicians and a devout Anglican, became a leading advocate for birth control despite the Anglican Church's official condemnation of artificial contraception. (The Anglican Communion was to give qualified approval to its use at a meeting of the Lambeth Conference in 1930.) As personal physician to the King and Archbishop of Canterbury, Dawson's endorsement of contraception seemed to convey approval at the highest levels of church and state and signal that a change in Anglican teaching on the matter was imminent.[33]

Catholic physicians who rallied to the bishops' call found themselves faced with an uphill battle. Widespread use of contraceptives coupled with support among prominent members of the medical community and Anglican establishment made opposition an almost futile cause. Nonetheless, a few Catholic physicians, including Halliday Sutherland, Letitia Fairfield and Frederick John McCann, sought to lay out the medical and moral arguments demonstrating the harmfulness of artificial contraception in books, pamphlets and short articles in *The British Medical Journal, The Lancet* and other leading medical papers.[34] Letitia Fairfield was a member of a special committee appointed by the National Council of Public Morals to examine the ethics of birth control. She was prominent among the signatories of a "note of reservation" appended to the report rejecting any sentences contained in it that in any way implied that artificial forms of contraception could be permissible.[35] Halliday Sutherland pointed out that Dawson was not a gynaecologist and that "his opinions cannot be accepted as that of an expert." Sutherland seized upon a remark in Dawson's speech for the Anglican Church Congress in 1921 that he found most curious. Dawson did not advise the use of contraceptives before the birth of the first child. Sutherland asked

"Why?" If artificial birth control is quite harmless, why not practise it from the beginning?"[36] When pressed this question by an Anglican priest who was sympathetic to contraceptive use, Dawson conceded privately that he had concerns that "the use of certain checks increases the chances of sterility."[37] Sutherland also seized upon the words of one of Dawson's defenders: "Lord Dawson has not stated that birth control is a good thing. He says it is here to stay, and no denunciations will abolish it."[38] Sutherland replied,

> Since when, may I ask, has it become necessary for any one, still less for every one, to accept a thing that is harmful merely because it is an established fact? Murder is an established fact. Although no denunciations will abolish either murder or birth control, there is no excuse for not telling the public the simple medical truth that contraceptive methods are harmful to men and women.[39]

McCann, one of the few gynaecologists involved in either side of the debate, argued "All known methods of contraception are injurious to the female, they only differ from being more or less so."[40]

Catholic physicians also sought to work through the Guild of SS. Luke, Cosmas and Damian ' a group numbering more than 400 ෙ in an effort to achieve wider publication of anti-contraceptionist views. Ernest Ware, President of the Guild, lectured to other physicians on the pathological evils of contraception and Mary Kidd, another prominent physician in the Guild, undertook to write directly to mothers.[41] The Guild's periodical, *The Catholic Medical Guardian*, also took up both the medical and moral aspects of contraception in frequent articles on the issue.[42]

Sutherland sought to combine medical and political arguments in an attack on Marie Stopes. He described her clinic and the devices she dispensed as "exposing the poor to experiment." He maintained that the ordinary decent instincts of the poor are against these practices and indeed they have used them less than any other classes. But owing to their poverty, lack of learning and helplessness, the poor are the natural victims of those who seek to make experiments of their fellows. In the midst of a London slum, a woman . . . has opened a birth control clinic where working women are instructed in a method of contraception described by Professor McIlroy as 'the most harmful method of which I have had experience.'[43]

Against the advice of the others, Stopes seized upon this attack as an opportunity to have a writ issued for libel.[44] (She was very envious of Margaret Sanger's capacity to engender publicity for the cause through legal proceedings.) Stopes lost the case. The Lord Chief Justice asked the jury if the words complained of by the plaintiff were "true in substance and in fact" to which they answered "Yes."[45] The case represented a considerable financial loss for Stopes though she was undeterred from her crusade. For Catholics, this case helped to provide a concrete opportunity to oppose the birth control movement. Cardinal Bourne, Archbishop of Westminster, personally helped to fund Sutherland's defense and eventually a national campaign was launched by influential Catholic laity. Individual Catholics and parishes from all over the British Isles and indeed some parts of the Empire, Europe and North America sent contributions.[46] Indeed, the campaign was so successful that over 1,000 remained after all the costs of the various appeals were paid.[47]

This victory may have lifted spirits in the Catholic community but the battle was far from won. The energy that had been mobilized by the Sutherland Appeal Fund was soon channeled into a new organization ∞ the League of National Life. This organization was founded in 1926 "to combat the theory and practice of Contraception (Birth Prevention); to oppose any form of State or Municipal assistance for the promotion of Contraception; and to uphold the honour and blessing of parenthood."[48] The League kept up a steady correspondence with the Ministry of Health in an effort to prevent the Maternity and Child Welfare Centres from distributing contraceptive information and devices.[49] Under the provisions of the Maternity and Child Welfare Act, 1918, these centers were the principal means by which women received obstetrical and gynecological care. Members of the League fought hard to prevent these centers from becoming government-funded birth control clinics. In 1926, Lord Buckmaster presented a motion in the House of Lords to allow for contraceptive information to be given at these centers. He cited several cases of women in extreme circumstances, often struggling to cope with several children who suffered severe birth defects. He acknowledged the fierce opposition on the part of Roman Catholics but concluded that "they have no power to impose their views upon us."[50] Viscount

FitzAlan, Ernest Ware, Letitia Fairfield and Frederick McCann were among those who spoke vehemently against the motion. These efforts did not succeed in blocking the motion. It was carried 57 to 44. However, it allowed contraceptive advice to be given only on a very limited basis to women whose lives would be endangered by another confinement.[51] The efforts of the League coupled with a Catholic Minister of Health undoubtedly delayed a wider directive allowing for the dissemination of contraceptive information. The Ministry ultimately capitulated in 1931 following the statements of Anglican bishops at the Lambeth Conference of 1930. Sutherland, in summing up the activities of the League, conceded "we failed. We witnessed the medical profession betray its trust; we saw the white flag hoisted over Lambeth Palace; we were at Whitehall in 1931 when the Ministry of Health first permitted advice on contraceptives to be given in ante-natal clinics."[52] The contraceptive issue did not require legislation for implementation and the major political leaders would not commit themselves either way on this question.

ORIGINS OF THE DEBATE
CONCERNING STERILIZATION OF THE "UNFIT"

The picture was to be somewhat different with regard to the sterilization of the "unfit." The efficacy and propriety of sterilizing the "unfit" had emerged in public discourse in the early 1920s. For example, G. Walmisley-Dresser, an Anglican priest in Exeter, issued a tirade against the cost of maintaining the mentally ill. He said: "It is high time to concentrate on prevention rather than cure, and the only certain means is the sterilization of all the obviously unfit."[53] Certainly, the issue arose on many occasions in the birth control clinics run by the Society for Constructive Birth Control.[54] Sterilization was an obvious corollary to the methods of contraception taught at the clinics and indeed permanent sterilization was preferred for many poor women who were not thought to possess the capacity to use contraceptives properly. The Council of the Eugenics Society laid out "An Outline of a Practical Eugenic Policy" in 1928. Among its premises was that no couple was to be "regarded as having an absolute right to parenthood if their circumstances are such as to be likely to prevent them from bringing up children without an exceptional amount of aid from the State."[55] While the document is in general quite cau-

tious, it does say that in the case of "definitely defective types," reproduction was to be prevented by either segregation or sterilization.
The Catholic Church had been quite clear in its moral condemnation
of sterilization as a "serious mutilation of the body."[56] This position
would soon be uncompromisingly re-asserted in *Casti Connubii.*[57]
However, Catholics proved quite adept at seizing upon the issue in
such a way as to forge a useful alliance with the Labour Party. A.
Gille, S.J., proclaimed that "the eugenists are growing candid at last
and airing their secret motives in the open . . . It is evidently cheaper
for the millionaire to sterilise the poor than to pay them better wages
and house them decently."[58] Sterilization operations were illegal in
Britain and the eugenicist lobby was divided on whether sterilization would actually solve the problem of racial degeneration. While
many believed that mental illness, feeble-mindedness, physical mal-
formation and alcoholism were inherited traits, there was considerable debate about the mechanism for inheritance.[59] Lord Dawson
warned the Eugenics Society, "I think we want to go forward with
the propaganda at a cautious pace, carefully selecting our ground."[60]
Just a couple months before the Lambeth Conference of 1930, when
Stopes smelled victory on the contraceptive question, she wrote privately to the Harley Street physician F. D. Saner to seek advice about
physicians who are able to perform sterilizations. She wrote:

Our Society, as perhaps you may know, is working for the elimina-
tion of the unfit in the race, and now our campaign for voluntary
birth control has almost obtained the desired effect we are turning
our attention to sterilization which has always been on our programme for general consideration but somewhat in abeyance as we
felt the time was not ripe for it.[61]

Saner indicated that there would be no difficulty finding physicians who would perform sterilizations despite the legal risks of doing so. Surgery for non-therapeutic reasons left the physician open to
possible murder charges should the patient die during the procedure.
Lord Dawson, who was by this point President of the Royal College
of Physicians, led a movement to allow for voluntary sterilizations.
He said "It is our aim to prevent disease and disability in our own
generation; why should we not aim to prevent them in the generations to follow? Sterilization would be a form of preventive treat-

ment in the interests of the race."[62] Dawson cast the procedure as a benevolent one, claiming that it brought "no after-regrets, and that relief is brought to suffering people, who are thereby helped to be better citizens."[63] To those who might have opposed the procedure on the grounds of individual liberty, Dawson said "law restrains liberty in matters of communal health, and when parents are ignorantly obstructive public medical services can act forcefully in the interests of children."[64]

CATHOLIC OPPOSITION TO LEGISLATION PERMITTING VOLUNTARY STERILIZATION

Cardinal Hinsley, successor to Bourne as Archbishop of Westminster, charged that sterilization was one of several "proposals of neopaganism" which armed "medical science with the means of death instead of life."[65] The Catholic community, numerically very small in Britain, seized upon sterilization and other issues to try to establish itself as a defender of the moral order in the wake of the Anglican retreat. Cora Hodson, the liaison officer to the Christian Churches on behalf of the Joint Committee on Voluntary Sterilization, indicated in a private letter to Cardinal Hinsley that "there is a real desire on all sides to avoid a political conflict with the Roman Catholic Church on this issue."[66] Ernest Ware and W. J. O'Donovan, leaders of the Guild of St. Luke, urged Cardinal Hinsley to make clear Catholic feeling on the sterilization issue in advance of the General Election in 1935. They felt sure that the Government would not pursue legislation if it became clear that Catholic laity along with their Bishops would strongly oppose such a measure.[67] The developments concerning sterilization were closely followed by the Vatican. The Guild provided reports on the situation and maintained a correspondence on the political maneuverings within Parliament on this issue with Cardinal Pacelli (the future Pius XII, then Vatican Secretary of State).[68] Letitia Fairfield and Henry Davis, S.J., were very active in setting out the Catholic position and they did so marshaling not only moral and medical arguments but also political ones that were very effective.[69] Unlike with the contraceptive issue, these campaigns required government legislation which could be rigorously opposed. The Westminster Catholic Federation, The Guild of St. Luke and the Archbishop of Westminster helped to compile, translate and circulate a comprehensive series of documents related to the situation in Germany.[70] Under Germany's Hereditary Health Law (1933), two million Germans were forcibly sterilized.[71] Unlike in the United States, the English public always opposed forceable sterilization and hence a discussion of what happened in Germany inevitably raised the specter of how a voluntary scheme might become coercive.

On the question of sterilization, Catholics were able to exert influence well beyond their numbers. The Minister of Health, Hilton Young, remained unresponsive to deputations of individuals seeking to promote sterilization schemes for fear of alienating Catholic voters in the run up to the General Election in November 1935.[72] Superintendents of privately-run hospitals sometimes withheld consent for the operations to take place for fear angering Catholic subscribers.[73] The political maturation of Catholics was clearly evident. Unlike their Anglican counterparts, they were able to defend their moral and doctrinal teachings in a way that made them a stronger political force. They did so by demonstrating that their teachings, far from being outdated religious dogmas, were indeed prophetic declarations of the rights of the poor. By casting them in such a light, they aligned themselves with larger political forces that helped to maintain and indeed enhance their political relevancy.

NOTES

[1.] The National Birth-Rate Commission found that there were 119 births per thousand married males under 55 among the upper and middle classes. The figures for skilled workmen and unskilled workmen were 153 per thousand and 213 per thousand respectively. G. R. Searle, *Eugenics and Politics in Britain 1900-1914* (Leyden: Noordhoff International Publishing, 1976), p. 26.

[2.] "Family Suicide. 'Breeding from Worst Stocks'" in *The Times*, 17 November 1920.

[3.] Rev. P. W. Vale to Marie Stopes, Cambridge, 14 July 1922. Marie Stopes Papers. London: British Library (BL) Additional Manuscript (Add MS) 58551 fol. 138r.

[4.] Ruth Hall (ed.), *Dear Dr. Stopes. Sex in the 1920s* (London: André Deutsch Limited, 1978), p. 75.

[5.] *Ibid.*, p. 71.

[6.] McLaren, *History of Contraception*, pp. 217-218. Mary Stocks, ⮞ The Story of Family Planning in C. H. Rolph [pseud.] (ed.), *The Human Sum* (New York: The Macmillan Co., 1959), pp. 51-54.

[7.]*Queen's Hall Meeting on Constructive Birth Control. Speeches and Impressions.* (London: G. P. Putnam's Sons, Ltd., 1921), p. 23.

[8.]*Ibid*, p. 32.

[9.]*Ibid*, p. 29.

[10.]*Ibid*, p. 8.

[11.]"The Church *versus* the Malthusian Evil" in *The Month*, Vol. CXL (August 1922), p. 173.

[12.]Vincent McNabb, "The Crime of Birth Control" in *Blackfriars*, Vol. II, No. 4 (July 1921), p. 216.

[13.]"The Church and Birth-control" in *The Month*, Vol. CXL (November 1922), p. 466.

[14.]See for example, E. J. Mahoney [Professor of Moral Theology at St. Edmund's College], *Christian Marriage* (London: Burns Oates & Washbourne Ltd., 1927), pp. 64-72.

[15.]W. R. Inge, "Religion and the States" in *The Hibbert Journal*, Vol. XVIII, No. 4 (1920), p. 647.

[16.]*Ibid.*, p. 648.

[17.]Harold Cox, *The Problem of Population* (London: Jonathan Cape, 1922), p. 5.

[18.]"The Fallacies of Eugenics" in *The Month*, Vol. CXXXV (January 1920), p. 84.

[19.]"Roman Catholic Criticism of Eugenics, With Reply From the President" in *The Eugenics Review*, Vol. 12 (April 1920), p. 49.

[20.]Henry Davis, *Eugenics. Aims and Methods* (London: Burns Oates & Washbourne, 1930), p. 15.

[21.]Thomas J. Gerrard, *The Church and Eugenics* (London: P. S. King & Son, 1912), p. 57.

[22.]*Ibid.*

[23.]*Ibid.*, p. 58.

[24.]"The Church and the Sacredness of the Human Soul' in *The Month*, Vol. CXL (August 1922), p. 174.

[25.]See for example, Edward Godwin, *Wise Words to Catholic Wives* (Birmingham: E. F. Hudson, Ltd, 1928), p. 9.

[26.]Lewis Watt, *Social Aspects of Birth Control* (Oxford: The Catholic Social Guild, [1927]), p. 6.

[27.]*Ibid.*

[28.]Letitia Fairfield, "Catholic Women and Neo-Malthusianism" A Speech delivered at the International Conference of Catholic Women's Leagues, held at the Hague, April 1928. Leititia Fairfield Collection. London: Contemporary Medical Archives Centre at the Wellcome Institute for the History of Medicine (CMAC). GC/193/E.3 pp. 2-3.

[29.]*Ibid.*, p. 3.

[30.] See for example, *"A City Full of Boys and Girls:" A Talk to Catholic Wives and Mothers By a Catholic Woman Doctor* (London: Catholic Truth Society, 1923).

[31.] See for example: Henry Davis, S.J., *Birth Control. The Fallacies of Dr. M. Stopes* (London: Burns, Oates & Washbourne Ltd., 1928). Mahoney, *Christian Marriage. A Grave Moral Evil. By the Archbishops & Bishops of Scotland* [A Lenten Pastoral for 1927] (Oxford: The Catholic Social Guild, 1928).

[32.] "Catholic Doctors and Birth Control. Conference at Glasgow" in *The Tablet*, August 5, 1922.

[33.] Lord Dawson of Penn, *Love ∽ Marriage ∽ Birth Control* (London: Nisbet & Co., Ltd, 1922).

[34.] See e.g.: Halliday Sutherland, *Birth Control. A Statement of Christian Doctrine against the Neo-Malthusians* (London: Harding & More Ltd, 1922), pp. 138-147. Letter from Halliday Sutherland in *British Medical Journal*, July 30, 1921, p. 169. Letitia Fairfied, "The State and Birth Control" in James Marchant (ed.), *Medical Views on Birth Control* (London: Martin Hopkinson & Co., Ltd, 1926), pp. 104-181. Frederick John McCann, *The Treatment of Common Female Ailments* (London: E. Arnold & Co., 1922). McCann, *The Effect of Contraceptive Practices on the Female Sexual Organs* (London: Simpkin, Marshall, Hamilton, Kent, 1928). McCann, *Contraception. A Common Cause of Disease* (London: Bale, Sons and Daniels, 1928).

[35.] *The Ethics of Birth Control. Being the Report of the Special Committee appointed by the National Council of Public Morals in connection with the investigations of the National Birth-rate Commission* (London: Macmillan and Co., 1925), pp. 29-30.

[36.] Halliday Sutherland, "Birth Control Dangers" in *Swindon Evening Advertiser*, 28 March 1922. Typescript. Marie Stopes Archive. CMAC. PP/MCS/H4a.

[37.] Corner is relaying the details of his correspondence with Dawson. Horace Corner to Marie Stopes, Abergavenny, 27 February 1922. Marie Stopes Papers. BL Add MS 58548 fol. 186r-187v.

[38.] Sutherland, "Birth Control Dangers."

[39.] *Ibid.*

[40.] McCann, *Treatment of Common Female Ailments*, p. 295.

[41.] "Catholic Doctors and Birth Control. Conference at Glasgow" in *The Tablet*, August 5, 1922, p. 187.

[42.] *The Catholic Medical Guardian, passim* 1923-1935.

[43.] Writ issued the 12th day of May 1922 between Marie Charlotte Carmichael Stopes vs. Halliday G. Sutherland and Harding & More Limited. High Court of Justice, King's Bench Division. 1922 - S - No. 2397. Marie Stopes Archive. CMAC PP/MCS/H.4a. For A. Louise McIlroy's views, see *The Lancet*, July 23, 1921, pp. 179-180.

44·See e.g. James Barr to Marie Stopes, Liverpool, 1 February 1923. Marie Stopes Papers. BL Add MS 58566 fol. 124.

45·"The Moral Problem of To-day. An Appeal to all Right-minded People." January 1924. Leaflet issued on behalf of the National Committee for the Sutherland-Wareing Appeal Fund. Bourne Papers. London: Archives of the Archdiocese of Westminster (AAW): Bo. 5/59. The author gratefully acknowledges the kind permission of the Archbishop of Westminster to cite material from the Archives.

46·Confidential Memo. Bourne Papers. AAW: Bo. 5/59. Letter to Cardinal Bourne, London, 3 January 1923. Bourne Papers. AAW: Bo. 5/59. Edward Eyre to Msgr. Jackman, 28 July 1922. Bourne Papers. AAW: Bo. 5/59. William Bodkin, S.J. to Cardinal Bourne, Stonyhurst College, 10 August 1923. Bourne Papers. AAW: Bo. 5/59. *The Tablet*, January 26, 1924, p. 118; March 22, 1924, p. 386; April 19, 1924, p. 538. *The Catholic Medical Guardian*, Vol. 1, No. 4 (October 1923), p. 91.

47·Various letters related to the Sutherland-Wareing Appeal Fund. Bourne Papers. AAW: Bo. 5/59. Hinsley Papers. AAW: Hi 2/16.

48·*National Life*, Vol. I, No. 1 (London, 1929), p. 1. Also see, *The Tablet*, November 6, 1926, pp. 599-600. *British Medical Journal*, November 6, 1926, p. 863.

49·*The Tablet*, December 4, 1926, p. 751. *The Lancet*, May 22, 1926, pp. 1008-1010; December 4, 1926, p. 1202; May 28, 1927, pp. 1140-1141. The Guild had also been active in this cause. See: Letter from Ernest Ware, 9 June 1926. Hinsley Papers. AAW: Hi 2/16.

50·*Birth Prevention is a National Danger* (London: League of National Life, 1926), p. 8. [Contains reprint of Speeches made by Lord Buckmaster in the House of Lords on April 28th, 1916.]

51·*The Lancet*, May 22, 1926, pp. 1008-1010. *British Medical Journal*, May 8, 1926, pp. 849-850. *Birth Prevention is National Danger*, pp. 10-11.

52·Halliday Sutherland, *Control of Life* (London, 1947; first published 1944), p. 104.

53·"Treatment of the Unfit" in *The Times*, 29 May 1923.

54·Marie Stopes to E. B. Turner, 30 October 1924. Marie Stopes Papers. BL Add. MS 58565 fol. 106.

55·*An Outline of a Practical Eugenic Policy 1928* (Approved by the Council of the Eugenics Society as a general indication of their aims, immediate and ultimate, though every item is not endorsed by all its Members.), p. 2. CMAC, SA/EUG J.17/13.

56·*The Month*, Vol. CXLVII (March 1926), p. 262. Also see, Henry Davis, S. J., *Eugenics. Aims and Methods*, pp. 40-41.

57·Pius XI, *Casti Connubii* (*On Christian Marriage*). Papal Encyclical, 31 December 1930. http://www.vatican.va/holy_father/pius_xi/encyclicals/documents/hf_p-xi_enc_31121930_casti-connubii_en.html. Also see,

Reflections on Sterilisation by a Catholic Priest (Croyden: Roffey & Clark, Ltd., 1933).

[58.]*The Catholic Medical Guardian*, Vol. I, No. 2 (April 1923), p. 35.

[59.]*Report of the Departmental Committee on Sterilisation* (London: H. M. Stationery Office, 1934). *The Lancet*, 28 July 1923, p. 181; 13 March 1926, p. 561; 27 March 1926, pp. 660-661; 4 May 1929, pp. 925; 21 June 1930, pp. 1380-1382. Lyndsay Andrew Farral, *The Origins and Growth of the English Eugenics Movement 1865-1925* (New York and London: Garland Publishing, Inc., 1985). G. R. Searle, *Eugenics and Politics in Britain 1900-1914* (Leyden: Noordhoff International Publishing, 1976). C. P. Blacker, "General Aspects of Hereditary Disease" in *The Practitioner*, October 1923, pp. 436-449.

[60.]Lord Dawson to M. D. Silcock, London, 15 September 1934. CMAC: SA/EUG D. 219.

[61.]Marie Stopes to F. D. Saner, London, 3 June 1930. Marie Stopes Papers. BL Add MS 58570 fol. 70.

[62.]Lord Dawson of Penn, *Address to York Medical Society on Medical Science and Social Progress*. (Reprinted from the British Medical Journal, November 2nd, 1935), p. 7. CMAC, SA/EUG C. 88.

[63.]*Ibid*, p. 11.

[64.]*Ibid*.

[65.]Cardinal Hinsley to Lord FitzAlan, n.d., Hinsley Papers. AAW: Hi 2/16.

[66.]Cora B. S. Hodson to Cardinal Hinsley, London, 22 October 1935. Hinsley Papers. AAW: Hi 2/16.

[67.]Ernest Ware and W. J. O'Donovan to Cardinal Hinsley, London, 21 October 1935. Hinsley Papers. AAW: Hi 2/16.

[68.]W. J. O'Donovan to Cardinal Pacelli, London, 5 October 1935. HP. AAW: Hi 2/16.

[69.]Letitia Fairfield, *The Case Against Sterilisation*. Third Edition. (London: Catholic Truth Society, 1939). Henry Davis, S.J., *State Sterilization of the Unfit* (London: Burns, Oates & Washbourne Ltd, 1931). It is clear that they were aided in their efforts by Pope Pius XI's unequivocal condemnation of sterilization in *Casti Connubii*. Prior to the publication of the encyclical, Davis was challenged in his presentation of the "Catholic" position by other Catholic writers who favored some measures of state sterilization.

[70.]*The Tablet*, January 27, 1934, pp. 110-111; July-November 1936, p. 463.

[71.]Andrea Tone (ed.), *Controlling Reproduction. An American History* (Wilmington, DE: Scholarly Resources, Inc., 1997), p. 169.

[72.]John Macnicol, "Eugenics and the Campaign for Voluntary Sterilization in Britain Between the Wars" in *Social History of Medicine*, 1989, p. 158.

[73.]*British Medical Journal*, 21 July 1934, p. 136.

THE SOCIAL EFFECTS OF CONTRACEPTION

JENNIFER ROBACK MORSE

This paper assesses the negative impact of contraception on society. Widespread use of contraception, both inside and outside of marriage, has had long term negative consequences that were not anticipated when first promoted and which do not receive the attention they deserve in the public square. It is hoped that this reflection will stimulate a long-overdue public discussion of this important topic.

Commentators from across the political spectrum agree that the introduction of the birth control pill marked the beginnings of a social revolution. Contraceptive technology had an impact on more than just fertility. Contraceptive technology affected both women and men, changing the way we view children, education, marriage, work and much more.

Many self-styled women's advocates consider the introduction of contraceptive technology to be an unambiguous good for women, and for society as a whole. The purpose of this paper is to offer an assessment of the negative impacts of contraception on society. My case in this paper is to show that the widespread use of contraception both inside and outside of marriage has had long term negative consequences that we may not have anticipated, and which do not receive the attention they deserve.

A re-examination of this question is necessary because many champions of contraception take credit for every positive social development that has occurred since the 1960's. These advocates claim credit not only for the ability of married women to space their pregnancies, but also for every woman who has gone to college and had a career. Very seldom, however, do advocates of contraception accept responsibility for any of the negative changes in social life that have taken place in the last thirty or forty years.

The technology of contraception is not an unmixed blessing comparable to the introduction of clean drinking water, or penicillin. Rather, contraception has been more like nuclear weapons: useful in extremely limited contexts, but so powerful that they need to be restrained. Contraception has been more than simply one item on a social menu, which opens up additional options for people who choose to use it. Instead, contraception has been accompanied by an ideology that has changed the whole context in which everyone makes their sexual and reproductive decisions. To use an analogy from economics, contraception as actually practiced in American has done more than simply offer consumers one more choice within a given competitive arena. The contraceptive ideology, combined with contraceptive technology, has changed the competitive terms for everyone, whether they like it or not, whether they chose it or not.

I hope to demonstrate that the question of whether and how to use contraception is not a "done deal," that requires no further thought. I hope to stimulate a long-overdue discussion of this important topic.

DEFINING THE CONTRACEPTIVE CULTURE AND ITS IDEOLOGY: THE ILLUSION OF CONTROL

There is much more to the contraceptive culture than simply the introduction of the birth control pill. There is also a distinct ideology which surrounds contraception. That ideology tells us what to value, what to avoid as unacceptable pain and what to pursue as desirable pleasures. That ideology tells us about human sexuality and its place in human society and in our individual lives.

The contraceptive ideology is that all adults are entitled to unlimited sexual activity without a live baby resulting. If we want a baby, we can have one. If we want to limit our sexual activity, that's fine too. But we are entitled to unlimited sex with only the number of live babies that we want. Although one could obviously find exceptions to this statement, and many people would deny that this what they believe, many people in our culture largely believe that they are entitled to sex without a live baby.

Obviously, this is not the only possible thing we could believe about contraception and its relationship to sexual behavior, reproduction and the rest of our lives. We might just conclude that contraception changes the odds of any sexual act resulting in a pregnancy and leave it at that. But in fact, our culture has gone much further than to incorporate the straightforward technological consequence of contraception into our personal decision-making calculus.

What made this belief possible? The U.S. Supreme Court played a key part in developing and legitimating this belief.

In *Griswold v Connecticut* (1965, 381 U.S. 479), the Supreme Court held that states could not constitutionally prohibit the flow of contraception information or the sale or use of contraceptive devices. The Court held that such prohibitions are unacceptable invasions of marital privacy. Contrary to widespread belief about this case, however, the Court specifically declined to find a right to use contraceptives. Instead, the Court simply held that the many goods of marital intimacy are damaged by exposure to others. The enforcement of the prohibition on marital contraception would expose the married couple to the scrutiny of outsiders, which would harm the relationship in ways the Court thought excessive (Bradley 2000, 732).

Obviously, *Griswold v Connecticut* does not, and cannot change the ultimate connection between sexual intercourse and pregnancy. That relationship is what it is due to nature's design. The link between pregnancy and sexual intercourse, while straightforward, is and has always been a roll of the dice. Sometimes intercourse results in a pregnancy, sometimes it doesn't. People have been taking their chances since time immemorial. A man might try to persuade himself and his partner with logic like this: "Come on honey, let's roll in the hay. I'll pull out in time, honest." A woman's version of a similar attempt to beat the odds might be something like this: "I won't get pregnant. Not today. It can't happen to me." And so forth. Improved contraception information and technology just allows people to roll the dice on slightly different terms.

Notice that I don't say, "on more favorable terms." Contraception changes the probability of pregnancy, of course; that is its purpose. But no contraception reduces the probability of pregnancy from a given sex act all the way to zero. Moreover, the use of any contraceptive method potentially changes other things about the couple's relationship and the sexual act itself. Some kinds of contraception interrupt the spontaneity of the sexual act. Some contraception methods have medical side effects, usually for the woman. If the use of contraception unambiguously improved the terms of sexual activity, everyone would use it all the time, for every act of intercourse. But some people decline to use it, for a variety of reasons that seem good to them. Therefore, if we say that contraception allows people to "roll the dice on improved terms," we are prejudging the situation to assume that reducing the probability of pregnancy is always and everywhere people's overriding concern. It is more neutral, and more fair, simply to say, contraception "changes the terms," rather than contraception "improves the terms."

If allowing people to change the terms on which they have sex is all that we held about sex and contraception, it would be an intellectually defensible position. But the social norms and constitutional interpretation around sex and conception have morphed into something quite different. The 1972 case, *Eisenstadt v Baird*, was crucial in this transformation.

This case disaggregated the married couple into an association of two individuals and found an individual right to obtain and use contraceptives. "Whatever the rights of the individual to access to contraceptives may be, the rights must be the same for the married and unmarried alike." It was this decision that covered immense social and legal ground in creating the illusion of reproductive freedom. The Court said,

> The marital couple . . . is an association of two individuals each with a separate intellectual and emotional makeup. If the right of privacy means anything, it is the right to be free from unwarranted government intrusions into matters so fundamentally affecting a person as the decision whether to bear or beget a child. (*Eisenstadt v. Baird* 1972, 405 U.S. 438, 453)

This statement by the Court exaggerates what any government is in a position to guarantee. Legal impediments to the flow of information may amount to "unwarranted government intrusion," into an admittedly very personal decision. However, allowing people full access to information is not the same thing as completely removing all barriers to the personal decision of "whether to bear or beget a child." All the information in the world about the most sophisticated forms of contraception does not assure that a person, either married or single, will be able to fulfill their reproductive plans. Contraception sometimes fails. People sometimes use it incorrectly, or intermittently. In these cases, the person's "decision" to avoid conception will not be fully realized. It is not any state interference, warranted or unwarranted, that thwarted the person's "decision," but simply the probabilistic connection between sexual activity, contraception and conception.

So it does not follow that we have a "right" to sexual activity, without conception. Nor did the Court discover such a right, although its language in *Eisenstadt* might mislead people into drawing the conclusion that such a right exists. It is a "right" that the state is not in a position to guarantee. The only way avoiding unwanted pregnancy while being sexually active is to have unlimited access to abortion. This is the only way the state could guarantee the right to have sex without having a live baby. Perhaps it is not surprising that *Roe v. Wade* followed a mere year after the *Eisenstadt* decision.

This is the illusory entitlement that the Supreme Court's jurisprudence on contraception created. People believe that an active sexual life, without the complication of unwanted children, is a good and desirable thing. We feel ourselves cheated if our desire for sexual activity is compromised by the undesired outcome of pregnancy. People have come to believe themselves entitled to unlimited sexual activity, without a live baby resulting.

Thus, the sea change in creating the contraceptive culture was more than simply the availability of the birth control pill. While it is certainly true that the availability of the Pill made the sexual revolution possible, the Pill did not necessarily make it inevitable. It was the legitimation and promotion of a particular set of ideas about the meaning and purposes of sexuality, and the meaning and purposes of freedom that propelled the whole sexual revolution. We have choices about how to utilize our knowledge of woman's fertility, her hormonal activity and our pharmaceutical skill, just as we have choices about how to use any technological knowledge. We still have those choices and we can make them differently. We need not continue to be in thrall to the Ideology of Contraception.

IMPACT ON RELATIONSHIPS BETWEEN MEN & WOMEN

The use of contraceptives has made sexual intercourse independent of parenthood, and the marriage of the future will be confined to those who seek parenthood for its own sake rather than as the natural fulfillment of sexual love. But under these circumstances who will trouble to marry? Marriage will lose all attraction for the young and the pleasure-loving and the poor and the ambitious. The energy of youth will be devoted to contraceptive love and only when men and women have become prosperous and middle-aged will they think of seriously settling down to rear a strictly limited family. (Dawson 1933)

CHANGING THE NORMS AROUND NON-MARITAL SEX AND CHILD-BEARING

Contraceptive ideology is only one part of the contraceptive culture. The relationships between men and women are changed in significant ways by the widespread use of contraception and the availability of abortion. These changes do not just affect the individuals who choose to use the technology. Contraceptive technology changes the terms on which everyone participates in the dating and mating game, even if they decline to use the technology. George Akerlof (Nobel Prize winning economist) and his colleagues provide a framework for discussion (Akerlof, et al. 1996). When sexual activity has a high probability of resulting in pregnancy, society develops a set of cultural norms for inducing men to commit to women they impregnate and their child. These norms, largely if informally enforced by women, include a strong social expectation that women will refuse sex outside of marriage. Women develop a set of socially acceptable ways to refuse sex, even with a man she genuinely likes. The norms also include the expectation that the man will marry a woman he impregnates. All these norms are designed to discourage casual sex and encourage fathers to commit to mothers.

When low-cost, highly effective contraception is introduced, these cultural norms no longer serve the same purpose and are likely to fade. A woman can not so easily refuse sex on the grounds that she might get pregnant: the probability of pregnancy is lower. A man can make birth control and sex the price of being in a relationship with him. Men can more easily find an alternative partner if she refuses. So even women who might ordinarily be inclined to abstain from pre-marital sex will find themselves under pressure to be sexually active, not only from men, but indirectly, from other women.

However, since no contraception is fool-proof, some pregnancies will still occur. What are the social norms about what people do about these unintended pregnancies? Akerlof and his colleagues argue that women are in a much worse position to insist that the man marry her.

As the social expectations shift toward permitting non-marital sex, women's bargaining power decreases. Akerlof and colleagues observe the decline of the "shotgun wedding" coincides with the introduction of birth control and abortion availability. As they put it, "The sexual revolution, by making the birth of the child the *physical* choice of the mother, makes marriage and child support a *social* choice of the father" (Akerlof 1996, 281).

If sex commonly results in pregnancy, women can refuse sex unless they receive an implicit or explicit promise of marriage in the event of pregnancy. As the connection between each sexual act and pregnancy weakens, women are less able to extract a promise of marriage in the event of pregnancy. If she asks for a promise, there is a high probability the man will exit the relationship and find someone who does not ask for a marriage promise. The "social compact" among women breaks down with even a small number of women who are willing to abort their children rather than carry a non-marital, unintended pregnancy to term.

Look at it this way. Women who are willing to terminate an unplanned pregnancy, will not ask the man for a promise to marry in the event of pregnancy: she considers abortion a simpler solution to her "problem" of an accidental pregnancy. Women who really want motherhood will keep the baby, even if the man refuses to marry her. Men presumably know this, so her attempts to persuade him to marry her are not credible. Therefore, in the presence of legalized abortion as a back-up to contraceptive failure, women will not insist on a promise of marriage in the event of unplanned pregnancy. To put it even more starkly, no woman will be in a position to demand such a promise, since there is no credible threat of social stigma or sanction that she can impose on him. The social norm that insists that men marry women they impregnate erodes quite quickly.

At the same time, we can see that this scenario of cheap contraception and abortion leads not only to an increase in sexual activity and abortion, but also to an increase in out-of-wedlock births. This was, in a sense, the puzzle of contraception. Why should low cost contraception lead to more children being born in less desirable, more difficult circumstances, namely out-of-wedlock, when the ability to prevent and terminate pregnancy increases?

It is precisely because so many women actually want babies. Many women want their babies, and don't want to have abortions. In bygone eras, these women would have had the support of the entire society in pressuring the father to marry them. But since having a baby is a "woman's choice," that pressure is greatly attenuated.

So, the overall birth rate has declined, the proportion of women married has declined and the proportion of babies born outside of wedlock has increased. From 1965 to 1989, the birth rate per thousand married white women declined from 119 per thousand to 90, while the birth rate per thousand unmarried white women doubled from 12 to 24 births per thousand over the same time period. At the same time, percentage of white women who married declined from 68% to 58%. The percentage of "shotgun marriages" declined from 60% to 42% for whites, while the ratio of adoptions to out-of-wedlock births declined from 49% to 20%.

In short, for women who had non-marital pregnancies, more kept the child to raise themselves. Fewer mothers married the father of the child or placed the child for adoption (Akerlof, et al 1996, 277-317, Tables I & II). The overall result is that fewer children are raised in married couple, two parent households. This is the family form most conducive to the welfare of children (Morse 2005, 19-43; George et al 2006).

TAKING SEX LESS SERIOUSLY

In addition to all this, contraception reduces the seriousness with which people take the sexual act. A sexual partner is not likely to become a partner for life, but only for an evening hook-up. It is not thought to be necessary to consider potential partners carefully in this environment. If you are unsure of the truth of this statement, I invite you to ask the following question of anyone you know who is engaged in a non-marital sexual relationship. "Would you be having a sexual relationship with this person if you thought there were a high probability of conceiving a child with them?" In many cases the person will say, not only "No," but "No Way."

So contraception does not just help married couples time and space their children. The contraceptive culture permits and even encourages sex that has no future. There are several problems with this recreational approach to sex. First, it takes up time and space that could be used by more mature sex. Women do not have forever to engage in procreative sex. Their fertility is limited. In effect, women are wasting time with recreational sex. I will discuss this more below.

Second, our bodies bond with each other during the sex act, whether we are serious about the other person or not. Cohabitation is a specific example of people not taking sex seriously (Morse 2005). Contraception makes the cohabitation option a more viable choice. A person can slide into living with someone, a few sleep-overs at a time, moving a few possessions in at a time. In an environment in which conceiving a child was likely, not many people would make the casual choice to live together.

Unfortunately, living together is not as good an option as it often appears. Cohabitation is not good preparation for marriage. Married couples whose marriages are preceded by cohabitation are more likely to get divorced (Krishnan1998). In addition, cohabitation increases the probability of divorce, and parental divorce increases the probability of cohabitation (Amato1996)

The idea that a couple can live together on a trial basis, so they can make an informed choice about whether they are right for each other turns out to be completely mistaken. We naturally attach to our sexual partners. Women attach through a hormone called oxytocin, which induces her to relax and connect with her sex partner. Male attachment tends to show up as possessiveness or jealousy, but can develop into loyalty, even heroic loyalty. This attachment process means that couples who live together, sleep together and are sexual with each other, attach to each other whether they are right for each other or not (Morse 2005, 44-58).

Finally, the most ironic fact about cohabitation is that the failure rate of contraception is higher among couples living together than any other group. Holding constant the age of the woman, the method of contraception, and broad income categories, cohabiting couples who say they are using contraception, experience a much higher failure rate than any other group. I suspect that many couples seriously underestimate this probability of contraceptive failure when they move in together (Fu, et al 1999). If they had more accurate information on this point, they might be more cautious about living together.

EARLY INITIATION OF SEXUAL ACTIVITY

One of the results of the introduction of the Pill and the ideology associated with it is the early initiation of sexual activity. In 1965, only 29 percent of college age freshmen females reported having had premarital intercourse, by 1985 that percentage had more than doubled to 63% (Robinson et al 1991, 216-220). Similarly, 14% of women reported having some sexual experience prior to age 16 in 1965. By 1989, that percentage had more than doubled to 33% (Akerlof et al 1996, 277-317, Table II). Let's trace some of the negative consequences of this change (Rector et al 2003).

• Girls who began sexual activity at age 13 are twice as likely to become infected by an STD as girls who started sexual activity after age 21.

• Nearly 40% of girls who commence sexual activity at ages 13 or 14 will give birth outside marriage. By contrast, only 9% of women who begin sexual activity in their twenties will give birth outside marriage.

• Women who become sexually active at age 13 or 14 are more than three times more likely to become single parents than are women who commence sexual activity in their early twenties.

• Girls who initiated sexual activity at ages 13 or 14 were less than half as likely to be in stable marriages in their thirties, when compared with women who began sex in their early twenties.

• Early sexual activity is linked to higher levels of child and maternal poverty.

The link between early sexual activity and higher probabilities of pregnancy can be partially explained by the fact that contraceptive failure is a function of age. That is, women are more likely to experience a contraceptive failure, the younger they are. This means that contrary to much popular opinion, contraceptive availability is no panacea against pregnancy, given early initiation of sexual activity.

For instance, consider the rate of contraceptive failure for the pill, widely considered the most reliable of all the reversible, non-long-acting contraceptive methods. The failure rate of the pill is 13% for poor married women under the age of 20, and declines to just under half that rate to 5.7%, for married poor women over 30. The age-specific failure rate is even more dramatic for cohabiting, but not married couples: for poor cohabiting women under age 20, the failure rate of the Pill is 48%, while for poor cohabiting women over age 30, the failure rate is a mere 10.8% (Fu et al 1999, 56-63, Table 2).

The link between early sexual activity and lower probability of successful marriage is in part, explained by the increased number of sexual partners. Multiple sexual partners prior to marriage is not good preparation for happy married life. People practice the "use and be used" or the "catch and release" philosophy of sexual relationships. People become jaded.

And of course, the higher probability of contracting STD's is related to the higher exposure. Having more sexual activity increases one's risk. So does having a larger number of partners. With or without successful contraception, increased sexual activity with multiple partners is a risk factor. Many of the most effective contraceptives, such as implants and the Pill, do not even claim to reduce exposure to STD's. Taken together, it is hardly surprising that the early initiation of sexual activity is associated with increased probability of contracting STD's.

THE DISRUPTION TO THE NATURAL RHYTHMS OF A WOMAN'S BODY

"DISAPPOINTED FERTILITY AMBITIONS"

It is safe to say that contraception is a key factor in the expansion of women's labor force participation at higher and more steady levels. The ability to postpone pregnancy without forgoing sex has made it possible for women to invest in more demanding careers, requiring more sophisticated training and deeper commitment to the labor force. At the same time, those same women can enjoy an active sex life without committing to a particular partner. The age at first marriage has risen steadily since 1965(Goldin and Katz 2002).

Most commentators treat this as an unambiguous good for women. Women have higher earning power, and more independence. More women are using their intellectual gifts in the paid workforce. So let us concede that contraception made possible the increase in education, career attainment and delay of marriage. I would argue that these are not an unambiguous goods in at least two senses. First, there are costs associated with these changes. An honest assessment of the impact of the pill needs to take these costs into account. Second, I argue that there are other ways for women to increase their investments in education and labor force participation. Some of the gains attributed to contraception could be attained by other means.

Women are rightly celebrated for having entered the labor force and succeeded in a man's world, largely on a man's terms. I agree with that assessment. But I believe that is the problem: the typical career path is geared toward the needs of men, not women. Many high-powered careers require intense investment in education at the beginning of one's working life. Pursuing a graduate or professional degree requires years of post-graduate education. Getting established in a career requires intense work for long hours. Career advancement may also require a willingness to travel or even relocate at the drop of a hat.

A few career paths are highly structured in an "up or out" fashion. If a person does not achieve a certain level of performance, they are not only passed over for advancement, they are kicked unceremoniously out of the organization. Getting tenure in a university has this structure. So does making partner in a professional firm.

The problem with this is that all this investment is required at exactly the time when women are at their peak fertility. Because they have jumped on the career ladder as established and maintained by generations of men, women's career ambitions are in conflict with their fertility ambitions, if they have any. Women who are ambitious for career advancement have to invest in education and career establishment when their bodies are ready to be investing in children. By the time they are "ready" socially and economically, their bodies are past being ready.

For many women in the first generation of high powered careers, fertility difficulties came as a rude awakening. They assumed they would be able to "have it all," literally. But there may be no good solution to a mid-life fertility crisis, particularly if the woman has not invested in finding a partner and maintaining a relationship with him. These women are extremely disappointed.

In 1998-99, Sylvia Ann Hewlett conducted a survey of high-achieving women, hoping to assess the factors responsible for their success. In the course of that survey, she noticed that *none of these women had children.* As she talked more with them, she discovered that *none of them had chosen to be childless.* That pair of observations led her to the research that resulted in her justly celebrated book, *Creating a Life: Professional Woman and the Quest for Children* (Hewlett 2002).

In a more systematic survey, she found that 33% of high-achieving women are childless at age 40. Among women in "Corporate America," defined as companies with over 5,000 employees, 42% of high-achieving women are childless at age 40. She also found that the vast majority of these women did not choose to be childless. Looking back on their early twenties, only 14% said they definitely did not want children. Among those women who did have children, a fourth of them wanted more children than they were ultimately able to have (Hewlett 2002, 86). Surely, these disappointed fertility ambitions must count for something in the calculus of career-advancement, claimed by contraception advocates as an unmixed good.

Many women believe that the combination of infertility treatments and adoptions will allow them to safely delay childbearing. However, these hopes may be misplaced. Hewlett found that 21% of high-achieving women in the 28-40 age group have themselves experienced infertility problems. But 89% of these women believe they will be able to get pregnant in their forties (Hewlett 2002, 89). Although adoption is a possible solution to infertility, women underestimate the difficulties of an older woman raising a possibly disturbed child, particularly if she is unmarried and must raise the child herself.

Not only is women's fertility compromised by delay, but her behavior and habits may change in ways that are unfavorable to motherhood. Ambitious women are asked to be aggressive and competitive at a time in their lives when their bodies cry out for reproduction and nurturing. According to Hewlett's surveys, many of the high-achieving women have spent years "hurting and being hurt."

There are so many high-income, high-achieving women who want to get married, that there is now a lively market for coaching women successfully toward that goal. The president of an organization called Lifeworks gives women an opening pep talk: "You may not know it, but you've developed a thick suit of armor that makes you cold and unapproachable." Another Lifeworks executive says, "A typical participant in one of our courses is a business executive who forgot to make time for a personal life. And between you and me, these are very prickly women. They've been wearing pants too long. Men like powerful women, but they don't want to be eaten alive." (Hewlett 2002, 163-166). Women come to these courses because they want to get married and have children. But the very traits that allowed them to be successful in their career-driven lifestyle actively hinder them in being successful in marriage and family.

AN ALTERNATIVE WAY TO 'HAVE IT ALL'

Contraception made it possible to postpone childbearing. Unfortunately, many women have unrealistic ideas about the costs of postponing childbearing: her reduced fertility and the changes to her own temperament. A more realistic way for women to use their educations and have careers is to spread her goals over her lifetime.

Women mature faster and succeed in school earlier. Women also live longer. We can take advantage of these facts to structure society so that women can completer their educations earlier than men, get married and have their babies while they are still young, fertile and energetic enough to enjoy them. After their fertility is completed, they can re-enter the workforce either as employees or as entrepreneurs. Women entrepreneurs, even high-achieving entrepreneurs, are more successful at combining career and childbearing than women in the highly structured labor market of corporate America. Only 22% of self-employed high-achieving women are childless, compared with 42% of high-achieving women in corporate America (Hewlett 2002, 89-90).

But to allow women to have children now and career later, society has to be structured around that goal. At least two things need to change. First, we need to change our idea of what counts as "pro-woman" labor market policies. Under the influence of Marxist feminism, we have structured society around their demands that the incomes men and women be equal at every point in their life cycles. So-called family friendly polices actually demand that women continue to work as nearly uninterrupted as possible. By contrast, policies that enhance adaptability to woman's changing needs over her life-cycle are more authentically pro-woman.

Second, we need to change our cultural attitude and social policies toward marriage. "Having it all eventually," requires that marriages be stable. For women to stay home with children, they have to believe that their husbands will not abandon them for a younger bride. For men to invest in a stay at home wife for his children, they have to believe that their wives will not leave him in a no-fault divorce, take the children and move in with another man. The current divorce law and the contraceptive culture reinforce each other.

Finally, we need to see the extremely unrealistic demands of that the pro-Career Woman, anti-child advocates have made on women. These self-styled advocates of women insist that work is the only place for an intelligent woman. If women insist on wasting themselves in motherhood, they should certainly only have one child. Any more than one child will certainly disrupt the all-important working life (see Hirschmann 2005). It goes without saying that this attitude would be impossible without contraception.

But look at how completely unrealistic this attitude is. These advocates are asking women to assume that work is their normal way of life and that motherhood is an unwarranted intrusion and disruption of that life. But what if one of your children is needy? Or your spouse becomes ill? Or a parent becomes ill? No one can safely assume that none of these problems will ever emerge in life. In fact, it is much safer to assume that eventually, they will. It is not realistic to think that a woman and the income she earns can manage all these things all by herself. Planning to have a working, on-going partnership with a husband is a much more realistic life plan, and one that does not seem to occur to our feminist champions.

THE SOCIAL CONSEQUENCES OF POSTPONING CHILDREN

"SMALLER NUMBER OF CHILDREN"

One of the key problems of declining fertility is the impact upon social insurance programs. The Social Security program, the Medicare program and now the prescription drug benefit, are taxpayer supported programs for the elderly. When the first of these programs was initiated in the 1930's, the birth rate was higher than it is now. One of the earliest economic justifications for the plan was that it was a good deal for all taxpayers, even though it was a "pay-as-you-go" program. It was a good deal if the birth rate was higher than the real rate of return on capital. Since the real rate of return on capital was historically something like 2%, responsible people thought that the growth rate of the population could support Social Security long term. Little did they realize that the birth rate was about to collapse.

Social Security is often described as the Third Rail of Politics. But I think that behind the Third Rail of Social Security is the *Real Third Rail* a subject so toxic, no one even wants to think about it. But if we could deal with this forbidden topic, the Social Security problem would largely solve itself.

That Real Third Rail, of course, is fertility. No one wants to mention that the insolvency of the Social Security system is a fertility crisis at least as much as a fiscal crisis. It is considered rude to mention that the collapse in the fertility levels, particularly striking among the most gifted women in society, is a contributing factor to the insolvency of our entitlement programs.

The total fertility rate peaked in 1957 at 3.68 babies per woman. Today, our fertility rate hovers right around the replacement rate of 2.1. The fertility of college educated non-Hispanic white women is now around 1.7 (Kotlikoff and Burns 2005, 19-22). Since these are the women whose children are most likely to become productive taxpaying citizens, their fall in fertility takes a particularly large toll on the future taxes paid into the Social Security system.

When Social Security was established, people got married and stayed married for a lifetime. Most women stayed home and raised children. At the end of their lifetimes, most married couples were still together.

In effect, both spouses made contributions to the Social Security system. The husband paid taxes. The wife raised children. When the family collected the pension, based on the husband's income, both spouses shared it.

As most people now realize, however, the husband's taxes don't go into a little account with his name on it. Those taxes go to pay the benefits of the currently retired generation. The children, raised by the wife, become the taxpayers who actually make the contributions which support the parents in their old age.

Today, the contraceptive culture is so far advanced that it is considered politically incorrect to mention the obvious contribution of motherhood. Feminism taught us to believe that motherhood is for ninnies, and that no self-respecting educated woman should be caught dead changing diapers. Public policies to encourage women to have more children are considered unacceptable infringements on women's freedom.

The most needed reform is that benefits should be based on both kinds of contributions, not just the financial contribution (see Longman 2004, 172-75). People who never have a child can still collect the taxes paid by other people's children. Ditto for people whose children are all losers, spend a lifetime "finding themselves" and never hold a job. The Social Security of the 1930's took for granted women's contribution of raising productive adult children. The result is fewer children: economists Isaac Ehrlich and Jian-Guo Zhong found that countries with generous social security systems have lower fertility rates, marriage rates and higher divorce rates (Ehrlich and Zhong 1998, 151-57). But these reforms, completely sensible from a fiscal point of view, are considered unmentionable in polite political company.

"FEWER CHILDREN GROW UP WITH SIBLINGS"

One of the obvious problems of declining fertility is that fewer children grow up with siblings. The sibling relationship is the most egalitarian of all the kinship relationships, witness the French Revolution slogan of "liberty, equality and fraternity." Brotherhood fits in with a basically egalitarian society in a way that fatherhood really doesn't.

Specifically, children with siblings learn sharing and cooperation in a way that only children do not. Children with siblings have each other. And parents of only children often become pre-occupied with that child in a way that can not be healthy for either the child or the parent.

Especially in large families, the children have a way of creating their own child-space that excludes adults to some extent. The children can plan and plot and scheme against the parents, while the parents for their part, look on with amusement. And, coincidently, the parents create a child-free space between the two of them. It is far better for children for their parents to have some space in their relationship that does not include them. It is not in the child's interest to be brought up into one adult's relationship and displace the relationship with the other parent. Having siblings is no guarantee against this particular pathology of course. But being an only child does increase its likelihood.

"LARGE GAP BETWEEN GENERATIONS"

Another problem with postponing childbearing is the increasing gap between generations. This can be a problem, independent of the number of children, but in fact, postponing usually involves a smaller family size. The large gap between generations, so common today, means that the family has two dependent generations at the same time: the elderly and the infant.

If a woman has her first child at forty, and her daughter does the same thing, the mother will be eighty when her daughter has her first child. That means the daughter will have an infant and elderly parents at the same time.

This in turn, can only mean impersonal or institutional care for the dependents. The family will not have enough members in the prime of their lives to take good, personal care of grandma, right at the time the new baby is born. The baby will be in day care or grandma will be in a nursing home, whether the family chooses it or not. There aren't enough hands on deck to deal with it. By contrast, if women have their children between the ages of 25 and 35, the kids will be out of diapers by the time the elderly parents need care.

Another problem of large gaps in the generations in that young people have positions of responsibility before they are parents. They are less likely to understand the concerns and needs of parents and children. Much of the entertainment business suffers from this defect. For instance, the creators of most video games are unmarried men, who have no clue about responsibilities and challenges parents face. Without the contraceptive culture, many of these men would have already been fathers, and would have developed a very different idea about what constitutes appropriate entertainment for the young.

CONCLUSION

I call this paper "The Cultural Contradictions of Contraception." It is now time to spell out these contradictions as explicitly as possible. On the one hand, contraception makes possible the widespread early initiation of sexual activity, as well as an increase in non-marital sexual activity. On the other hand, this has not been accompanied by the natural consequence of sex, which is babies. So everyone, male and female, young and old, is stimulated to do what the body does, namely to think about sex and have sex, without ever following through and experiencing what the sex drive is supposed to produce, namely a new baby and an increased connection between the parents.

On the one hand, contraception was supposed to "level the playing field" between men and women, by making it possible for women to compete on equal terms in the market place. On the other hand, contraception has produced incredible competitive pressure on women to compete in the market place and ignore or denigrate the home front. A couple of eighteen year olds who want to get married and stay married, who want to have children and have the mother care for them, this couple is at an extreme disadvantage in our modern world.

The gender equality created by contraception is only in the market place. Contraception makes it possible for women to "choose" to be childless or to have few children. But it cannot make it possible for women to "choose" to have more children or many children, once they have exercised their right to postpone childbearing until their thirties. It makes men and marriage seem less necessary. By giving women the "choice" to control their sexuality, it may create a "non-choice" in which women live increasingly alone, unattached or only weakly attached.

For all these reasons, the impact of contraception on society is a question that deserves serious attention. We should no longer assume that the widespread availability and social acceptability of artificial birth control has been an unambiguous good.

SOURCES CONSULTED

Akerlof, George A., Yellen, Janet L. and Katz, Michael L. May 1996. An Analysis of Out-of-Wedlock Childbearing in the United States. *Quarterly Journal of Economics* 111 (2): 277-317.

Amato, Paul R. August 1996. Explaining the Intergenerational Transmission of Divorce. *Journal of Marriage and the Family* 58 (3): 628-640.

Bradley, Gerard V. 2000. Same-Sex Marriage: Our Final Answer? *Notre Dame Journal of Law, Ethics and Public Policy* 14 (2): 732.

Dawson, Christopher. 1933. *The Dynamics of World History*. New York: Sheed and Ward.

Eisenstadt v. Baird. 1972. 405 U.S. 438, 453.

Ehrlich, Isaac and Zhong, Jian-Guo. May 1998. Social Security and the Real Economy: An Inquiry into Some Neglected Issues. *American Economic Review: Papers and Proceedings.* 88 (2): 151-57.

Fu, Haishan, Darroch, Jacqueline, Haas,Taylor and Ranjit, Nlini. 1999. Contraceptive Failure Rates: New Estimates from the 1995 National Survey of Family Growth. *Family Planning Perspectives* 31(2): 56-63.

George, Robert P. and Elshtain, Jean Bethke. Eds. 2006. *The Meaning of Marriage: Family, State, Market and Morals.* Dallas: Spence Publishing.

Goldin, Claudia and Katz, Lawrence F. 2002. The Power of the Pill: Oral Contraceptives and Women's Career and Marriage Decisions. *Journal of Political Economy.* 110 (4): 730-770.

Griswold v. Connecticut. 1965. 381 U.S. 479.

Hewlett, Sylvia Ann. 2002. *Creating a Life: Professional Woman and the Quest for Children.* New York: Talk Miramax Books.

Hirschmann, Linda. December 2005. Homeward Bound. *The American Prospect* at: http://www.prospect.org/web/page.ww?section=root&name =ViewWeb&articleId=10659

_____. 2006. *Get to Work: A Manifesto for the Women of the World.* New York: Viking Press.

Kotlikoff, Laurence J. and Burns, Scott. 2005. *The Coming Generational Storm: What You Need to Know about America's Economic Future.* Cambridge MA: MIT Press.

Krishnan, Vijaya. 1998. Premarital Cohabitation and Marital Disruption. *Journal of Divorce and Remarriage* 28 (3-4): 157-170.

Longman, Phillip. 2004. *The Empty Cradle: How Falling Birthrates Threaten World Prosperity and what to do about it.* New York: Basic Books.

Morse, Jennifer Roback. 2005. *Smart Sex: Finding Life-long Love in a Hook-up World.* Dallas: Spence Publishing.

Rector, Robert, Johnson, Kirk, Noyes, Lauren and Martin, Shannan. 2003. *The Harmful Effects of Early Sexual Activity and Multiple Sexual Partners among Women.* Washington DC: The Heritage Foundation.

Robinson, Ira, et al. 1991. Twenty Years of the Sexual Revolution, 1965-1985: An Update. *Journal of Marriage and the Family* 53: 216-220.

THE OXFORD CONCEPTION
STUDY METHODS OVERVIEW

CECILIA PYPER, LISE BROMHALL, SARAH DUMMETT,
DOUGLAS G. ALTMAN, PAT BROWNBILL &
MICHAEL F.G. MURPHY

No randomized, controlled trials have investigated whether couples who are provided with information about the woman's fertile time will change their sexual behavior and increase their likelihood of achieving a pregnancy. Therefore, there was a need for a large trial that collected precise markers of the fertile time and accurate information about intercourse patterns in order to address this question. We recognized that such a study would have the potential of also clarifying further the findings from smaller prospective observational studies regarding factors affecting fertility (e.g., Wilcox et al. 1995, 2000; Dunson et al. 1999; Gnoth et al. 2003).

The Oxford Conception Study is a randomized, controlled trial designed to investigate whether information about the potential fertile time will increase the conception rate in women wishing to conceive. Three different versions of a fertility monitor were developed for the study. The monitor measures urinary estrogen metabolites (estrone-3-glucuronide, or E3G) and luteinizing hormone (LH). The monitor display indicates high or low fertility.

One third of women were randomly assigned to receive information from the fertility monitor about the early fertile time, one third received information about the late fertile time, and one third did not receive any information from the fertility monitor but still did all the urine tests (the last group was the control group).

The study commenced at the end of 2002. Recruitment was finalized in January 2006. A total of 1,453 women were recruited into the study. All the women tested their urine on days 6 through

25 of the menstrual cycle. All the women were followed up for six cycles or until they were pregnant, whichever came first. The design and recruitment experience of the trial have been described in more depth in a previous paper, (Pyper et al. 2006).

The primary analysis will compare the pregnancy rates between each of the groups of women but other pregnancy outcomes are measured. The data from this study will allow many additional factors that may affect fertility to be assessed, including patterns of sexual intercourse and changes in intercourse patterns with feedback about the fertile days; menstrual cycle function; stress; exposure to tobacco products, alcohol, caffeine, and medications. Time-specific conception probabilities will also be estimated from sexual intercourse information recorded in 12-hour intervals.

INTRODUCTION

A large amount of research has focused on the study of reduced fertility—also known as "subfertility"—and its treatment, while less research has focused on investigating behavioural and lifestyle factors that influence fertility, such as patterns of sexual intercourse and changes in intercourse patterns with feedback about the fertile days; menstrual cycle function; stress; exposure to tobacco products, alcohol, caffeine, and medications. While most reproductive health promotion is targeted at avoiding unintended pregnancies, investigations that address avoiding unintended subfertility or infertility are often neglected. In the United Kingdom, the National Health Service is allowing limited access to fertility treatments to couples with subfertility problems. Many of these treatments and services use intensive resources. It is, therefore, important to target those limited services to couples who require it, while the couples who require only behavioral and lifestyle changes can make those changes on their own without using National Health Service treatments. The data from this study will help to determine whether behavioral or lifestyle changes are likely to alter the time taken for a couple to achieve a pregnancy.

In a literature review carried out in 2002, Stanford et al. reviewed the markers of fertility, including basal body temperature, calendar-based calculations, cervical secretions, and hormone measurement in urine. They stated that measuring basal body temperature is of little value to couples trying to conceive because it is a retrospective and imprecise marker of ovulation. They also stated that the calendar calculation is an inaccurate marker because many women have greater cycle variability than is accommodated by a calculation. They stated that, although cervical secretions are more accurate in identifying the fertile time, they require an educational intervention. Stanford et al. also suggested that devices that measure only luteinizing hormone (LH) may not identify the days of highest probability of conception. However, devices that measure estrone-3-glucuronide (E3G), a metabolite of estrogen, together with LH in the urine identify the complete fertile time accurately and are easy to use.

Public information leaflets, such as WellBeing of Women's "Preparing for Pregnancy" (WellBeing of Women 2004), urge couples to "make love at least every other day, especially during the 'fertile' time of the month." The Royal College of Obstetricians and -Gynaecologists guidelines for conception currently state, "People who are concerned about their fertility should be informed that sexual intercourse every 2 to 3 days optimises the chance of pregnancy. Timing intercourse to coincide with ovulation causes stress and is not recommended." (Royal College of Obstetrician-Gynaecologists 1998). An "every other day" strategy is well above the national average for sexual intercourse. A survey conducted by the National Centre for Social Research in 1990 found that the average frequency of intercourse was 5.8 times per month, with reduced intercourse frequency as age increased (Johnson et al. 1994).

This is the background to the trial we conducted.

METHODS

TRIAL DESIGN

The trial had three groups. The women were randomly assigned, in equal numbers, to the two intervention groups and the control group. Each group received different information from the fertility monitor, as illustrated in Figure 1:

> 1. For the late fertile time group, the monitor displayed high fertility from the first appearance of urine LH and for the next two days. It then shows low fertility until the end of the menstrual cycle.

2. For the early fertile time group, the monitor displayed high fertility from the first appearance of E3G and low fertility from the first appearance of LH until the end of the menstrual cycle.

3. For the control group, the monitor revealed no information about the fertility status, although participants still performed urine tests.

Both women and their partners provided informed consent to participate in the study. Ethics approval for the Oxford Conception Study was obtained in September 2002 from the Central Oxford

Figure 1. Study flow diagram

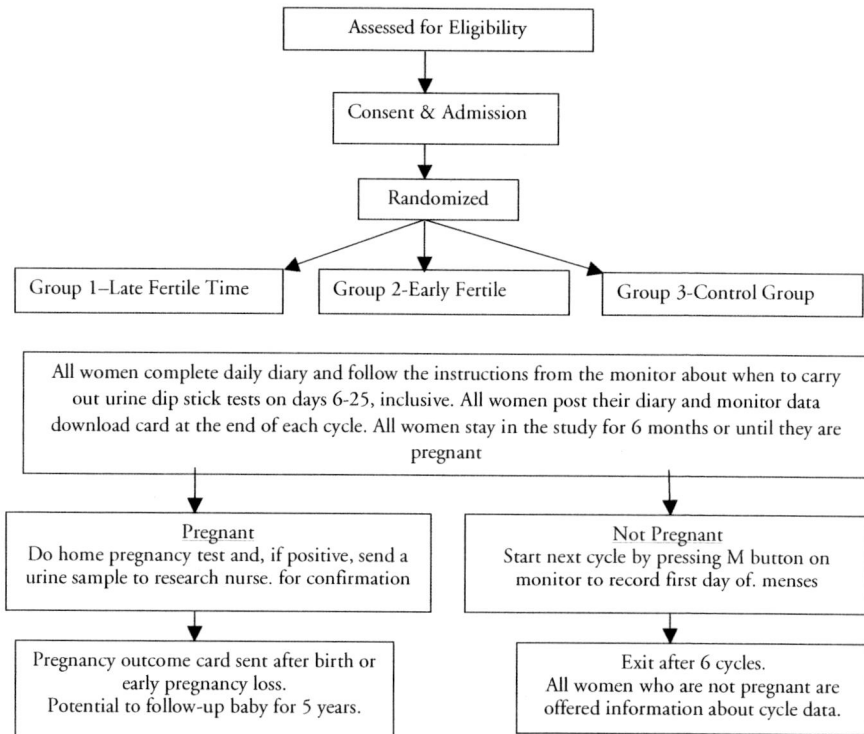

| Assessed for Eligibility |

| Consent & Admission |

| Randomized |

| Group 1–Late Fertile Time | Group 2-Early Fertile | Group 3-Control Group |

All women complete daily diary and follow the instructions from the monitor about when to carry out urine dip stick tests on days 6-25, inclusive. All women post their diary and monitor data download card at the end of each cycle. All women stay in the study for 6 months or until they are pregnant

Pregnant
Do home pregnancy test and, if positive, send a urine sample to research nurse. for confirmation

Not Pregnant
Start next cycle by pressing M button on monitor to record first day of. menses

Pregnancy outcome card sent after birth or early pregnancy loss.
Potential to follow-up baby for 5 years.

Exit after 6 cycles.
All women who are not pregnant are offered information about cycle data.

Ethics Committee CO1.282 (Sep 02). The study is registered as a controlled trial and can be reviewed at http://www.controlled-trials.com/ISRCTN69465542.

After randomization, all groups completed the same schedule of follow-up assessments. Women remained in the study until pregnancy or until six cycles were completed, whichever came first. There was follow-up for pregnancy outcomes.

SAMPLE SIZE

The sample size was based on the primary study objective, which was to compare the cumulative three-cycle pregnancy rate between women from the late fertile time group and the control group. After allowing for a 15% non-pregnancy dropout rate, the calculation was based on detecting a difference of 10 percentage points between the three-cycle pregnancy rate of the late fertile time group (50%) and that of the control group (40%). We calculated that a sample size of 450 women per group (1,350 women in total) was required for 80% power with a significance level of 5%.

The recruitment period was extended by 3 months to allow for additional women to be recruited into the OCS in order to take into account entrants whose data was to be excluded. Data from 125 OCS trial entrants will be excluded from the analysis. These entrants were 59 women who were already early pregnant prior to recruitment into the OCS, but were unaware of the fact at recruitment, plus 66 "re-entry events" when women who had previously been recruited into the study entered the OCS more than once, (either following a study miscarriage or planning a subsequent pregnancy.) Of those 66 "re-entry events", 59 women entered the study twice and 7 women entered the study three times. Therefore although there were a total of 1,453 entrants into the OCS, the total number of women who participated in the OCS was 1,387.

THE FERTILITY MONITOR

The study used the Clearblue Easy fertility monitor manufactured by Unipath, Ltd., in Bedford, United Kingdom. The monitor package, which is shown in Figure 2 (next page) and which was not available commercially in the United Kingdom until early 2006, consists of a handheld, battery-powered monitor and disposable urine test sticks that have been designed for use by women whose menstrual cycle normally lasts between 21 and 42 days. The fertility monitor identifies a woman's fertile period by the levels of E3G and LH in urine.

An independent study has demonstrated the accuracy of the monitor in relation to serum estradiol, serum LH, and follicular ultrasound (Behre et al. 2000).

For the purpose of this trial, the fertility monitor was modified from the commercially available system so that the daily result for potential fertility would be displayed or not displayed according to the randomised allocation. In addition all the monitors were modified to remind all the women to test their urine on 20 days of every

Figure 2. Fertility monitor

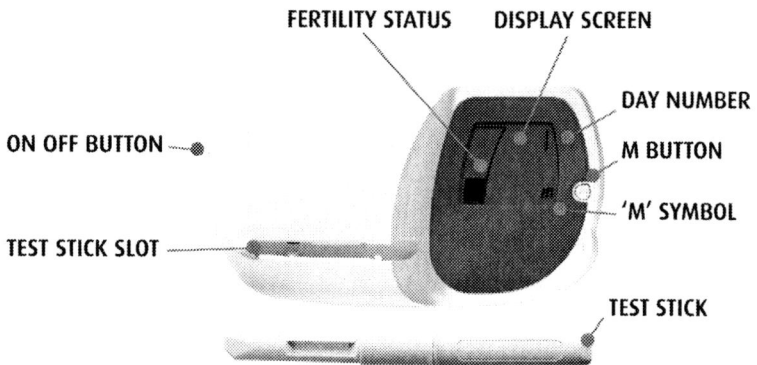

cycle, from day 6 to day 25, inclusive. For the early fertile group, the change from displaying low fertility to high fertility was triggered by the detection of elevated E3G concentrations and ended at the LH surge. For the late fertile group, the change from displaying low fertility to high fertility was triggered by the detection of the elevated LH surge and remained high for the next two days. For the control group, the monitors offered no information about fertility.

Each monitor was designed to store the serial information obtained about the E3G and LH levels over several cycles. At the end of each cycle, the women pressed the menses button and inserted a credit-card-sized data card into the monitor to download the information. The women then sent the card and their completed diary to the research centre. A data card reader and computer software enabled the information to be transferred to a computer for analysis.

ELIGIBILITY

The inclusion criteria for the Oxford Conception Study were as follows:

- Women aged 18 to 40 years who are having sexual intercourse with a regular partner

- Trying to conceive for less than three cycles

- Menstrual cycle length of 21 to 39 days for the past three cycles

- Willing to record all medication use and sexual intercourse during the study

- Willing to complete recruitment session in person or by telephone

- Willing to be randomized into one of three groups and

- Willing to have a baseline pregnancy test to ensure that they are not pregnant at entry.

The exclusion criteria for the Oxford Conception Study were as follows:

- Either partner has a history of infertility or is currently undergoing infertility treatment

- Either partner is using any form of contraception

- Woman is breastfeeding

- Woman has used hormonal contraception during the past three menstrual cycles

- Woman has used emergency contraception in the past two menstrual cycles and

- Woman has used injectable contraceptive in the past year.

The women were recruited at the time of their menses to ensure as often as possible that they were not already at an early stage of pregnancy. All of the couples enrolled and randomised had been trying to achieve a pregnancy for fewer than three cycles and had no past history of subfertility.

DATA COLLECTION

The variables recorded at admission for the couple included age; occupation; previous fertility investigations; dietary supplements; medical history; smoking; and alcohol, caffeine, and medication consumption. Additional information collected from the women included gynecologic and general medical history, contraceptive history (including last method of contraception used and time from last use of contraception), parity, weight, height, and the Hospital Anxiety and Depression (HAD) questionnaire (Bjelland et al. 2002).

During the trial the women were asked to record in a daily diary the following information: intention to conceive that cycle; days of menses; frequency of protected or unprotected intercourse in 12-hour intervals; cigarette, alcohol, and caffeine consumption; vitamins, mineral supplements, or any medication taken; and comments about any other details relevant to trying to get pregnant. The women were asked to make a daily mark for each item rather than leaving the space blank (e.g., a line to indicate no smoking, or no alcohol, or no intercourse) in order to avoid any ambiguity about missing data. In addition, all women were asked to complete the HAD questionnaires again at the end of each cycle.

All women were supplied with home pregnancy tests, which they were instructed to use if their menses were delayed. If the test was positive, they were instructed to send a urine sample to the research nurse, who performed an additional pregnancy test to confirm the pregnancy. The women who did not get pregnant after six cycles exited the study. At this stage, women in all three groups were offered additional information from their fertility monitor. This additional information was in the form of a simple graphic printout showing their E3G and LH levels and likely time of ovulation.

PLANNED ANALYSES

The primary question to be addressed was whether the pregnancy rate was higher for women in the late fertile group than for women in the control group. Conception rates were also to be compared between each of the three groups. The analysis will adjust for other characteristics and exposures, including woman's age, man's age, woman's body-mass index, alcohol or caffeine intake, and smoking.

Daily physiological conception probabilities will be estimated using two methodologies: those of Royston and Ferreira (1999), and the Bayesian methodologies described by Dunson and Weinberg (2000), and Dunson and Stanford (2005). The data from this study will allow many additional issues to be addressed, including the time-specific probabilities of clinical pregnancy in 12-hour intervals, changes in intercourse patterns with feedback about the fertile days, and other issues in relation to menstrual cycle function, sexual intercourse, other exposures, fertility, and pregnancy outcomes.

RESULTS

RECRUITMENT EXPERIENCE

The sources for recruiting couples and the rate of recruitment shifted substantially over time in response to changes in the recruiting strategy.

The recruitment strategy in 2002 was to recruit 120 to 150 couples every three months. Poster advertisements were sent to primary health care centers in Oxford. Poster advertisements were also sent to local nurseries, with requests that the staff place the posters on the notice boards. In addition, advertisements were regularly placed in local newspapers and magazines. Despite the efforts and publicity, the recruitment rates initially were lower than desired.

By mid-2003, the recruitment strategy was changed into targeted local radio advertisements. This strategy almost doubled recruitment during the first six months, but the impact was not sustained.

By the beginning of 2004, the response rate from the radio advertisements had declined. However, at this time, it was also observed that an increasing number of women were being recruited via the Internet. Therefore, from the beginning of 2004, the recruitment strategy concentrated on placing advertisements about the study on websites dedicated to information about pregnancy and babies. In addition, over time the number of women who heard of the study by word of mouth increased steadily.

The Oxford Conception Study is now fully recruited, and enrolment has closed.

Women have been recruited from all regions of the United Kingdom. In future reports from this study, the characteristics of the women will be reported in detail. The total number of 1,453 entrants into the OCS resulted in 818 pregnancies. A total of 100 pregnancies will be excluded from the main trial analysis; 59 of the pregnancies will be excluded because the women were early pregnant prior to the trial and 41 pregnancies will be excluded because the women had re-entered the study. There are therefore 718 eligible trial pregnancies. Of these women, 10 women had twin pregnancies, 156 women had an early pregnancy loss and 5 women had a late pregnancy loss. There have been 536 births, including 3 stillbirths. There has been one maternal death not related to her pregnancy. Data from 26 pregnant women is currently outstanding.

DISCUSSION

There is an expanding market in home-testing devices that claim to assist women in conceiving by monitoring their fertile time and advising couples how to target intercourse (Braat et al. 1998). Many of these devices are widely available on the Internet, but up until now, all of them have lacked clinical trial evaluation of efficacy. The Oxford Conception Study now provides a definitive epidemiologic assessment of a device which uses a mechanism that is already supported by a body of physiological research.

The Oxford Conception Study is one of the largest prospective studies of its kind, collecting detailed information on up to six menstrual cycles from 1,453 entrants, with accurate hormonal references and sexual intercourse data in 12-hour intervals. The study has sufficient power to determine whether targeting intercourse during the fertile time increases the pregnancy rate.

The Oxford Conception Study will enable more accurate estimates to be made about the precise length of the fertile interval of the menstrual cycle, which has previously been measured in days, or approximate 24-hour intervals. The data from this trial will also allow replication of many analyses made with previous prospective pregnancy studies and will be useful for addressing many issues related to menstrual cycle function, sexual behavior, day-specific probabilities of conception, fertility, and pregnancy outcomes (WellBeing of Women 2004; Johnson et al 1994; Lynch et al 2006; Buck et al 2004.)

We found that a large number of women are willing to use the Internet for enrolling in a clinical study of means to assist conception. This finding is important because the successful recruitment of volunteers is an increasingly difficult aspect of many clinical trials. The inability to recruit volunteers often causes significant delays in amassing robust evidence and in getting that new evidence translated into clinical practice. The experience of the Oxford Conception Study has been that website recruitment increased the recruitment rate efficiently, with high retention rates. Thus, the Oxford Conception Study suggests a major role for Internet-based recruiting for future studies.

Because many of our participants were Internet users, they may not be representative of all couples planning a pregnancy. We recognize that care must be taken to reach and communicate with patients from a variety of socioeconomic, educational and racial backgrounds, and that recruiting via the Internet could theoretically influence our ability to generalize our findings. Hospital-based or clinic-based trials face similar problems with regard to selection of participants and the question of whether or not they are representative, but nevertheless are regarded as providing important evidence to answer clinical questions.

ACKNOWLEDGMENTS
We thank Patrick Royston, Bill Collins, Jeff Spieler, Virginia Lamprecht, and Bill Ledger for their assistance in the study design. We thank Camilla Allbrook for her support with data management. A UK National Health Service Executive Primary Care Career Scientist Award supported the development of the study and Dr. Pyper's salary. The DLM Charitable Trust supported the salaries of the research staff. The Childhood Cancer Research Group supported development and maintenance of the study database. Unipath provided partial support for salaries of two of the research staff. The UK National Health Service research and development funding supported some recruitment from primary care.

The National Perinatal Epidemiology Unit is funded by the Department of Health in England. The views expressed in this paper are those of the authors and do not necessarily reflect the views of the Department of Health.

"The Childhood Cancer Research Group receives support from the department of Health and the Scottish Ministers", and therefore the views expressed don't necessarily reflect either of their views.

SOURCES CONSULTED

Behre, H. M., J. Kuhlage, C. Gassner, B. Sonntag, C. Schem, H. P. Schneider, and E. Nieschlag. 2000. Prediction of ovulation by urinary hormone measurements with the home use ClearPlan® Fertility Monitor. *Human Reproduction* 15(12): 2478-82.

Bjelland, I., A. A. Dahl, T. T. Haug, and D. D. Neckelmann. 2002. The validity of the Hospital Anxiety and Depression Scale: An updated literature review. *Journal of Psychosomatic Research* 52(2): 69-77.

Braat, D. D., J. M. Smeenk, A. P. Manger, C. M. Thomas, S. Veersema, and J. M. Merkus. 1998. Saliva Test as ovulation predictor. *Lancet* 352(9136): 1283-4.

Buck, G. M., C. D. Lynch, J. B. Stanford, A. M. Sweeney, L. A. Schieve, J. C. Rockett, S. G. Selevan, and S. M. Schrader. 2004. Prospective pregnancy study designs for assessing reproductive and developmental toxicants. *Environmental Health Perspectives* 112(1): 79-86.

Dunson, D. B., D. D. Baird, A. J. Wilcox, and C. R. Weinberg. 1999. Day-specific probabilities of clinical pregnancy based on two studies with imperfect measures of ovulation. *Human Reproduction* 14(7): 1835-9.

Dunson, D., and C. R. Weinberg. 2000. Modeling human fertility in the presence of measurement error. *Biometrics* 56(1): 288-92.

Dunson, D. B., and J. B. Stanford. 2005. Bayesian inferences on predictors of conception probabilities. *Biometrics* 61(1): 126-33.

Gnoth, C., D. Godehardt, E. Godehardt, P. Frank-Herrmann, and G. Freundl. 2003. Time to pregnancy: Results of the German prospective study and impact on the management of infertility. *Human Reproduction* 18(9): 1959-66.

Johnson, A., J. Wadsworth, K. Wellings, and J. Field. 1994. *Sexual Attitudes and Lifestyles*. Oxford: Blackwell Scientific Publications.

Lynch, C. D., L. W. Jackson, and G. M. B. Louis. 2006. Estimation of the day-specific probabilities of conception: Current state of the knowledge and the relevance for epidemiologic research. *Paediatric and Perinatal Epidemiology* 20(s1): 3-12.

Pyper C, Bromhall L, Dummett S, Altman DG, Brownbill P, Murphy M. The Oxford Conception Study design and recruitment experience. Paediatric and Perinatal Epidemiology 2006; 20 (Suppl. 1): 51–59.

Royal College of Obstetrician-Gynaecologists. 2004. *Fertility: assessment and treatment for people with fertility problems.* London: Royal College of Obstetrician-Gynaecologists Press.

Royston, P., and A. Ferreira. 1999. A new approach to modelling daily probability of conception. *Biometrics* 55(4): 1005-13.

Stanford, J. B., G. L. White, and H. Hatasaka. 2002. Timing intercourse to achieve pregnancy: Current evidence. *Obstetrics and Gynecology* 100(6): 1333-41.

WellBeing of Women. 2004. *Preparing for Pregnancy.* London. http://www.wellbeing.org.uk/docs/pdf/Preparing%20for%20Pregnancy_22032005.pdf, accessed April 4, 2006.

Wilcox, A. J, C. R. Weinberg, and D. D. Baird. 1995. Timing of sexual intercourse in relation to ovulation: Effects on the probability of conception, survival of the pregnancy, and sex of the baby. *New England Journal of Medicine* 333(23): 1517-21.

Wilcox, A. J., D. Dunson, and D. D. Baird. 2000. The timing of the "fertile window" in the menstrual cycle: Day specific estimates from a prospective study. *British Medical Journal* 321(7271):1259-62.

USEFULNESS OF ELECTRONIC HORMONAL FERTILITY MONITORING FOR AVOIDING PREGNANCY

RICHARD J. FEHRING

Couples wishing to achieve or avoid pregnancy can now use an electronic hormonal fertility monitor to aid home fertility monitoring. The Clearplan Easy Fertility Monitor (CPFM) is a handheld monitor designed to help couples achieve pregnancy. It provides information on three levels of fertility (low, high, and peak) based on urinary threshold levels of estrogen and luteinizing hormone (LH). The monitor can be used as an aid to avoid pregnancy when used with another marker of fertility. We conducted an efficacy study to determine the effectiveness of using the monitor along with cervical mucus monitoring with 215 couples seeking to avoid pregnancy and found a correct-use unintended pregnancy rate of 2.0% per annum and a total pregnancy rate of 13.0% per annum. These same couples rated the monitor easy to use and helpful based on a ten-item survey. Overall, the monitor is not perfect, but can be useful for couples who wish to have an objective device for fertility monitoring.

In 1990, Carl Djerassi, one of the developers of the first hormonal contraceptive pill, published an article in *Science* magazine stating that in the future there will be what he called Jet Age natural family planning (NFP) (Djerassi 1990). In the article, he described a method of NFP whereby women would be able to measure reproductive hormones in their urine to estimate the fertile phase of the menstrual cycle. Six years later, Unipath scientists introduced a handheld fertility monitor, called Persona, which was designed to read test strips impregnated with antibodies from two reproductive hormones (estrone 3 glucuronide and luteinizing hormone, i.e., E3G and LH) and provide the user with an indication of fertility (with a red light) and infertility (with a green light) (May 1997). A prototype of Persona was tested as a contraceptive device in

Europe and, with an adjustment of its internal algorithm, is now sold in Europe but not in the United States.

A similar device called ClearPlan (or ClearBlue) Easy Fertility Monitor (CPFM) is sold in the United States as a device to help couples achieve pregnancy (May 2001; Spieler and Collins 2001). Like Persona, the CPFM is a handheld device that measures threshold levels of urinary E3G and LH. However, unlike Persona, the CPFM provides three levels of fertility—low, high (based on reaching a threshold of E3G), and peak fertility (based on reaching a threshold of urinary LH) (May 2001; Unipath Diagnostics 2001). Since the device is designed to enhance the ability to achieve pregnancy, it does not always cover the beginning of the fertile phase of the menstrual cycle. To be used as a device for avoiding pregnancy, not only does it need to be "used in reverse" (i.e., avoiding intercourse on the high and peak days) but it also needs to be used along with another marker for the beginning and sometimes end of the fertile phase.

The purpose of this paper is to provide evidence for the usefulness of the CPFM as an aid for avoiding pregnancy when used with another marker of fertility. In order to accomplish this evidence will be provided for: (1) the accuracy of the CPFM, (2) the effectiveness of the CPFM when used along with cervical mucus monitoring as a means to avoid pregnancy, and (3) evidence for satisfaction with and ease of use of the CPFM. The satisfaction and ease-of-use results include both quantitative and qualitative data. The conclusion will illustrate how the monitor can be used effectively for special reproductive circumstances, such as the anovulatory state of breastfeeding, long menstrual cycles, and peri-menopause.

EVIDENCE FOR ACCURACY OF THE CPFM

Accuracy data for the CPFM comes from the manufacturer and two independent studies, one by researchers in Germany and the other by researchers in Japan. The CPFM is designed to detect the rising level of E3G and the surge in urinary LH. The CPFM is based on urinary hormonal immunoassay techniques. Detection of urinary metabolites of urinary estradiol (E3G) has been recognized by the World Health Organization (WHO) as a reliable marker for the beginning of the fertile phase of the menstrual cycle (Spieler and Collins 2001). Product testing has shown the ClearBlue monitor to be

98.8% accurate in detecting the LH surge. The CPFM detected the LH surge in 169 of 171 cycles from 88 women, in agreement with a quantitative radioimmunoassay for LH (Unipath Diagnostics 2001). In a study with 90 women who each used the CPFM for 1–4 cycles, in 352 cycles with an LH surge, the first day of high fertility (i.e., the day of the first rise in E3G) was 3.01 ± 2.33 days before the LH surge (May 2001; Unipath Diagnostics 2001).

German researchers conducted an independent study to determine the accuracy of the CPFM (Behre et al. 2000). They monitored 53 female volunteers to detect daily serum levels of LH and estradiol and employed transvaginal ultrasound to ascertain the precise day of ovulation. The 53 women contributed 150 cycles of data with use of the CPFM, of which one cycle was determined to be anovulatory. Of the remaining 149 cycles, there were 135 cycles (90.6%) in which the CPFM detected an LH surge and there was an ultrasound-confirmed ovulation. In those 135 cycles, ovulation occurred 97.0% of the time during a three-day period that included the two "peak" days plus the next day "high" on the CPFM. There were no ultrasound-detected ovulations before the monitor "peak" days. The researchers also found that, in 92% of the cycles, the first "high" reading on the monitor coincided with the serum estradiol rise day.

Another study with 30 healthy female volunteers showed that a Japanese-made version of the CPFM, called the Clearview Primera Fertility Monitor (made by Mitsui Pharmaceuticals, Inc., in Tokyo, Japan), indicated up to five days of "high" fertility readings in 58.6% of the cycles (i.e., 17 out of 29 cycles) before the CPFM "peak" reading and in 82.8% of the cycles (i.e., 24 of 29 cycles) before a laboratory determined urinary LH peak (Tanabe et al. 2001). The authors of that study concluded that the device will allow couples to use the information to time intercourse for the best prospects of achieving pregnancy.

EFFICACY OF THE CPFM AS AN AID TO NFP

No published studies have reported on the efficacy of the CPFM as an aid to avoid pregnancy. However, researchers from Germany, Ireland, and the United Kingdom collaborated on a study to determine the effectiveness of a prototype of the Persona monitor (Bonnar et al. 1999). This study is relevant because the early prototype of the Persona had the same threshold levels for detecting E3G and LH as the current CPFM. The Persona study involved 710 female volunteers (median age 30 years, with regular menstrual cycles) who were asked to use the fertility monitor (without any formal training) for the purpose of avoiding pregnancy for a one-year period. At completion of the study and 7,209 cycles of use, there were 67 method-related pregnancies (i.e., pregnancies that resulted from having intercourse on a "green light" day), 92 user-related pregnancies (intercourse on "red light" days), and 3 pregnancies of uncertain timing. A 13-cycle life table analysis yielded a method (i.e., correct use) pregnancy rate of 12.1%. Theoretically, the algorithm used in the current CPFM alone would provide this level of efficacy if used in reverse without other markers for the beginning and end of the fertile window.

MARQUETTE EFFICACY STUDY OF THE CPFM

In 2001, researchers at Marquette University initiated an efficacy study of using the CPFM as an aid to NFP for the purpose of avoiding pregnancy (Fehring et al. 2007). A method was developed in which the use of the CPFM was paired with self-observation of cervical mucus. Cervical mucus (both appearance and sensation) was rated on a 1–8 scale, with 1 being no mucus and dry sensation, and 8 being wet and slippery sensation. The beginning of the fertile phase was either the presence of mucus or a high reading on the monitor (whichever came first), and the end of fertility was three full days past the peak on the monitor.

Our study enrolled 225 couples from four cities—Atlanta, Madison, Milwaukee, and St. Louis. Of the 225 couples, 195 contributed data for the analysis, and 30 were lost to follow-up and did not return data or the monitors. Mean age of the 195 female participants was 29.4 years (SD = 5.8, range 19–42), and mean age of the male partners was 31.1 years (SD = 6.2; range 18–49). The participants were primarily Caucasian, Catholic, and at least high-school educated, had a mean of 1.4 children, and had combined household incomes greater than $50,000. None of the participants were on hormonal contraception or breastfeeding for at least three months before enrolling in the study. All participants agreed to avoid pregnancy with use of the CPFM for 12 months.

There were a total of 22 unintended pregnancies, of which three occurred with correct use, and a total of 1,795 documented months of use. The 12-month correct-use survival rate was 0.98, meaning an unintended pregnancy rate of 2.0 per annum (95% CI = 0.96–1.00). The total (typical use) survival rate at 12 months was 0.86, meaning an unintended pregnancy rate of 14.0 per annum (95% CI = 0.82–0.94). After that study was completed, another 20 couples met the criteria for the study and were added to the data set for this paper. So we now had a total of 215 couples and 22 unintended pregnancies, of which three were achieved with correct use, and a total of 1,850 documented months of use. The correct-use unintended pregnancy rate was still 2.0 per annum with a 98% effectiveness and a total use pregnancy rate of 13.0%, or an 87% survival rate effectiveness. (See Table 1.)

Table 1: Twelve-Month Correct and Typical Unintended Pregnancy Rates with Use of the CPFM Plus Cervical Mucus Monitoring (*N* = 215 couples)

Months of Use	# Preg	Correct Use Rate	# Preg	Typical Use Rate
3 months	1	0.995	8	0.962
6 months	0	0.995	5	0.922
9 months	1	0.988	4	0.896
12 months	1	0.980	5	0.871
Total	3		22	

The 215 participants contributed a mean of 8.6 months of use (SD = 3.9; median of 11 months), and 122 (56.7%) remained in the study for the agreed 12 months. Of the remaining 93 participants, 30 were lost to follow-up, 19 left to achieve a pregnancy, 18 left for personal reasons, and 3 left for health reasons. Of the 19 participants who intended to achieve a pregnancy, 12 did so in the first cycle of trying.

SATISFACTION WITH THE USE OF THE CPFM AS AN AID TO AVOID PREGNANCY

In order to determine the satisfaction and usefulness of the CPFM, we mailed a 10-item satisfaction survey to the 195 participating couples of our prospective study. The 10-item survey was a shortened form of a satisfaction questionnaire developed by Severy for evaluating the Persona fertility monitor (Severy 2001). The 10 items are ranked on a scale from 1 to 7, with bipolar negative and positive adjectives. (See Table 2 for the content of each item.)

The survey was mailed anonymously to the 195 couples (husband and wife) in the study after completion of the efficacy phase. Of the 195 surveys mailed, 65 were returned with undeliverable addresses. Of the 130 couples who received the questionnaires, 77 of the female forms (59.2%) and 71 of the male forms (54.6%) were returned. As seen in Table 2, the mean scores for the women ranged from

Table 2: Ease of Use and Satisfaction with the ClearPlan Easy Fertility Monitor*

Item	Female (*N* = 77)		Male (*N* = 70)	
	Mean	SD	Mean	SD
Ease of including monitor in daily routine	5.70	1.48	5.87	1.35
Ease of performing urine test	6.23	1.02	6.13	1.33
Understanding monitor information	6.55	0.78	6.21	1.13
Overall opinion of CPFM	6.15	1.00	5.93	1.28
CPFM increased ability to avoid pregnancy	5.99	1.46	6.01	1.39
CPFM decreased anxiety about pregnancy	5.68	1.42	5.67	1.34
Ease of using the CPFM	6.11	1.04	5.86	1.21
How do you like the CPFM	5.92	1.30	5.89	1.28
Compared to other methods, how improved	6.25	1.61	6.07	1.69
Chances of avoiding pregnancy	5.98	1.23	6.10	1.09

* Rating based on 1–7 scale, with 7 being the highest rated score for each item.

5.68 to 6.55 and for the men ranged 5.67 to 6.21. The highest rated item of the 10 for both the women and the men was "understanding the information the monitor provided." The lowest ranked item for both the women and the men was "to what degree has the use of the CPFM has decreased your anxiety about becoming pregnant." Overall, ease of use, information provided, and the ability to use the monitor to avoid pregnancy were ranked very high by both the husbands and the wives.

The survey also included a section for open-ended comments. There were comments from 25 of the respondents. The most frequent responses were (1) the test strips were too expensive, (2) the monitor did not always provide a warning of peak, and (3) the monitor was useful in objectively defining the peak day. Following is an example response saying that the test strips were too expensive:

> *After the birth of our third child we used the monitor briefly to avoid pregnancy, however, it was difficult to obtain the test sticks at various Walgreen's in our area. Additionally, the cost of the sticks was a fact to continue with the monitor.*

Following is an example from another couple:

> *The sticks are too expensive and we have found another method using saliva that we like better.*

Following is an example response saying that there was no warning of the peak of fertility:

> *The monitor generally did not register before my peak ovulation day. I had to rely completely on mucous observations pre peak. It was helpful identifying my peak day.*

Following is an example from another couple:

> *Two days ago the monitor read a peak with no sign by mucus or monitor of rising fertility.*

Following is an example response saying that the monitor helped to clarify the peak:

> *Even if I saw mucus post peak I knew for sure I had ovulated thus reducing confusion.*

Following is an example from another couple:

> *It only helps make rhythm a little clearer because it marks a certain ovulation.*

DISCUSSION OF EFFICACY AND SATISFACTION

Researchers have recommended using urinary hormonal markers (i.e., urinary metabolites of estrogen, progesterone, and LH) as indicators of the fertile phase for helping women/couples to avoid pregnancy (Martinez et al. 1995; Martinez 1997; Crosignani and Rubin 2000). However, there have been no published studies on how effective urinary LH indicators or the use of the CPFM could be to help women/couples avoid pregnancy. The current study is the first efficacy study of using the CPFM as an adjunct to self-observation of cervical mucus as a means to avoid pregnancy.

The low correct-use unintended pregnancy rate of 2% found is similar to efficacy rates found with other NFP methods. Like other NFP methods, the CPFM plus cervical mucus self-observation overestimates the fertile phase. Most of the overestimation in this study was due to estimating fertility by use of self-observation of cervical mucus (Fehring, Raviele, and Schneider 2004). The mean number of days of fertility, as estimated by self-evaluation of cervical mucus based on the 1,300 NFP charts collected for this study, was 11.1 (SD = 3.7), and the total days of fertility estimated by the CPFM was 6.1 (SD = 3.2).

Although the Marquette researchers hoped to have a lower unintended pregnancy rate, the 12–14% per annum unintended pregnancy rate found in this study was not unexpected. This rate is lower than the overall typical unintended pregnancy rate of 20–25% for NFP methods as reported in the literature (Trussell 2004). The lower typical pregnancy rate could be because of the homogenous characteristics of the sample, the higher education and social class of the sample used in this study, or the accuracy and ease of use of the fertility monitor.

In an earlier effectiveness study of a mucus-only method at Marquette University, researchers found a correct-use 12-month unintended pregnancy rate of 2.0 and a use-effectiveness rate of 15.2 among 242 couples (Fehring, Lawrence, and Philpot 1994). In comparison, the current study had a use-effectiveness pregnancy rate of 11.2%. The participants for both of these studies were demographically similar. The correct-use rates are similar, but the use rates from the monitor plus mucus seem to be slightly better. So a question could be asked whether the monitor actually adds to the efficacy of using mucus-only NFP methods. This question could be answered only by a randomized comparison study.

Comparison of the results of this study could also be made with two other recent efficacy studies of NFP methods—a calendar-based method called the Standard Days Method (SDM) and a simplified version of cervical mucus monitoring called the TwoDay Method (TDM) (Arévalo, Jennings, and Sinai 2002; Arévalo et al. 2004). The correct use per annum pregnancy rates for the SDM and TDM were 5.60 and 4.50, respectively, and the typical or total pregnancy rates were 12.0 and 14.0, respectively. Although the correct-use unintended pregnancy rate of 2.0% for the current study is lower than these two studies, the differences could well be due to the poorer and less educated participants in the SDM and TDM studies and/or to the accuracy of the fertility monitor. The typical-use unintended pregnancy rates of the current study are similar to the SDM and TDM rates. However, the accuracy of the CPFM used in the current study might be lost when it is paired with cervical mucus observations. Furthermore, having two markers of fertility made the use of the CPFM plus mucus method much more complex than the simpler instructions for use of the SDM and TDM. Finally, the pregnancy rates for the SDM and TDM rates were determined on cycles of use rather than months of use.

RELATED SATISFACTION AND EASE-OF-USE STUDIES
In a similar study on the acceptability of the CPFM, Severy (2001) assessed the acceptability of the Persona monitor with 220 U.S. women who recorded their acceptability and ease of use of the fertility device on a 7-point scale, with 1 being the least acceptable (and most difficult to use) and 7 the most acceptable (and the easiest to use). The 220 women were between the ages of 18 and 35, were in monogamous relationships, were sexually active, were not intending to have a child in the next year, and used the device for at least six months. The mean rating of "ease of use," like in the current study, was around 6, and the mean acceptability score was close to 6. The investigator concluded that the Persona fertility monitor was highly acceptable to volunteer couples and that the monitor had a positive

effect on the women's reproductive functioning, the women's health, and the couples' relationships.

In a related study, researchers from Family Health International and the University of Florida conducted a study to determine the psychological impact of using the CPFM with 52 couples from Florida and North Carolina who used the monitor for four consecutive cycles to achieve pregnancy (Severy et al. 2006). The couples also were provided with a multiple-item, paper-and-pencil tool to measure dimensions of acceptability for their family planning method. Acceptability of the monitor and having fertility-focused intercourse were more favorable at baseline among the couples who eventually achieved a pregnancy. For couples who did not achieve pregnancy, acceptability declined over time, and relationships became more strained.

The researchers concluded that their research findings suggested that fertility monitoring does not have a negative influence and may even have a positive influence on the couples' relationship, in particular in enhancing communication. Although gaining knowledge of fertility initially helped to keep stress and anxiety at a minimum, stress and anxiety entered the relationship for couples that did not achieve a pregnancy.

Finally, Severy and Robinson (2004) also found high acceptability and reproductive knowledge among 60 couple users of the CPFM across time (i.e., 13 cycles of use). The acceptability was higher among couples who became pregnant within the first three months of use. There have been no studies to determine the acceptability and ease of use of the CBFM as a device to monitor fertility and avoid pregnancy along with a double-check of the fertile window (i.e., a fertility algorithm).

LIMITATIONS IN USING THE CPFM
PLUS MUCUS OBSERVATION

The obvious limitation of the efficacy portion of this study was that the sample was not compared with a random selection of participants using another method of family planning. Therefore, the results could be influenced by many factors, including biases of the researchers and clinicians contributing to the study (Grimes et al. 2005; Trussell 2004).

Another limitation is that use of two markers of fertility adds to the complexity of teaching and using this method of NFP. Furthermore, at times the two markers of fertility confused the participants (e.g., when there was a low reading on the monitor and cervical mucus present, when the peak in the monitor and the peak in mucus did not coincide, or when there was no peak reading for the monitor). The confusion with the two markers was also reflected in the satisfaction results when several couples mentioned they did not experience any high days before the peak reading of the monitor. Some couples would incorrectly ignore the mucus reading when they had a low reading on the monitor.

Although the couple participants agreed to avoid pregnancy for 12 months with the use of the monitor and mucus observations, some of the young couples discontinued the study prematurely to achieve a pregnancy or started to test the ends of the estimated fertile window without declaring that they were trying to achieve a pregnancy. We have observed that the decision to achieve a pregnancy does not always begin with a 100% effort. Unintended intercourse patterns reveal that there is often a first testing of the ends of the estimated fertile phase. Furthermore, although the frequency of intercourse, among the participants, was similar to previous studies, there was an underreporting of intercourse during the fertile time. This was apparent when a number of participants would reveal this several months after the pregnancy interview. The average frequency of intercourse per cycle for this study was 3.85 (SD = 3.32; range 1–24), but many of the cycles (16%) had missing data or no recorded intercourse due to uneasiness of sharing that information.

RECOMMENDATIONS

A conservative recommendation from this study would be that when using both cervical mucus monitoring plus the CBFM, couples should be consistent in monitoring both markers and avoiding intercourse when either marker indicates a fertile day. Waiting for three full days after the peak in the monitor or mucus (i.e., resuming intercourse on the evening of the fourth day past either peak) is recommended. The intercourse patterns in this study showed that unintended pregnancies tended to occur at the end and just outside of the end of the estimated fertile phase. In fact, with 13 of the unintended pregnancies, intercourse occurred on either the third or fourth day past the last peak reading on the monitor.

Another recommendation is to simplify the method and to use only the monitor as an indicator of fertility along with a simple algorithm (Fehring 2005). The algorithm is based on using the earliest peak on the monitor from the last six cycles of charting minus six days as a double-check for the beginning of the fertile phase. European researchers have demonstrated good efficacy results with a double-check method of NFP using the basal body temperature shift, cervical mucus, and a calendar-based formula (Frank-Hermann et al. 2005). Hopefully, simplifying the use of the monitor as a means to avoid pregnancy would make it easier for the couple and help to lower unintended pregnancies.

A final recommendation is to conduct a randomized control trial of the CPFM comparing the recommended fertility algorithm with the use of cervical mucus alone as a method of avoiding pregnancy. The monitor could also be compared with the use of basal body temperature (BBT) as a marker of fertility or other developed methods of NFP.

USE OF THE CPFM WITH SPECIAL CIRCUMSTANCES

In order to be useful as a method of NFP, the CPFM needs to be able to adapt to, and provide estimates for, fertility during special reproductive circumstances. These special circumstances include long cycles, breastfeeding, and the peri-menopausal years. The CPFM is designed to be able to track menstrual cycles that vary from 21 to 42 days in length. This variability in length should capture most menstrual cycles, since at least 95% fall within 21–35 days in length (Fehring et al. 2006). However, menstrual cycles longer than that pose a problem. When menstrual cycles are longer than that on a consistent basis, we have the women retrigger the monitor and fast forward to day 5. The monitor will then test for elevated levels of E3G and LH for the next 20 days.

Marquette University researchers have designed a protocol for women who are breastfeeding and not ovulating. The protocol entails creating artificial 26-day cycles. To do this, a woman fast forwards the monitor to day 5 every 20 days. The monitor starts asking for a test on day 6 and continues testing for E3G and LH for the next 20 days. The woman creates these artificial 26-day cycles until a peak reading is recorded followed by a menses. Results of using the protocol were recently reported from the first 10 breastfeeding users (Fehring, Schneider, and Barron, 2005). The researchers found that only 17% of the days during the ovulatory breastfeeding duration leading to the first menses were considered fertile by the monitor, compared with the estimated 50% of the days by self-observation of cervical mucus (t = 3.64, p < 0.01). Furthermore, the peak (LH reading) gave a clear estimate of the first ovulation before the first menses.

Although the Marquette researchers do not have a protocol developed for women experiencing peri-menopausal variability, they have been tracking the use of the monitor with women who fall into this category of fertility. For the most part, the monitor is able to track the variability in length and estimated time of fertility. When the variability between long and short cycles gets too great, the monitor might miss the fertile phase in the very short or long cycles. However, when this happens, the woman is probably not fertile. Taffe and Dennerstein (2002) have demonstrated that once the running range between the longest and shortest menstrual cycle among peri-menopausal women is greater than 42 days, there will be fewer than 20 menstrual cycles left.

CONCLUSION

Although the CPFM was designed for couples to achieve pregnancy, when used along with another marker of fertility, it can be a very effective means of avoiding pregnancy. Marquette University researchers found that it is at least as effective as, if not more effective than, current NFP methods. For the most part, couples using the monitor found that it was easy to use, provided good information about the menstrual cycle, and helped to objectively estimate the fertile phase. Further studies need to be conducted to compare use of the monitor to avoid pregnancy with other methods of NFP. Finally, simplification of using the monitor as a method to avoid pregnancy could be accomplished by using a simple fertility algorithm to have a double-check for the beginning and end of the fertile phase. However, the monitor could be designed with the current threshold level of the Persona monitor and thus used without another marker of fertility.

Both the current Persona and the CPFM (with another marker of fertility) need to be further investigated for their efficacy in helping couples to avoid pregnancy and achieve pregnancy. Protocols for use of the CPFM with special reproductive circumstances, such as monitoring fertility while breastfeeding and not ovulating, continue to be developed.

ACKNOWLEDGEMENTS

I wish to acknowledge the following health professionals who contributed data charts to this study and input into the development of the cervical mucus/hormonal method of NFP: Kathleen Raviele, MD, Atlanta; Julie Krause, RN, Madison, Wisconsin; Mary Schneider, MSN, ARPN; Susana Crespo, RN, Peggy McIntyre, RN, Cynthia Jones-Nosacek, MD, Milwaukee, Wisconsin; Susan Lepak, Oklahoma City, Oklahoma; and Mary Lee Barron, MSN, ARPN, PhD (c).

SOURCES CONSULTED

Arévalo, M., V. Jennings, M. Nikula, and I. Sinai. 2004. Efficacy of the new TwoDay Method of family planning. *Fertility and Sterility* 82: 885–892.

Arévalo, M., V. Jennings, and I. Sinai. 2002. Efficacy of a new method of family planning: The Standard Days Method. *Contraception* 65: 333–8.

Behre, H. M., J. Kuhlage, C. Gassner, B. Sonntag, C. Schem, H. P. G. Schneider, and E. Nieschlag. 2000. Prediction of ovulation by urinary hormone measurements with the home use Clearplan Fertility Monitor: Comparison with transvaginal ultrasound scans and serum hormone measurements. *Human Reproduction* 15: 2478–82.

Bonnar, J., A. Flynn, G. Freundl, R. Kirkman, R. Royston, and R. Snowden. 1999. Personal hormone monitoring for contraception. *British Journal of Family Planning* 24: 128–34.

Crosignani, P. G., and B. L. Rubin. 2000. Optimal use of infertility diagnostic tests and treatments. *Human Reproduction* 15(3): 723–732.

Djerassi C. 1990. Fertility awareness: Jet-age rhythm method? *Science* 248: 1061–2.

Fehring, R. 2005. New low and high tech calendar methods of family planning. *Journal of Nurse Midwifery and Women's Health* 50(1): 31–38.

Fehring, R. J., D. Lawrence, and C. Philpot. 1994. Use effectiveness of the Creighton Model ovulation method of natural family planning. *Journal of Obstetric, Gynecologic, and Neonatal Nursing* 23: 303–312.

Fehring, R., K. Raviele, and M. Schneider. 2004. A comparison of the fertile phase as determined by the Clearplan Easy Fertility Monitor™ and self-assessment of cervical mucus. *Contraception* 69: 9–14.

Fehring, R., M. Schneider, and M. Barron. 2005. Protocol for determining fertility while breast-feeding. *Fertility and Sterility* 84(3): 805–7.

Fehring, R., M. Schneider, and K. Raviele. 2006. Variability in the phases of the menstrual cycle. *Journal of Obstetric, Gynecologic, and Neonatal Nursing* 35:376-384.

Fehring, R. J., M. Schneider, K. Raviele, and M. L. Barron. 2007. Efficacy of cervical mucus observations plus electronic hormonal fertility monitoring as a method of natural family planning. *Journal of Obstetric, Gynecologic, and Neonatal Nursing* 36(2):152-160.

Frank-Hermann. P., C. Gnoth, S. Baure, T. Strowitski, and G. Freundl. 2005. Determination of the fertile window: Reproductive competence of women—European cycle databases. *Gynecology and Endocrinology* 20: 305–312.

Grimes, D. A., M. F. Gallo, V. Grigorieva, K. Nanda, and K. F. Schulz. 2005. Fertility awareness-based methods for contraception: Systematic review of randomized controlled trials. *Contraception* 72: 85–90.

Martinez, A. R. 1997. Prediction and detection of the fertile phase of the menstrual cycle: An overview. *Advances in Contraception* 13: 131–38.

Martinez, A. R., M. J. Zinaman, V. H. Jennings, and V. M. Lamprecht. 1995. Prediction   and detection of the fertile period: The markers. *International Journal of Fertility* 40: 139–55.

May, K. 1997. Monitoring reproductive hormones to detect the fertile period: Development of Persona—The first home use system. *Advances in Contraception* 13: 139–141.

———. 2001. Home monitoring with the ClearPlan Easy Fertility Monitor for fertility awareness. *Journal of International Medical Research* 29 (Suppl. 1): 14A–20A.

Severy, L. J. 2001. Acceptability of home monitoring as an aid to conception. *Journal of International Medical Research* 29 (Suppl. 1): 28A–34A.

Severy, L. J., C. T. Klein, and J. McNulty. 2002. Acceptability of personal hormone monitoring for contraception: Longitudinal and contextual variables. *Journal of Social Psychology* 142: 87–96.

Severy, L. J., and J. Robinson. 2004. Psychological aspects of achieving or avoiding pregnancy. In *Integrating Faith and Science through Natural Family Planning,* ed. R. J. Fehring and T. Notare, 111-133. Milwaukee, WI: Marquette University Press.

Severy, L. J., J. Robison, C. Findley-Klein, and J. McNulty. 2006. Acceptability of a home monitor used to aid in conception: Psychological factors and couple dynamics. *Contraception* 73: 65–71.

Spieler, J. M., and W. P. Collins. 2001. Potential fertility—Defining the window of opportunity. *The Journal of International Medical Research* 29 (Suppl. 1): 3A–13A.

Taffe, J. R., and L. Dennerstein. 2002. Menstrual patterns leading to the final menstrual period. *Menopause: The Journal of The North American Menopause Society* 9(1): 32–40.

Tanabe, K., N. Susumu, K. Hand, K. Nishii, I. Ishikawa, and S. Nozawa. 2001. Prediction of the potentially fertile period by urinary hormone measurements using a new home-use monitor: comparison with laboratory hormone analyses. *Human Reproduction* 16(8):1619-1624.

Trussell, J. 2004. Contraceptive failure in the United States. *Contraception* 70: 89–96.

Unipath Diagnostics. 2001. *Professional Information: Clearplan Easy Fertility Monitor.* Princeton, NJ: Unipath Diagnostics Company.

EFFECTIVENESS OF VARIOUS APPROACHES TO NFP & BEYOND SCIENTIFIC CHOICE OF NFP METHODOLOGY

PETRA FRANK-HERRMANN, C. GNOTH, U. SOTTONG, E. TOLEDO, S. BAUR, G. FREUNDL, T. STROWITZKI

It was the aim of the German NFP working group and its scientific committee to select, further develop, and evaluate NFP guidelines that are evidence-based and practicable and meet the high efficacy expectations of women in European countries. The outcome of the review and research process was to use a symptothermal methodology that determines the onset as well as the end of the fertile time according to the double-check principle.

To determine the onset of the fertile time, the minus-8 rule (based on the earliest temperature rise) is more precise than the calculation rules based on cycle length (i.e., minus-20 rule). The onset of the fertile time should be double-checked by mucus observation, but further guidelines like abstaining from intercourse during bleeding or on every other day are not necessary.

To determine the end of the fertile time, the rules chosen to interpret the temperature rise—again, double-checked by mucus observation—are more precise and therefore demand less abstinence than the traditional means of determining the temperature shift, the temperature spike rules, and other temperature guidelines. The German NFP working group rules also render a high percentage of interpretable charts and are less complicated than some other guidelines.

INTRODUCTION

Up to the beginning of the 1980s, modern Natural Family Planning (NFP) methods were not very well known in Germany. There was some use of Rötzer's Symptothermal Method (STM) and Döring's Temperature Method, but the use was not extensive. In addition, the Billings Ovulation Method (OM) was known by gynecologists, but not used by women. Many NFP methods have been developed historically with pioneer NFP users. Furthermore, there is a lack of scientific evidence in the acceptance or rejection of rules for the various NFP systems. Today, although NFP methods are better known, the efficacy of NFP methods to avoid pregnancy is seen differently by different researchers (European Natural Family Planning Study Groups 1999, Barbato and Bertolotti 1988, Frank-Herrmann et al. 1997, Howard and Stanford 1999, Hilgers and Stanford 1998, Kambic 1999, Grimes et al. 2004). Oral contraceptives and the IUD play a much greater role in Germany than in the United States. This difference in cultural preference is one of the reasons why efficacy in European countries is the major issue in family planning choice, as shown by a representative public opinion poll undertaken in 1985 (Döring et al. 1986).

On the basis of international scientific and empirical knowledge and our own research, the German NFP working group assumed responsibility for selecting, further developing, and evaluating NFP guidelines that are evidence-based and practicable and that meet the high efficacy expectations of women in European countries. This process lasted from 1982 until 1990. The aim of this paper is to explain the rules of the NFP method of the German NFP working group, the reasons for choosing these rules, and the corresponding scientific results.

DEVELOPMENT IN GERMANY SINCE 1980

In 1980, Döring and his students were the only people engaged in the field of NFP research in Germany. Between 1979 and 1982, two of Döring's students collected extensive international NFP literature (1,500 references), often by correspondence. They compared the different NFP methods of Rötzer, Thyma, SERENA Canada, Kippley, Flynn, Billings, CLER, and so forth, as well as the existing scientific results. This literature search was discussed and published for the first time in 1982 and updated several times in the following years (Raith et al. 1999).

At about the same time as Döring's research was being published and updated, the German Catholic Bishops' Conference established a working group and a scientific committee to support NFP teaching and research. Utilizing the literature review and considering the German situation, the scientific committee decided that the double-check variation of the Symptothermal Method (STM) was the most suitable natural method for the cultural context when taking into account the high efficacy expectations of many women in industrialized countries.

The scientific committee decided to choose only those rules that were necessary to get at the same time a maximum of practicability and a correct interpretation of the charts, and to develop standardized NFP teaching materials. From the very beginning, a pilot study was started to investigate the practicability of NFP.

From 1984 onward, based on first results, the German Catholic Bishops' Conference, together with the German Ministry of Family and Health, financed a six-year prospective observational study in order to investigate effectiveness, practicability, and psychological aspects and to further develop and evaluate the teaching approach (Arbeitsgruppe NFP 1988, 2006). In 1990, there were some minor modifications of the STM method on the basis of the results of the project. The database that was established during these years has been continued until today. It now represents the German Database, with 1,599 women and 35,996 cycles.

Today, the former scientific committee is acknowledged by the German Association of Obstetrics and Gynecology as an expert group for "natural fertility." The NFP teachers are organized by Malteser Arbeitsgruppe NFP under the roof of the German Association of the Malteser Order.

THE GERMAN STM METHODOLOGY

The double-check variation of the STM consists of recording cervical mucus patterns and changes of basal body temperature and applying calculation rules. Both the beginning and the end of the fertile phase are identified by two parameters according to the double-check principle, as shown in Figure 1. For the first year of application, there is a rule of transition to determine the onset of the fertile phase.

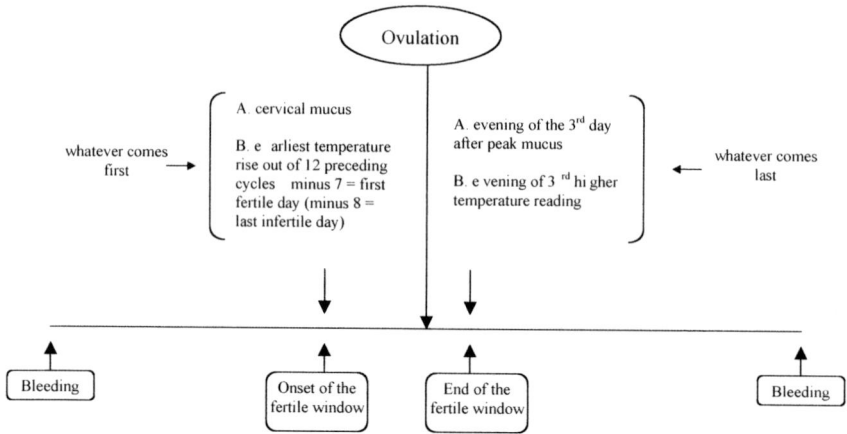

Ovulation

whatever comes
first →

A. cervical mucus

B. e arliest temperature
rise out of 12 preceding
cycles minus 7 = first
fertile day (minus 8 =
last infertile day)

A. evening of the 3rd day
after peak mucus

B. e vening of 3 rd hi gher
temperature reading

← whatever comes
last

Bleeding

Onset of the
fertile window

End of the
fertile window

Bleeding

FIGURE I:

DETERMINATION OF THE FERTILE PHASE

ACCORDING TO THE STM

DETERMINATION OF THE INFERTILE DAYS
AT THE ONSET OF THE CYCLE (FIG. 2)

As soon as at least 12 temperature curves have been recorded, the minus-8 rule is used: The day of the earliest first higher temperature reading (out of at least 12 temperature charts) minus 8 days equals the last infertile day at the beginning of the cycle.

The beginner, however, who lacks knowledge of 12 previous cycles, considers the first five days of the cycle infertile. If the lengths of the last 12 cycles are known (by a menstruation calendar), it can be determined whether the infertile phase at the beginning of the cycle can be extended according to the calculation rule: the shortest cycle length out of at least 12 cycles minus 20 equals the duration of the infertile period at the beginning of the cycle. This number of days (five or more) is fixed once and remains the same during the first year of NFP use with one restriction: if, during the first year of NFP use, the minus-8 rule (which is to be checked after each cycle) already reduces the infertile phase at the beginning of the cycle, the minus-8 rule is applied at once.

These guidelines are only valid if they are double-checked by mu-cus observation according to the double-check principle (i.e., what-ever comes first is considered the beginning of the preovulatory in-

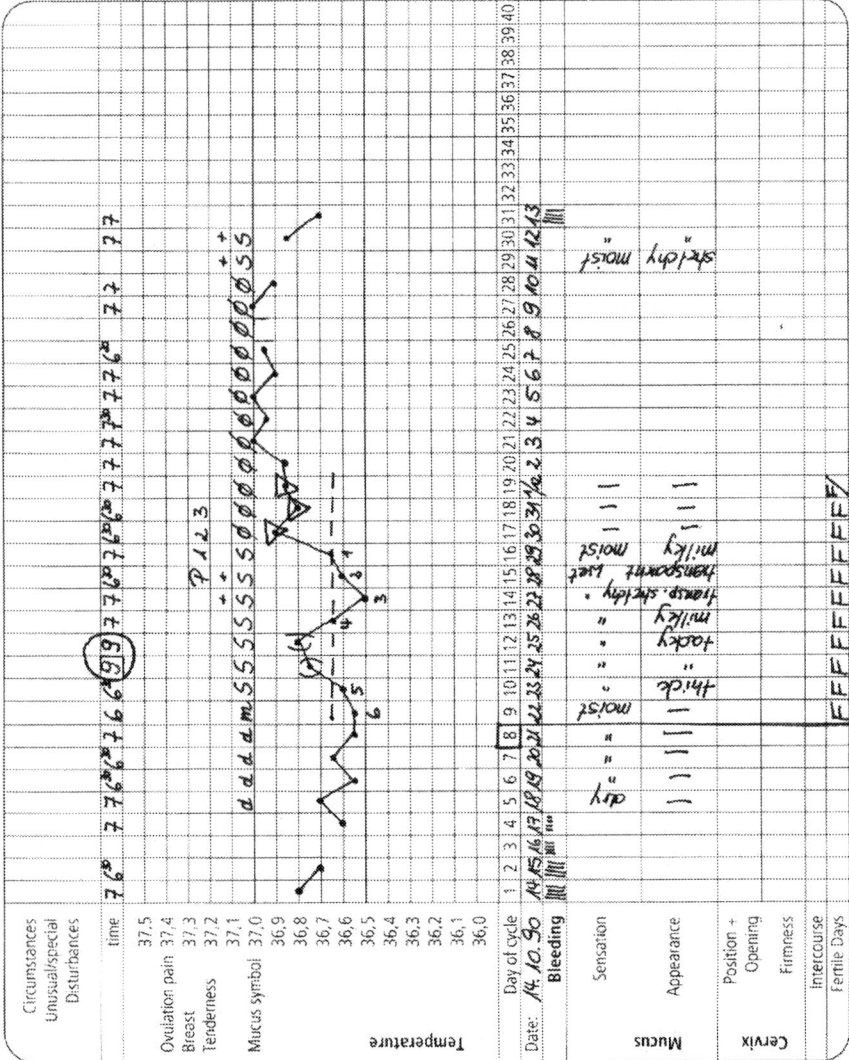

FIGURE 2: CHARTING ACCORDING TO THE STM

fertile period). In addition, there must have been at least three higher temperatures in the previous cycle.

DETERMINATION OF THE POSTOVULATORY INFERTILE DAYS

The postovulatory infertile phase starts either in the evening of the third day after peak mucus symptom or in the evening of the third higher temperature reading, whichever comes last.

The peak of the mucus symptom is the last day on which a woman observes mucus of the individually best quality.

A temperature rise has taken place when there are three consecutive temperature readings that are all higher than the previous six. The third raised temperature should be at least 0.2°C (two squares on the chart) above the highest of the six previous temperatures.

There are two exceptions to the temperature rule:

1. If the third higher temperature is not 0.2°C (two squares) higher than the six low temperatures, one has to wait for a fourth temperature reading. This does not have to be 0.2°C higher, but simply higher than the six low temperatures.

2. Among the three necessary higher temperatures, one reading may drop under or upon the line (drawn through the highest of the previous six low temperatures). This reading can be ignored.

SCIENTIFIC ARGUMENTATION OF METHOD RULES

The basis of the decision for this specific NFP method was the literature search in 1982, the German pilot study between 1982 and 1984 (439 women, 2,276 cycles), the six-year ministry project from 1985 to 1990 (689 women, 9,945 cycles), and the German Database (which is a continuation of the ministry study through the present).

END OF THE FERTILE PHASE

DETERMINATION OF THE TEMPERATURE RISE.

The temperature rise often is more a rise than a shift and may last several days. Accordingly, there are many different recommendations on how to determine it (Frank and Raith 1985).

In 1966, the WHO recommended the "three higher than the previous six" principle of Holt for recognizing the temperature rise. This principle is the most common principle in Europe for recognizing temperature increase. On the contrary, in Anglo-American countries, the coverline method is more widely used. The coverline covers nearly the whole hypothermic phase. McCarthy and Rockette analyzed 8,496 cycles showing that 11% more cycles could be interpreted with the "three higher than the previous six" rule than with the coverline rule (McCarthy and Rockette 1983). Our own data yielded nearly the same result: the "three higher than the previous six" principle yielded 12% more interpretable curves in 2,276 cycles (Socher 1987). It was concluded that there is no more need for the classical coverline rule.

The definition of the height of the three higher temperature readings varies among NFP methods. However, it has mostly become more flexible than the definitions in the 1960s of the WHO, Döring, CLER, and others (Raith et al. 1999). With the former strict rules that all three consecutive temperature readings have to be at least 0.2°C higher than the previous six, the end of the fertile phase could be determined only in 22% out of 9,128 cycles, as shown in Table 1 (Rosmus 1994). Rötzer was the first to develop and evaluate the set of rules that only the last of the three higher readings has to be 0.2°C higher than the previous six, plus the above cited two exceptions to that rule—provided that the temperature is double-checked with the second parameter, cervical mucus. Out of 9,945 cycles, 94.5% were interpretable according to this set of rules as biphasic or monophasic cycles, 2.9% were monophasic ones, and 5.5% were not interpretable (3.1% were not interpretable because of too many missing temperature readings in the periovulatory phase, 1.5% were not interpretable because of disturbances, and 0.9% were not interpretable according to the rules). If periovulatory temperature readings were charted completely, only 2.4% were not interpretable.

Table 1: Characteristics of the Temperature Rise (n = 9,128 cycles with interpretable temperature charts)

Source of rule	Rule for determining the temperature rise	Percentage of cycles in which the temperature rise could be determined
1960s Döring/WHO	All 3 higher readings ≥ 0.2°C	21.7 %
Our set of rules	3rd higher reading ≥ 0.2°C	67.2 %
	+ First exception rule	+ 22.8 %
	+ Second exception rule	+ 10.0 %

In view of these results, even Döring agreed to accept this new set of rules. Already very early, it seemed to be clear that the Temperature Method (TM) is a very effective natural method: The pioneers of the TM analyzed several large retrospective databases (Vincent 1967, Döring 1967) and three prospective studies (Marshall 1968, Vollman 1975, Rice, Lanctot, and Garcia-Devesa 1981). They found no pregnancy from intercourse from the third higher temperature reading onward up to the end of the cycle, except for one case of Vincent and some cases of Marshall, who at that time determined the temperature rise only with three low values and demanded only a rise of 0.1°C (Frank and Raith 1985, Raith et al. 1999).

CERVICAL MUCUS SYMPTOM.

In the 1960s, Billings and Rötzer, independently from each other, advanced the mucus symptom from a minor parameter to a main parameter, being equivalent to the temperature (Billings 1964, Rötzer 1965). Observation techniques and descriptions of the mucus qualities are similar in the methods of both researchers and in our STM. Billings, Rötzer, and others use very similar peak day definitions. Some NFP methods prefer the free description of cervical mucus observations; others use symbols or categories. We offer both; the woman may decide after the learning phase to stick to only one procedure. Because we did not like the misleading terms "fertile-type mucus" and "infertile-type mucus," we chose the symbols S (secretion corresponds to infertile-type mucus) and S+ (secretion corresponds to fertile-type mucus), as shown previously in Figure 2.

To evaluate the quality of our mucus rules and the teaching of those rules, we analyzed the data of the ministry project: In 94.6% of the charts, a peak day was registered. Only 2.9% out of 689 women had never or rarely mentioned the mucus symptom (Rosmus 1994). This compares favorably with the WHO data (WHO 1981a).

DOUBLE-CHECK FOR THE END OF THE FERTILE PHASE.

The double-check of Thyma and others evaluates both parameters (cervical mucus and temperature) independently from each other. Rötzer interprets the temperature in relation to the mucus peak, marking the three higher temperature readings always after the mucus peak. The disadvantage of that procedure is that in case the peak occurs after the temperature rise, a somewhat complicated extra rule is needed. Therefore, we decided to use the independent double-check approach—the fertile phase nevertheless ends on the same cycle day.

Determining the end of the fertile phase depends not only on physiology, but also on how well both NFP parameters correlate. There are different ranges of gaps according to different sets of rules. In our study (n = 8,756 cycles with mucus peak and temperature rise), on the average, the peak day was 1.1 days before the first higher temperature reading. In 78.1% of the cycles, the peak day occurred in between three days before and the day of the first higher temperature reading itself (Rosmus 1994).

Because ovulation may already happen up to three days before the peak, pregnancies are to be expected if less than three days are waited for after the peak, as shown in Table 2.

Table 2: Distance of Peak Day of Mucus Symptom to Objective Ovulation (= day 0)

Method	Average distance to ovulation[1] (days)	Range (days)
Billings et al. 1972 (n = 22 cycles)	-0.9	-3 to +2
Flynn and Lynch 1976 (n = 29 cycles)	+0.5	-2 to +1
Hilgers et al. 1978 (n = 64 cycles)	-0.3	-3 to +3
Gnoth et al. 1996 (n = 62 cycles)	-0.3	-3 to +2

[1] Ovulation day was determined by hormonal analysis in the first three studies and by daily ultrasound and LH in the last one.

BEGINNING OF THE FERTILE PHASE

Our decision to use a double-check approach to determine the beginning of the fertile phase and not only mucus (like the groups of Billings, Hilgers, and some STM groups like CLER and others) derives from correlation studies between the symptoms and the objective ovulation and from effectiveness studies. Table 3 shows that there are women who observe their mucus symptom only very shortly before ovulation in all groups, possibly too shortly considering the length of sperm survival.

The data of effectiveness studies confirm these results. If the onset of the fertile window is identified by mucus observation alone, efficacy is reduced (European Natural Family Planning Study Groups, 1999). The WHO five-country study is commonly referred to as

Table 3: Distance from the Beginning of Mucus Symptom to Objective Ovulation

Method	Average distance to ovulation[1] (days)	Range
Billings et al. 1972 (*n* = 22 cycles)	6.2	3-10
Flynn and Lynch 1976 (*n* = 29 cycles)	5.2	3-12
Hilgers et al. 1978 (*n* = 64 cycles)	5.9	0-15
Gnoth et al. 1996 (*n* = 62 cycles)	7.8	1-17

[1] Ovulation day was determined by hormonal analysis in the first three studies and by daily ultrasound and LH in the last one.

evidence of the efficacy of the OM. While the pregnancy rate of the OM was very low in the three participating developing countries, it was much higher in the two industrialized countries (3.4% pregnancy rate in one year in Ireland and 6.3% in New Zealand) (WHO 1981b). The small Australian study of Ball (1976) found a pregnancy rate of 2.9% (all method-related pregnancies were due to intercourse on preovulatory dry days), while the American study of Klaus et al. (1979) found a pregnancy rate of 1.0% (most of the pregnancies were due to intercourse on the last day before the onset of mucus). In the Australian study of Johnston et al., (1978) there was a pregnancy rate for the preovulatory dry days between 3.7% and 9.8%. Only few European data exist on mucus methods, mainly because mucus methods are not largely used in Europe. Barbato et al. (1988) found in their prospective study on the STM (8,140 cycles, 460 women) that all of the 12 method-related pregnancies occurred when determining the fertile window with mucus observation only. This shows that pregnancy sometimes occurs due to intercourse on the so-called dry days.

Therefore, with our STM, the beginning of the fertile phase is determined by cervical mucus observation combined with the minus-8 rule. In the first year of NFP use, cervical mucus observation is used together with the transition rule (see the information for beginners in the previous section, "Determination of the Infertile Days at the Onset of the Cycle").

In the 1990s, the discussion with the calculation rules centered on how many previous cycles women have to consider. Tietze and Potter

(1962) found that the risk of conception increases up to sevenfold if only 6 instead of 12 cycles are considered. At the same time, they found that a database of less than 12 cycles cannot be compensated by a stronger calculation (e.g., minus 21 instead of minus 20), contrary to what is recommended by several NFP groups. We confirmed those results with our database (Rosmus 1994).

In our effectiveness study, there was no method failure for the double-check with "minus 20" or "minus 8"; however, three pregnancies occurred due to intercourse on the fifth cycle day (Frank-Herrmann et al. 1997). Considering the high fertility of women with short cycles, we modified the 5-day rule: If, during the first year of NFP use, the first higher temperature reading happens on day 12 or earlier, the minus-8 rule is applied at once.

THE GERMAN NFP EFFECTIVENESS STUDY

The effectiveness of a family planning method has to be measured in real rates of unintended pregnancies—that is, method-related pregnancy rates and use-related pregnancy rates.

Why is a method-related pregnancy rate of 2% to 3% (using the Pearl Index or a 12-month life-table value) not a particularly good rating for a family planning method? A Pearl-Index (PI) of 2 to 3 means that not only will two to three out of 100 women become pregnant within one year, but also another two to three out of the remaining 97 to 98 women will get pregnant in the following year, and still another two to three women will get pregnant in the next year, and so on. After 10 years, 20% of the original group will probably have become pregnant (probably not 30%, because it is not possible to extrapolate the PI in a linear way because the risk of conception will decrease in the remaining population with time). To be rated as highly efficient, a family planning method needs to have a PI (or 12-month Life Table) of 0.3% to 0.5%, so that only one unintended pregnancy occurs out of 100 women over two to three years, or only one pregnancy in 3,600 cycles, or four to five pregnancies in 10 years.

To estimate true method effectiveness, pregnancy rates have been calculated in relation to sexual behavior using the "perfect/imperfect-use" model of Trussell and Grummer-Strawn (1990, 1991). In the German database (758 NFP beginners avoiding pregnancy), the pregnancy rate was 0.4% to 0.6% per year when no intercourse occurred in the fertile phase. The overall pregnancy rate was 2.2%, showing a fairly good use effectiveness in the German setting (Frank-Herrmann et al. 1997).

DISCUSSION

In order to promote NFP in Germany, it is necessary to have an easy-to-learn method with an efficacy comparable to that of the oral contraceptive pill.

During 15 years, starting in the 1980s, the German NFP working group and its scientific committee established an NFP method that is evidence-based and practicable and that meets the high efficacy expectations of women in European countries. The resulting variant of the STM has been shown to be highly effective. Today, our STM is used in a number of European countries.

NECESSARY RULES

It is necessary to use the double-check to determine the onset as well as the end of the fertile phase. Furthermore, it is necessary to learn mucus observation and interpretation of the peak mucus day, the minus-8 rule, and a certain sound and easy rule to interpret the temperature rise.

UNNECESSARY RULES

Because the minus-8 rule is more precise and sometimes requires less abstinence than the minus-20 rule or other cycle-length-based calculation rules (short cycles due to anovulation or luteal phase insufficiency prolong the fertile phase unnecessarily), calculation rules are no longer necessary. Even in the first year of NFP use, the calendar is used—if at all—only once at the beginning to see if the user may consider more than five days at the onset of the cycle as infertile. From the beginning, the fixed number of preovulatory infertile days is controlled by the minus-8 rule. To avoid using many different and therefore confusing rules to determine the onset of the fertile phase seems to us to be very important also from a pedagogical point of view.

Other unnecessary rules that prolong abstinence are the classical coverlines, abstaining during the menstrual bleeding, and abstaining every other day. Rötzer's rule of the premature temperature rise is unnecessarily complicated. Furthermore, all rules that interpret the temperature rise very late in the postovulatory phase, thereby prolonging considerably the fertile phase, are unnecessary. In this sense, one can also do without the spike rule of Marshall (in the described so-called second exception rule, the spike becomes the first higher temperature reading).

To conclude, in our cultural context, there is a need to inform users about the most reliable methodology in order to enable them to choose responsibly how they are going to use it. NFP users are intelligent enough to adapt the method to their personal requirements of efficacy (i.e., in certain situations, they may rely on mucus observation only or just look on the calendar). However, to be able to make an informed choice, it is necessary to learn the most effective method that the users themselves may modify. There might be a different situation especially for developing countries. Some NFP methods developed recently are simplified modifications intended for use in developing countries, where continuation has a higher priority than efficacy (Arévalo et al. 2004, Thapa et al. 1990, Jennings and Sinai 2001).

ACKNOWLEDGEMENTS
The authors cordially thank Richard Fehring and Theresa Notare for their intensive and encouraging support, their patience and their extremely valuable comments.

SOURCES CITED
Arbeitsgruppe NFP. 1988. *Natürliche Methoden der Familienplanung. Schriftenreihe des Bundesministeriums für Jugend, Familie, Frauen und Gesundheit, Band 239.* Kohlhammer, Stuttgart, Berlin, Köln.

Arbeitsgruppe NFP. 2006. *Natürlich und Sicher.* Trias, Stuttgart.

Arévalo, M., V. Jennings, M. Nikula, and I. Sinai. 2004. Efficacy of the new TwoDay Method of family planning. *Fertility and Sterility* 82(4): 885-892.

Ball, M., 1976. A prospective field trial of the "ovulation method" of avoiding conception. *European Journal of Obstetrics, Gynecology and Reproductive Biology* 6:63-66.

Barbato, M., and G. Bertolotti. 1988. Natural methods for fertility control: A prospective study. *International Journal of Fertility* Supplement, 48-51.

Billings, J.J., 1964. *The Ovulation Method.* Advocate Press Pty. Ltd., Melbourne, Australia.

Billings, E.L, J.J. Billings, J.B, Brown, and H.G. Burger. 1972. Symptom and hormonal changes accompanying ovulation. *The Lancet* 1:282-284.

Döring, G.K., 1967. On the reliability of the temperature method in contraception. *Deutsche Medizinische Wochenschrift* 92:1055-1061.

Döring, G,, S. Baur, P. Frank, G. Freundl, and U. Sottong. 1986. Results of a representative survey of family planning behavior in West Germany 1985. *Geburtshilfe Frauenheilkd* 46(12):892-7.

European Natural Family Planning Study Groups. 1999. European multicenter study of natural family planning: Efficacy and drop-out. *Advances in Contraception* 15(1): 69-83.

Flynn, A.M., and S. S, Lynch, 1976. Cervical mucus and identification of the fertile phase of the menstrual cycle. *British Journal of Obstetrics and Gynecology* 83:656-59.

Frank, P., and E. Raith. 1985. *Natürliche Familienplanung Heute.* Springer, Berlin, Heidelberg, New York.

Frank-Herrmann, P., G. Freundl, C. Gnoth, E. Godehardt, J. Kunert, S. Baur, and U. Sottong. 1997. Natural family planning with and without barrier method use in the fertile phase: Efficacy in relation to sexual behavior. *Advances in Contraception* 13(2–3): 179-189..

Freundl, G. 1993. The Europen Natural Family Planning Study Groups. Prospective European multi-center study of natural family planning (1989-1992): interim results. *Advances in Contraception* 9:269-283.

Gnoth, C., P. Frank-Hermann, M. Bremme, G, Freundl, and E. Godehardt. 1996, How do self-observed cycle symptoms correlate with ovulation? *Zentralbl Gynakol* 118(12):650-654.

Grimes, D. A., M. F. Gallo, V. Grigorieva, K. Nanda, and K. F. Schulz. 2004. Fertility awareness-based methods for contraception. *Cochrane Database of Systematic Reviews* 18(4): CD004860.

Hilgers, T.W., G.E. Abraham, and D. Cavanagh. 1978. Natural family planning I. The peak symptom and estimated time of ovulation. *Obstetrics and Gynecology* 52(5): 575-82.

Hilgers, T. W., and J. B. Stanford. 1998. Creighton Model NaProEducation Technology for Avoiding Pregnancy: Use effectiveness. *Journal of Reproductive Medicine* 43(6): 495-502.

Jennings, V., and I. Sinai. 2001. Further analysis of the theoretical effectiveness of the TwoDay Method of family planning. *Contraception* 64(3): 149-153.

Johnston, J., D, Roberts, and R, Spencer. 1978. *A Survey Evaluation of the Effectiveness and Efficiency of Natural Family Planning Service and Methods in Australia: Report of a Research Project.* St. Vincent's Hospital, Syndney, Australia.

Kambic, R. T. 1999. The effectiveness of natural family planning methods for birth spacing: A comprehensive review, pp 63-90. In: Girotto, S., and F. Bressan (eds): *Human fertility regulation—Demographic and statistical aspects.* Edizioni libreria cortina, Verona.

Klaus, H., J.M. Goebel, B. Muraski, M.T. Egizio, D. Weitzel, R.S.Taylor, M.U. Fagan, K. Ek, and K. Hobday. 1979. Use-effectiveness and client satisfaction in six centers teaching the Billings Ovulation Method. *Contraception* 19(6):613-29.

Marshall, J., 1968. A field trial of the basal body temperature method of regulating births. *Lancet* 2(7558):8-10.

McCarthy, J. J., and H. E. Rockette. 1983. A comparison of methods to interpret the basal body temperature graph. *Fertility and Sterility* 39(5): 640-646.

Raith, E., P. Frank, and G. Freundl. 1999. *Natürliche Familienplanung Heute.* Springer, Berlin, Heidelberg, New York.

Rice, F. J., C. A. Lanctot, and C. Garcia-Devesa. 1981. Effectiveness of the sympto-thermal method of natural family planning: An international study. *International Journal of Fertility* 26(3): 222-230.

Rosmus, T. 1994. Selbstbeobachtung der Frau durch die sympto-thermale Methode unter besonderer Berücksichtigung von Zyklusparametern und Praktikabilität der Methode. Medical thesis, University of Düsseldorf.

Rötzer, J. 1965. *Family Size and Loving Marriage: A Guide to the Regulation of Conception.* Herder, Vienna, Austria

Socher, K. 1987. Untersuchung der fruchtbaren und unfruchtbaren Tage im Menstruationszyklus aufgrund der Basaltemperatur und des Zervixschleimsymptoms. Medical thesis, University of Munich.

Thapa, S., M.V. Wonga, P.G. Lampe, H. Pietogo, and A. Soejoenoes. 1990. Efficacy of three variations of periodic abstinence for family planning in Indonesia. *Studies in Family Planning* 21:327-334.

Tietze, R., and R.G. Potter. 1962. Statistical evaluation of the rhythm method. American *Journal of Obstetrics and Gynecology* 5:692-698.

Trussell, J., and L. Grummer-Strawn. 1990. Contraceptive failure of the ovulation method of periodic abstinence. *Family Planning Perspectives* 22(2): 65-75.

Trussell, J., and L. Grummer-Strawn. 1991. Further analysis of contraceptive failure of the ovulation method. *American Journal of Obstetrics and Gynecology* 165(6 Pt2): 2054-2060.

Vincent, B. 1967. *The Temperature Method and Contraception: Medical and Psychological Approaches.* Masson et Cie, Paris, France.

Vollman, R.F. 1977. *The Menstrual Cycle.* WB Saunders Co., Philadelphia.

World Health Organization (WHO). 1981a. A prospective multicentre trial of the ovulation method of natural family planning. I. The teaching phase. *Fertility and Sterility* 36(2): 152-158.

World Health Organization (WHO). 1981b. A prospective multicentre trial of the ovulation method of natural family planning. II. The effectiveness phase. *Fertility and Sterility* 36(5): 591-598.

DIFFERENT METHODS FOR DIFFERENT NEEDS: PERCEPTION, BEHAVIOR, AND EFFECTIVENESS

IRIT SINAI

In choosing a Natural Family Planning method, a couple can only choose a method that is available and that the couple knows about and finds acceptable. This paper explores some of the determinants of availability and acceptability, including method effectiveness, of several Natural Family Planning methods: the Billings Ovulation Method, two versions of the Sympto-Thermal Method, the TwoDay Method, and the Standard Days Method. All these methods are highly effective, but some are somewhat more effective than others on specific cycle days relative to ovulation. Where the Billings Ovulation Method and the Sympto-Thermal Method are more precise, the TwoDay Method and the Standard Days Method require shorter counseling and enable a faster route toward autonomy. They also involve less time commitment from teachers. These and other characteristics of the methods and of couples contribute to the availability of methods and to couples' perceptions of them.

Before a couple can begin to use a family planning method, several things need to happen. First, the method should be offered in a setting that is accessible to them. Second, they need to be aware of the method and know where they can receive information on how to use it. Third, the couple needs to choose to use the method. A multitude of factors affect each of these components, including characteristics of the method itself and of the couple. This article compares several Natural Family Planning (NFP) methods with a view to what it takes for these methods to be available to couples and for couples to choose these methods and then continue using them. The focus is on using NFP to prevent pregnancy.

The umbrella term "NFP" covers several methods with many variations. Some methods involve monitoring the biological symptoms of fertility and ovulation; other methods require monitoring cycle days. Four methods will be compared in this article:

• **The Billings Ovulation Method.** This method requires that the woman monitor her cervical secretions and distinguish between different types of secretions.

• **The Sympto-Thermal Method.** This method, which is offered in different programs with variations, requires that the woman monitor several symptoms of fertility (secretions, basal body temperature, and sometimes the position of the cervix), as well as the cycle day.

• **The TwoDay Method.** Like the Billings Ovulation Method, this method is based on observing cervical secretions. However, users do not need to distinguish between types of secretions.

• **The Standard Days Method.** The fertile period is on days 8-19 for all users in all cycles (the method is most effective for women with cycles that usually range 26-32 days).

The characteristics of these methods that may affect the ability and willingness of programs to offer them and of instructors to teach them will be compared, including the time it takes couples to learn to use the method and to reach autonomy and what is required for a provider to learn how to teach these methods. Other method characteristics that may affect the couple's perception of the method—in-

Method	Menses	Pre-ovulatory infertile days	Beginning of the fertile window	End of the fertile window
Billings Ovulation Method	The woman considers herself fertile during menses	The woman avoids intercourse every other dry day to avoid confusion between secretions and semen	The first day the woman notices fertile-type secretions	Four days after peak day
Sympto-Thermal Method			The first day the woman notices fertile-type secretions	Using the 3-over-6 rule for basal body temperature
Double-check variation of the Sympto-Thermal Method			The first day the woman notices fertile-type secretions or shortcycle-19, whichever comes first	Using the 3-over-6 rule for basal body temperature, or four days after peak day, whichever is later
TwoDay Method			The first day the woman notices secretions of any type	The first day that the woman noticed no secretions for that day or the day before
Standard Days Method			Day 8 of the cycle	Day 19 of the cycle

Table 1: Days Considered Fertile by the Various NFP Methods

cluding effectiveness, number of days considered fertile, whether the fertile window is fixed or changing each cycle, and the need to monitor symptoms—will also be discussed.

Because NFP methods are offered with many variations in various settings, it is important to define exactly the rules for identifying the fertile days that I used for the comparisons. These are summarized in Table 1.

The Billings Ovulation Method (BOM) requires that women avoid intercourse during menses. After their period ends, they avoid intercourse every other dry day until the onset of mucus secretions (i.e., a sensation of dampness or wetness detectable at the vulva). They consider themselves fertile from that point until the evening of the fourth day after the Peak Day (the Peak Day is the last day on which fertile-type mucus is recognized, or the last day on which the wet or lubricative sensation is felt) (WHO 1981).

The Sympto-Thermal Method (STM) is offered in many countries with variations. This analysis includes two variations, which I term the STM and the STM with Double-Check. Users of both versions do not consider themselves fertile during menses. After menses, they consider themselves fertile from the onset of fertile-type cervical secretions. They read their basal body temperature daily and determine the end of the fertile window using the 3-over-6 rule—the first time in the cycle that three temperatures are recorded, all of which are above the level of the six daily temperature readings immediately preceding the first elevated temperature (Colombo and Masarotto 2000). This variation of the method is taught in many NFP centers in various countries. The STM with Double-Check is taught mostly by NFP centers in Germany, Austria, and several other European countries. To determine the beginning of the fertile window, the woman keeps track of her cycle length for 12 months and determines the length of her shortest cycle. She subtracts 19 from that cycle length. The result is the first fertile day. But if she observed fertile-type cervical secretions first, then that is the beginning of the fertile day (note that some users prefer to monitor the first day of temperature increase for the previous 12 cycles and subtract 7 from that figure instead of using the short cycle minus 19 days formula). The end of the fertile period is determined using the 3-over-6 rule and the Peak Day plus 4 days rule—whichever comes later (Frank-Herrmann et al. 2005).

Users of the TwoDay Method follow an algorithm to determine when they are fertile. Each day, they ask themselves two questions: "Did I note any secretions today?" and "Did I note any secretions yesterday?" If the answer to either question is "yes," the woman considers herself fertile today. If the answer to both questions is "no," the woman does not consider herself fertile today (Arévalo et al. 2004).

Users of the Standard Days Method consider themselves fertile on days 8-19 (inclusive) of the menstrual cycle (Arévalo et al. 2002). The same rule is followed by all users in all cycles.

THE PROGRAM PERSPECTIVE

Couples can only choose to adopt a method that is available to them—that is, a method that a program or teacher in their area offers. The program can be a dedicated NFP program, a family planning program, a program at a health clinic, or a community-based program. Programs usually operate with limited resources. Since different methods require different amounts of resources, the program needs to balance its available resources with the resource needs of the method to determine if the program can offer the method. Methods have many requirements. Two that I focus on here are the time it takes to teach a method and the number of visits required before a client can reach autonomy.

Each program has its own protocol. Generally speaking, however, couples learning the Billings Ovulation Method (BOM) and both versions of the STM need to attend one or two group sessions that can last anywhere from 45 minutes to an hour or more. They also need to attend at least one or two individual follow-up sessions during the first several months of use. Compare this to the TwoDay Method and the Standard Days Method, which require only one counseling session, lasting 20-30 minutes. The woman (or couple) is considered autonomous after that one session, although most programs do offer the opportunity for a subsequent visit for those who choose it. Clearly, the BOM and the STM use more personnel resources then the TwoDay Method and the Standard Days Method.

It is not enough that the program offers a method—couples in the area need to be aware that the method is offered. To accomplish this, programs should promote the methods they offer. Different promotional strategies can work better in various settings—community meetings, mass media, and brochures, for example. Each program should consider carefully the approach that is best suited for the location, the population, the program, and the method.

THE TEACHER PERSPECTIVE

For a method to be available, teachers should also be ready, willing, and able to teach it. There are many necessary ingredients for a teacher to be ready to teach the method, including, for example, the availability of support materials. The basic requirement, however, is that the teacher needs to be trained.

Different programs have different protocols for training their teachers. Generally speaking, however, to learn to teach the BOM and the STM, a teacher needs to participate in a workshop that takes three or four days. Once the training program is complete, the teachers must complete a supervised practicum with a specified number of clients whom they need to teach and follow. The practicum often lasts about six months, sometimes followed by another workshop.

Compare this to the teacher training requirements for the TwoDay Method and the Standard Days Method. The length and intensity of training for these methods depend on the type of provider—physicians and nurses learn more quickly than community volunteers. Providers can therefore be taught how to provide the TwoDay Method or the Standard Days Method in a training that lasts between two hours and a day, depending on the level of the provider. It is recommended that providers participate in a refresher training two or three months later to reinforce what they know, but this is usually done in the context of routine supervision, so there is no need for the providers to attend another training session. The TwoDay Method and the Standard Days Method require less time to train providers than the BOM and the STM because the former are much less complicated to use than are the latter.

Teachers who provide methods are often volunteers, or they work in settings with many competing demands on their time. Therefore, the time that it takes to teach the method can be an important determinant of their willingness to teach the method to couples after they themselves are trained. As shown above, the BOM and both versions of the STM require more time commitment from teachers than the TwoDay Method and the Standard Days Method.

In an ideal world, when a program offers more than one method, it should be the couple's choice which method to use. But we do not live in an ideal world. When a teacher is trained in a specific method, it is often difficult for her or him to feel comfortable teaching a different method. Multi-method programs should be aware of this phenomenon. They should either train different providers in different methods or undertake programs to help providers adjust to teaching more than one method.

THE COUPLE PERSPECTIVE

When the method is available and couples are aware of it, they also need to be able to find the method acceptable. Severy and Newcomer (2005) define method acceptability as the voluntary sustained use of a method in the context of alternatives. This section examines some of the characteristics of methods and couples that can affect the acceptability of the methods to the couple.

METHOD EFFECTIVENESS

For couples seeking to avoid pregnancy, effectiveness can be an important characteristic of NFP methods. Studies have shown that the methods I compare here are all highly effective (see, for example, Arévalo et al. 2002, 2004; Frank-Herrmann et al. 2005 and 2007; WHO 1981). However, the nuances of the rules used to identify the fertile days make some methods somewhat more effective than others.

I use a unique data set to compare the effectiveness of the various methods on different days relative to ovulation. The data were collected by the Quidel Corporation as it was testing an ovulation prediction device that never made it to market. The data set is not large—107 women, ages 19-45, who were experienced NFP users in European centers contributed 326 cycles—but it is very detailed. Participants charted both cervical secretions and basal body temperature. They also collected daily samples of early morning urine for quantitative analysis of estrone-3-glucuronide (E1-3-G), pregnanediol-3-alpha-glucuronide (Pd-3-α-G), luteinising hormone (LH), and follicular stimulating hormone (FSH). Transvaginal ultrasonography was used to monitor each ovulation (Ecochard 2005). Therefore, the data include all necessary information to determine whether current use of each of the methods would have prevented pregnancy for the study participants on any given day relative to ovulation (determined objectively by sonogram).

Using these data, I determined what the probability of pregnancy would have been for these women, in these cycles, if they had been using the four methods that I focus on here. As I did this, I used another piece of information—the results from a study by Wilcox et al. (1998) that show the probability of pregnancy from intercourse on different days relative to ovulation. Because of the viability of sperm, intercourse six or more days before ovulation rarely results in pregnancy. However, the probability of clinically detected pregnancy increases progressively, from about 4% if intercourse occurs five days before ovulation, to 29% two days and 27% one day before ovulation, declining to 8% if intercourse occurs on the day of ovulation and zero thereafter. Intercourse one or more days after ovulation can rarely result in pregnancy (Wilcox et al. 1998).

I took the Wilcox et al. probabilities and multiplied them by the percentage of cycles in the data in which that day relative to ovulation was not considered fertile by the method. The results are depicted in Figure 1. Each line represents a method and shows the theoretical probability of pregnancy from intercourse on that day relative to ovulation for users of this method. The levels are not speci-

Figure 1: Probability of Pregnancy on Days Relative to Ovulation

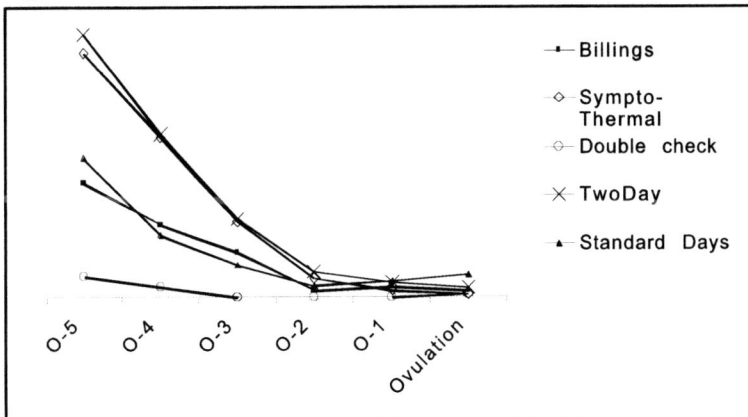

fied in the figures because these are not actual effectiveness levels and do not reflect actual method failure. Yet they represent the comparative failure of the methods relative to each other. All the methods are highly effective, as shown in effectiveness studies. Note that Figure 1 was stretched vertically to magnify the small differences between the methods.

The STM with Double-Check is somewhat more effective then the other methods. The BOM is slightly more effective in the early part of the fertile window than the other cervical secretions-based methods (the STM and the TwoDay Methods) because it is the only one that both considers a woman fertile during menses and also includes the every-other-dry-day instruction. The Standard Days Method also appears to be quite effective.

OTHER METHOD CHARACTERISTICS

The effectiveness of the method in helping the couple avoid pregnancy is an important determinant of the acceptability of the method to the couple, but it is not the only method characteristic that may influence acceptability. Among factors that can influence acceptability are the time it takes to learn the method and to reach autonomy, which I discussed above, as well as the number of days in each cycle

Table 2: Method Characteristics

	Median Non-fertile days	Fertile Window	Monitoring	Charting	Commodities
Billings	11*	Varied			Charts
Sympto -Thermal	17	Varied			Thermometers Charts
Sympto -Thermal Double-check	15	Varied			Thermometers Calendars Charts
TwoDay	18	Varied			Charts
Standard Days	16	Fixed			CycleBeads Charts

* The Billings Ovulation Method considers days with menses as potentially fertile. After menses every other dry day is considered fertile until the fertile window starts.

that the method considers fertile (so that the couple needs to avoid intercourse when attempting to postpone pregnancy), the commodities required to use the method, whether the fertile window is fixed or variable between cycles, and the need to monitor symptoms. I compare the methods along these characteristics in Table 2.

The length of the fertile window determines when during the cycle the couple can have intercourse to either achieve or avoid pregnancy. A recent study found that couples using NFP do not have intercourse less frequently than users of other methods—they simply time it differently in the cycle (Sinai and Arévalo 2006). Yet the length of the fertile window can affect the couple's perception of the method.

The Billings Ovulation Method, both versions of the Sympto-Thermal Method, and the TwoDay Method identify a fertile window that is variable. Couples cannot know exactly when that window will start during each cycle and how long it will last. The Standard Days Method, on the other hand, identifies a fixed fertile window for all users in all cycles. Couples can, therefore, plan around it.

Monitoring and charting for use of the Standard Days Method and the TwoDay Method are much simpler than the monitoring and charting required to correctly use the BOM and the STM. From simplest to most complex, the methods require the following monitoring and charting:

- **The Standard Days Method** requires that the woman mark the first day of her period on a calendar. This is the only charting. The user monitors her CycleBeads each day by moving a rubber ring one bead per day. When the ring is on white beads, she is considered fertile. On all other days, she is not. There is a special bead to alert the woman if her cycle was shorter than 26 days. If she completed CycleBeads and does not start her period by the next day, her cycle was longer than 32 days. This method requires the use of a commodity (CycleBeads).
- **The TwoDay Method** requires that the woman follow the algorithm described above. The woman monitors her cervical secretions daily by asking herself if she noted secretions of any type on that day or the day before. She does not need to distinguish between different types of cervical secre-

tions or identify the Peak Day. To chart, she only notes daily whether or not she had cervical secretions of any type that day.

- **The Billings Ovulation Method** also requires that the woman monitor cervical secretions. However, the woman needs to distinguish between different types of cervical secretions, identify changes in cervical secretions, and determine the Peak Day. The woman needs to chart in her calendar the type of cervical secretions she notices each day and count four days after the Peak Day.
- **The Sympto-Thermal Method** has similar monitoring and charting requirements as the BOM with regard to cervical secretions. In addition, the woman needs to read her basal body temperature each morning, chart it, and calculate when the fertile window will end, using the 3-over-6 rule. This method also requires a commodity (a basal body temperature thermometer), which is available in most places, but may be harder to obtain in more remote areas.
- **The Sympto-Thermal Method with Double-Check** has all of the above requirements of the STM, as well as the requirement that the woman keep track of her cycle length in the previous 12 months, determine which cycle was the shortest, and subtract 19 from the length of that cycle.

COUPLE CHARACTERISTICS

Acceptability is also determined by characteristics of the woman and the couple. Different people have different needs. Among other factors, these needs are determined by biology, life circumstances, and religious beliefs.

Cycle regularity is one biological characteristic that can make a difference in method choice. To use the Standard Days Method, a woman should have cycles that usually range 26-32 days. Cycle regularity is also important for women who wish to use the Sympto-Thermal Method with Double-Check, because the more variability they have in their cycle length, the longer the identified fertile window will be. In addition to cycle length, a variety of factors can make cervical secretions or basal body temperature harder for some women to interpret.

Age, parity, age of youngest child, and level of literacy are examples of life circumstance characteristics that can influence couples' preference for a specific method.

Conventional wisdom suggests that NFP is a method for Catholic couples. However, recent experience with the Standard Days Method and the TwoDay Method in many countries in Asia, Africa, and Latin America show that while different traditions and beliefs can play a role in method preference, NFP can serve the needs of many couples worldwide for an effective, natural, and acceptable method, regardless of their religion.

CONCLUSION

The Billings Ovulation Method, two different versions of the Sympto-Thermal Method, the TwoDay Method, and the Standard Days Method are all highly effective NFP methods. They have some differences, however, that make programs, teachers, and users find one method more acceptable than the others.

The good news is that there are several effective natural methods and that the differences among them can meet the different needs of a wide range of couples. Programs that offer more than one method may be able to meet these needs better. If the goal is to help more couples use NFP, then the differences between different methods must be considered.

ACKNOWLEDGMENTS

The author thanks Dr. René Ecochard for permission to use the Quidel data and for his invaluable assistance with the analysis. Support for the analysis and preparation of this paper was provided by the Institute for Reproductive Health, at Georgetown University, Washington, DC, which is funded under cooperative agreement HRN-A-00-97-00011-00 with the U.S. Agency for International Development (USAID). The views expressed by the author do not necessarily reflect the views or policies of USAID or Georgetown University.

SOURCES CONSULTED

Arévalo, M., V. Jennings, M. Nikula , and I. Sinai. 2004. Efficacy of the new TwoDay Method of family planning. *Fertility and Sterility* 82: 885-892.

Arévalo, M., V. Jennings, and I. Sinai. 2002. Efficacy of a new method of family planning: The Standard Days Method. *Contraception* 65: 333-338.

Colombo, B., and G. Masarotto. 2000. Daily fecundability: First results from a new data base. *Demographic Research* 3: Article 5 (www.demographic-research.org/Volumes/Vol3/5).

Ecochard, R. 2005. Heterogeneity: The masked part of reproductive technology success rates. *Rev Epidemiol Sante Publique* 53: 2S107-2S117.

Frank-Herrmann, P., C. Gnoth, S. Baur, T. Strowitzki, and G. Freundl. 2005. Determination of the fertile window: Reproductive competence of women—European cycle databases. *Gynecological Endocrinology* 20: 305-312.

Frank-Herrmann, P., J. Hail, C. Gnoth, E. Toledo, S. Baur, C. Pyper, E. Jenetzky, T. Strowitzki, and G. Freundl. 2007. The effectiveness of a fertility awareness based method to avoid pregnancy in relation to a couple's sexual behaviour during the fertile time: a prospective longitudinal study. *Human Reproduction* 22(5):1310-1319. Available at: http://www.oxford-journals.org/eshre/press-release/freepdf/dem003.pdf

Severy, L. J., and S. Newcomer. 2005. Critical issues in contraceptive and STI acceptability research. *Journal of Social Issues* 61: 45-65.

Sinai, I., and M. Arévalo. 2006. It's all in the timing: Coital frequency and fertility awareness-based methods of family planning. *Journal of Biosocial Science* 38: 763-777.

Wilcox, A. J., C. R. Weinberg, and D. D. Baird. 1998. Post-ovulatory aging of the human oocyte and embryo failure. *Human Reproduction* 13: 394-398.

World Health Organization (WHO). 1981. Prospective multicenter trial of the Ovulation Method of Natural Family Planning. II. The effectiveness phase. *Fertility and Sterility* 36: 591-598.

A RANDOMIZED CONTROL TRIAL OF TEEN STAR

PILAR VIGIL, MANUEL E. CORTÉS, HANNA KLAUS

The Teen STAR (Sexuality Teaching in the context of Adult Responsibility) program avoids the two extremes of sexuality education—abstinence-only or "comprehensive"—as it balances the facts of fertility with the emotional, cognitive, social, and spiritual aspects of human sexuality.

A primary and secondary program was initiated to prevent sexual activity among Chilean teens aged 12–18 years old. Among the females who participated in the program, only 3.4% transitioned from virginity to intercourse, compared with 12.4% of control females who did not participate in the program. Among the males who participated in the program, only 8.8% transitioned from virginity to intercourse, compared with 17.6% of control males who did not participate in the program. Twenty-one percent of sexually active program subjects discontinued intercourse, compared with 9% controls. Of those program subjects who discontinued intercourse, none resumed activity at the end of one year, whereas 11.7% of control subjects did resume sexual activity.

Pregnancy rates were studied among female students who participated in Teen STAR versus female students who did not participate in the program (i.e., the control group). Average pregnancy rates per year were 0.87% in the program group and 4.87% in the control group during the follow-up period.

INTRODUCTION

During the last twenty-five years, there have been extensive efforts to reduce the consequences of risky adolescent sexual behaviors by programs classified either as abstinence-only or as comprehensive sexuality (also known as abstinence-based education, safer-sex, secular, or abstinence-plus programs) education programs (Thomas 2000, Silva 2002). The first kind of program—

abstinence-only sex education programs, which the United States government defined under Section 510 of the 1996 Social Security Act—can be perceived as inherently coercive in the sense that they do not promote free choice on the part of the teen participant. They can also be seen as authoritarian in approach. The second kind of program—comprehensive sexuality education—also promotes abstinence as the first and best choice for preventing pregnancy and sexually transmitted diseases (STDs), including Human Immunodeficiency Virus (HIV), but it also provides education and sometimes services regarding all contraceptive methods. These comprehensive sexuality education programs are designed to assist students in becoming well-informed decision makers (Pittman 2006), but these programs sometimes view the consequences of sexual behaviors mechanistically, or isolated from social and individual values.

Although controlled randomized evaluation has been scant for both approaches (Silva 2002), the available evidence suggests that adolescent sexual behavior is a complex phenomenon and that addressing it requires an integrated, sophisticated approach that is not unduly bound by ideological simplicity (Kirby 2001).

The Teen STAR (Sexuality Teaching in the context of Adult Responsibility; see: www.teenstar.cl and www.teenstarprogram.org.) program began twenty-seven years ago in an attempt to offer a program of education in human sexuality that encompasses the whole person. In so doing, the program has avoided the two extremes of abstinence-only and comprehensive sexuality education programs.

Teen STAR is an interactive, holistic education program in human sexuality leading to the acceptance of one's own sexuality and fertility. It involves feelings as well as intellect, requires that fertility patterns be learned through observation, and demands both parental participation and teacher-student confidentiality. Learning through observation challenges teens to integrate their biological capacity to be fathers or mothers into all aspects of their lives, i.e., social, emotional, intellectual, spiritual, and physical aspects of their sexuality (Vigil 2004a; de Malherbe 2005). Adolescence can produce a temporary "deafness" to the teachings that adults would like to transmit to young people (Hall et al. 2004). Teens need to make decisions about their own behavior, make their own discoveries, and reach their own conclusions. Adolescents are immersed in the task of establishing their own ego identity. This requires at least a theoretical distancing from the "parental ego". Knowledge of their fertility helps them understand their sexuality (Vigil et al. 2006a, 2006b), as well as their capacity to procreate. Experiencing their body's messages about fertility and its potential for procreation is a source of intellectual learning for teens. Additionally, it allows teens to choose to express this potential with total freedom and to save it for a committed relationship: marriage (Vigil et al. 2002a). At the same time, parental involvement is still an important component of the Teen STAR program. Other studies have also shown that parental participation in interventions appears to be associated with a higher tendency toward abstinence (Silva 2002).

To reach these goals, Teen STAR develops the following areas:

1. Improving self-identity and self-esteem. Adolescents need to know who they are, so they are encouraged to become aware of themselves as free, if limited, persons.

2. Valuing their freedom and decision-making ability. Teens are informed about free and responsible choices. Self-control is a prized fruit that feeds on self-knowledge.

3. Building a feeling of respect for the gift of life. Human life is a gift, received to be given. Only those teens who value their own life will be able to present it as a gift to others. If youngsters despise themselves, they will despise life and will not consider their possible surrender as a precious gift.

PURPOSE OF THE STUDY

The objective of the present review is to analyze the results obtained with the Teen STAR program in two randomized, controlled trials: (1) a study conducted to evaluate the effect of Teen STAR on sexual behaviour among Chilean female and male adolescents (Vigil et al. 2005a) and (2) a study conducted to evaluate the effect of Teen STAR on teenage pregnancy rates in Chilean adolescent girls (Cabezón et al. 2005).

METHODOLOGY

TEEN STAR TEACHER TRAINING

Teachers from different schools voluntarily participating in the study were trained in a five-day seminar-workshop at the Pontifical Catholic University of Chile (PUC), Santiago. They were prepared to develop all units of the Teen STAR program with the students and hold effective meetings with parents. Teen STAR has different developmental curricula, differentiated on the basis of age, sex, and school class. Each curriculum has 14 units (Cabezón et al. 2005):

1. Initial session and introduction to the program

2. Differences between genders

3. Identification of prejudices on female and male's features

4. Anatomy and physiology of human reproductive system

5. Puberty, fertility in women, and fertility in men

6. Fertility awareness, registration of fertility records (classes distributed along the course)

7. Knowing emotions and controlling behaviors

8. The manipulation of sexuality in media

9. Self-assurance and maintaining decisions

10. Marriage, family, and parenthood

11. Beginning of life, value of human life

12. Family planning methods, contraception

13. Pregnancy, delivery, breastfeeding

14. Final session and feedback

The units are delivered in one or more 45–90 minute sessions. Progression depends on satisfactory completion of each unit by the students before passing to the next unit.

Teachers were trained to maintain fluent communication with parents, while at the same time respecting the confidentiality of communications with students. Personal interviews with the students are an integral aspect of the program, so teachers were also trained in counseling skills. Each teacher received a Teen STAR manual including the curricula and supplementary articles and audiovisual materials, such as posters, videotapes, and CDs.

STUDY OF THE EFFECT ON
ADOLESCENT SEXUAL BEHAVIOR
The study on Teen STAR's effect on adolescent sexual behavior (Vigil

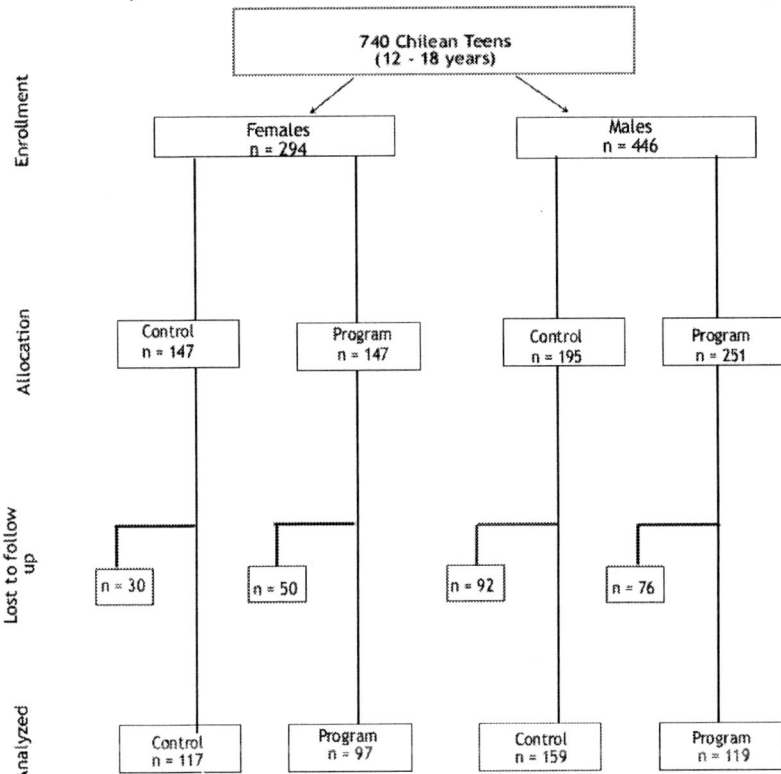

Figure 1: Flow of Participants through Each Stage of the Study of the Effect of Teen STAR on Adolescent Sexual Behavior

et al. 2005a; 2005b) included 740 Chilean white teens (12–18 years old) attending 10 basic schools or high schools (Figure 1). The study and control groups consisted of students in the same grade in classes of 30 to 40 students. They were randomly divided into program and control groups by drawing the letter of the class from a black bag. The program group (*n* = 147 females, 251 males) consisted of those teens who participated in the Teen STAR program with parental consent. A trained Teen STAR teacher who was part of the school's staff and had voluntarily agreed to participate in the training workshop worked with the program group over eight months. The program's curricula, differentiated on the basis of age, sex, and school class, were offered twice a week during school hours. In addition, at least one personal interview was conducted with each student as part of the program. The intervention with parents consisted of three meetings along the school year, which described the characteristics of the program and physical and psychological development of teens and requested parents' feedback. Program impact was assessed by means of anonymous pre- and post-program questionnaires administered to study and control subjects (Vigil et al. 2005a).

The control group (*n* = 147 females, 195 males) comprised students with similar characteristics (same age, sex, and socioeconomic and educational levels) from parallel classes at each school who did not participate in the Teen STAR program and received the regular school education. These students also completed the pre- and post-program questionnaires. Questionnaires were given at the same time to control and program students. The questionnaires for both groups were identified by a name chosen by each student and known only to him or her. The completed questionnaires were placed into a special box, which was sealed in front of the students. The box was then submitted to a statistician. The pre- and post-program responses of the control group and the program group were compared. The surveys contained 135 questions about diverse topics. Their analysis allowed evaluation of the impact of the Teen STAR program on the teens' sexual activity via rates for (1) primary abstinence, (2) discontinuation of intercourse, (3) resumption of sexual activity, and (4) influence of the curriculum on abstinence (Vigil et al. 2005a).

The study was approved by the directing councils of all participating educational establishments, as well as by the Ethics Committee of the Faculty of Biological Sciences of the Pontifical Catholic University of Chile, Santiago.

The study included all those teenagers willing to take part who had their parents' consent. Before the initiation of the study, all adolescents younger than 12 and older than 18 years of age (both ends of the normal distribution curve) were excluded. Also excluded from the outcome analysis were all those students whose pre- and posttests either were missing identifiers (e.g., missing date of birth) or had internal inconsistencies or unreliable data, (e.g., noncorrelated questionnaires in terms of date of birth and ID code, omitted questions, or noncorrelated answers to paired questions in the questionnaire). For certain variables, exclusion criteria were lack of answer or dissenting replies (e.g., saying he/she had intercourse in pre-program questionnaire and saying he had not in post-program questionnaire) to a specific question (Vigil et al. 2005a).

The statistical study employed a student's t-test and analysis for sample homogeneity for dropouts in both groups.

STUDY OF THE EFFECT OF TEEN STAR ON TEENAGE PREGNANCY

A randomized, controlled study to evaluate the efficacy of the program in preventing adolescent pregnancy (Cabezón et al. 2005) was conducted that compared intervention with the Teen STAR program with no intervention in a public girls school in San Bernardo, a peripheral community of Santiago, Chile. The trial included a total of 1,259 Chilean white girls, 15 to 16 years old at the time they joined the study, who were divided into three cohorts depending on what year they started high school: the 1996 cohort of 425 students, in which no one received intervention; the 1997 cohort, in which 210 students received Teen STAR and 213 (control group) did not; and the 1998 cohort, in which 328 students received Teen STAR and 83 (control group) did not (Cabezón et al. 2005; Rev. Pan. 2005) (Figure 2 [next page]). As in the previous study, participants were randomly divided into program and control groups by drawing the letter of the class from a black bag. The classes each had 30 to 35 girls. The 1998 cohort included more girls in the program group. This was because initial results obtained with the 1997 cohort showed a decrease in pregnancy rates, so we were asked to expand the program group. Eight teachers were available, so the program group included eight classes (328 girls) for the 1998 cohort. All cohorts were fol-

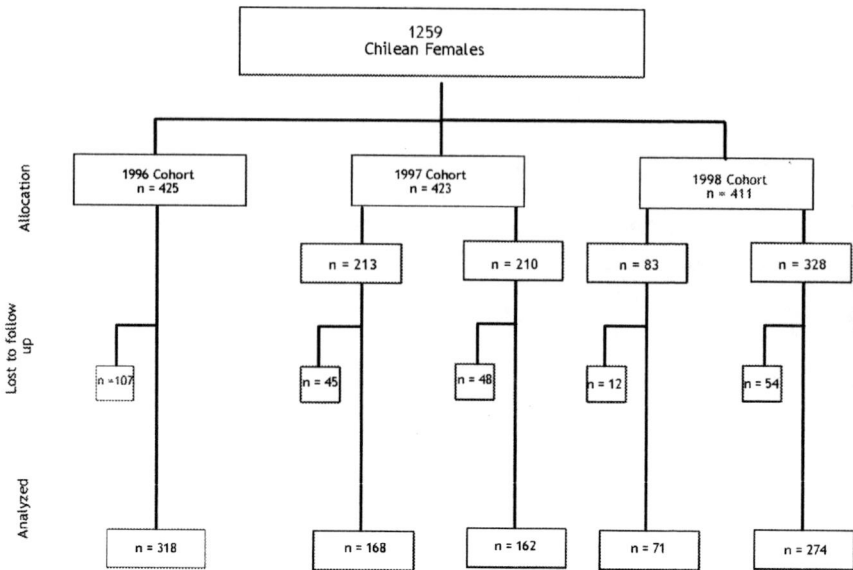

Figure 2: Flow of Participants Through Each Stage of the Study of the
Effect of Teen STAR on Teenage Pregnancy Prevention

lowed for four years; pregnancy rates were recorded for program and
control groups. Pregnancy rates were measured, and risk ratio (RR)
with 95% confidence interval (CI) was calculated for program and
control groups in each cohort. The homogeneity test consisted of the
application of the chi-square (χ^2) test (Cabezón et al. 2005).

RESULTS

EFFECT ON ADOLESCENT SEXUAL BEHAVIOR

In the program group, 8.8% of virgin males and 3.4% of virgin females transitioned to sexual activity, versus 17.6% of virgin males
and 12.4% of virgin females in the control group ($p = 0.004$) (Vigil
et al. 2005a; 2005b) (see Figure 3 [next page]). The delay observed in
the initiation of sexual activity within the program group was similar for females and males (V-square = 0.32; $p = 0.571$; V-square is a
corrected χ^2 value obtained from a 2 x 2 table) (Cortés et al. 2006).
Within the group of sexually active students, 20.5% of program
students discontinued sexual activity (i.e., had no act of intercourse
within the final three months), compared with 9% of students in the

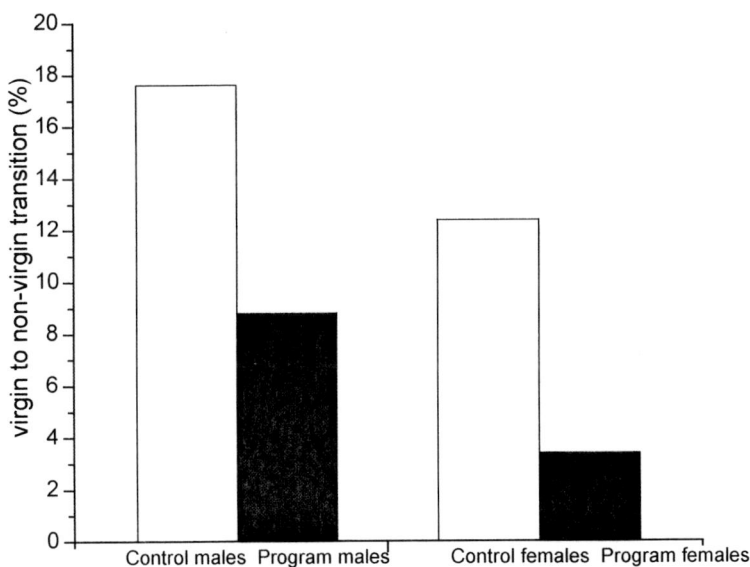

Figure 3: Transition Rates of Sexual Activity in Program and
Control Students for Males and Females

control group who discontinued sexual activity ($p \leq 0.03$). Among students who had initiated sexual activity before the intervention, but who were sexually inactive at the time the study began, 11.7% of the control group resumed intercourse during the period of the study, while none of the students in the program group did (Vigil et al. 2005a). Adolescents participating in the program exhibited an increase in the number of reasons for not having intercourse, or "maintaining abstinence," from one reason at the beginning of the program to three reasons at the end of it (Vigil et al. 2005a).

EFFECT ON TEENAGE PREGNANCY

Over the four-year follow-up, 6 pregnancies occurred in the program group and 35 in the control group. Average pregnancy rates per year were 0.87% for the program and 4.87% for the control group during the follow-up period. For the 1996 cohort (no intervention), the pregnancy rate was 14.7%. For the 1997 cohort, the pregnancy rates were 3.3% and 18.91% for program and control groups, respectively (RR: 0.17619, CI: 0.0759–0.4086). For the 1998 cohort, the pregnancy rates were 4.43% and 22.66% for program and control

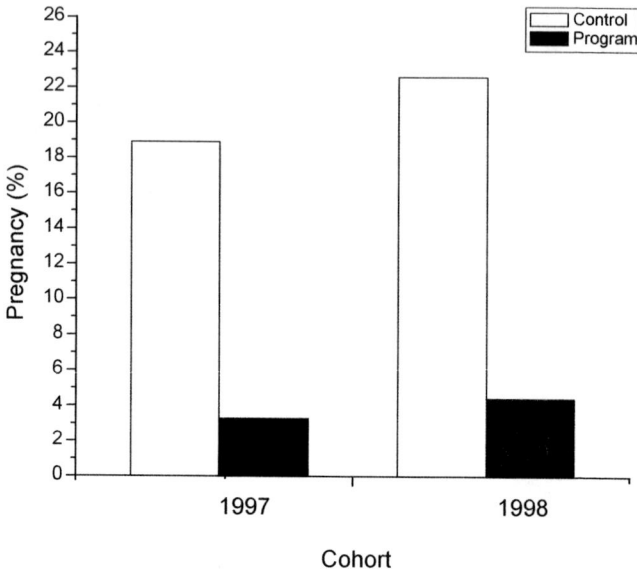

Figure 4: Overall Cumulative Pregnancy Rates over 4-Year Follow-Up for the 1997 and 1998 Cohorts

groups, respectively (RR: 0.19574, CI: 0.0995–0.3848) (Cabezón et al. 2005; Rev. Pan. 2005) (see Figure 4). Program adolescents also exhibited a significant change in their reasons for abstinence, particularly "I can't seem to find the right person" and "I don't feel ready," suggesting an internalization of their locus of control. They pointed out that they felt less prepared to have sexual intercourse. A reverse trend was found in the control group adolescents for the second of the above reasons (being one year older, they felt better qualified to initiate sexual activity), while choices for the first reason remained unchanged (Cabezón et al. 2005).

DISCUSSION

Although many sex education programs have been conducted and lavish amounts of money have been spent, it is well known that teenage pregnancies continue to be a significant problem. In Chile,

15.6% of all live births in the 1996–1998 period involved mothers younger than 20 years. Therefore, in Chile, about 40,000 teens become mothers every year (Vigil et al. 2005a), and this does not consider illegal abortions or pregnancies starting at 19 and ending at 20 years (Álvarez et al. 1990; Delpiano and Aguilera Reyes. 2001).

In countries such as the United States, teenage pregnancies have decreased during the last 15 years, but still about 800,000 adolescents give birth each year. It should be noted that the decrease in teenage pregnancy rates is different according to ethnic groups. Currently, the highest pregnancy rates are within the Hispanic groups (Brindis 2006).

Adolescents are at high risk of contracting STDs: nearly one half of new reported cases occur among 15 to 24 year old people (Brindis 2006). Teens' perceptions of invulnerability (Hall et al. 2004), teen pregnancies, and the increasingly earlier initiation of sexual activity signal an urgent need to provide effective sex education programs to this age group.

DiCenso's meta-analysis (DiCenso et al. 2002) of primary prevention strategies found that provision of contraception, even while acknowledging that abstinence is preferable, did not delay the initiation of sexual intercourse or improve use of birth control among young men and women. Nor was there a reduction in pregnancies among young women, while the interventions increased pregnancies in partners of male participants.

Other studies, in addition to ours, have demonstrated that sexual education programs can have an impact in the delay of initiation of sexual activity and teen pregnancies (Olsen et al. 1991; Darroch et al. 2000; Sather and Zinn 2002; Rev. Pan. 2005). These programs promote a person's sense of worth, together with free and informed decision making, and appear to have greater impact on teens. A program that embraces all aspects of the human person leads to satisfactory outcomes. Teen STAR is such a program. It has resulted in (a) increased tendency toward abstinence, (b) discontinuation of sexual activity, and (c) taking personal responsibility for decisions about when to give oneself to another. An additional factor to be considered is parental involvement. Our program included three meetings with parents. A positive correlation between parental involvement and delay in initiating of sexual activity has been shown (Klaus et al. 1987). For this reason, we believe that including and integrating parents is a key factor in the success of the program.

Attitudes precede behavior change; hence, changes in attitude toward primary (decides to abstain from intercourse without having had it previously) or secondary abstinence (decides to abstain from intercourse having had it previously) are significant. When these changes settle in, a holistic perception and transformation of life can be expected. Understanding the following factors helps Teen STAR foster changes in attitude:

> 1. **The psychological underpinnings of the increased tendency toward abstinence.** Teen STAR's anthropological rationale encourages the free decisions not only by adolescents (our first and foremost goal) but also by anyone who says yes to the program. The above data show that the values people get in touch with work both through their innate appeal and through group interaction (i.e., increased awareness of one's own dignity and the value of freedom).

> 2. **Causes for discontinuation of sexual activity.** The participants' post-test responses appear to show that they stopped activity as a result of a changed perception of themselves, rather than out of boredom or peer pressure.

> 3. **Strong personal decisions, reached through internalized understanding of one's procreative capacity.** The focus on personal decisions shows the value of the Teen STAR program as a proposal with a future—with firm roots. The program is based on convictions and adherence to values.

This study showed a decrease in initiation of sexual activity, along with an increase in discontinuation of sexual activity. Analysis of the long-term effects of this type of intervention is important and has not been done sufficiently. Preliminary studies indicate that continued observation and attention to the girls' fertility patterns reinforces their decision to remain, or return to, abstinence. The reduction in pregnancies was sustained in the groups of girls who participated in the program. However, the goal of long-term follow-up of these students to assess behavior after high school still needs to be met.

We believe that the effectiveness of the Teen STAR program is mainly based on certain characteristics that make it substantially different from both abstinence-only and comprehensive sexuality education programs. Fertility awareness, coupled with placing a high value on possessing fertility, in terms of both future procreation and present understanding of their bodily processes, makes the program a whole-person experience whose impact may well last for the rest of participants' lives. Generally, self-esteem and self-confidence result from integrating what one understands of oneself into making one's own decisions about all behaviors.

For teens, recognizing their fertility not only leads to better knowledge of themselves but also can become a tool for them to recognize various endocrine-metabolic pathologies. Specifically, among girls, certain gynecological problems can be discovered through the charting of their fertile period by the observation of the different patterns of cervical mucus, as well as the regularity of their menstrual cycles (Vigil et al. 2006a, 2006b). Some disorders, such as polycystic ovarian syndrome, can be suspected in patients who have noticed abnormal cervical mucus patterns, as well as an abnormal distribution of adipose tissue in the body. Symptoms of other pathologies, such as ovarian and adrenal tumors, problems in the hypothalamo-hypophyseal-gonadal axis, and autoimmune diseases, could also be identified from the cervical mucus patterns, a tool that every woman should be familiar with (Vigil 2004b). In the case of males, appropriate learning of their anatomy and physiology could help them to discover emerging problems at their juvenile stages, such as obesity, hypo- and hyperandrogenism, abnormal development of their genitals, growth dysfunctions, and STDs such as *Chlamydia trachomatis*, an infection that can impair the fertility of men as well as women (Vigil et al. 2002b; Gonzales et al. 2004; Vigil and Cortés 2006). Prompt recognition of abnormalities would hasten medical diagnosis and treatment.

Today's challenge for educators is to help young people to perceive sexuality as a whole, including all dimensions of one's human experience. Reason, freedom, and emotions should be integrated into sex education programs. Programs should overcome the tendency to separate affections and emotions from bodily requirements, as well. Personal actions such as precocious sexual activity not only can cause undesirable consequences, e.g., unintended teen pregnancies and the contraction of STDs, but also have an impact on the adolescent's psyche and emotions.

CONCLUSIONS

The Teen STAR program delayed sexual initiation among virgins and facilitated discontinuation of sexual activity among sexually active students: program students found more reasons to maintain sexual abstinence than control students (Vigil et al. 2002a; Vigil et al. 2005a). The program was also effective in preventing unintended adolescent pregnancies (Cabezón et al. 2005; Rev. Pan. 2005). Properly trained high school teachers proved to be efficient in delivering the program. Teen STAR has shown an impact on pregnancy prevention that extends for at least the four years of high school when begun during the first year of high school (Cabezón et al. 2005).

ACKNOWLEDGMENTS

We thank Paulina del Río and Professor María Angélica Kaulen (from the Faculty of Letters, PUC), for their help with the preparation of the English version of this manuscript. Also, we thank Ana R. Godoy, *BSc (Biochem)*, for her technical help with the preparation of the figures.

SOURCES CONSULTED

Álvarez, M. L., A. Mauricci, and S. Muzzo. 1990. Información sexual de los adolescentes según sexo. *Revista Chilena de Pediatría* 61(2): 102-108.

Brindis, C. D. 2006. A public health success: Understanding policy changes related to teen sexual activity and pregnancy. *Annual Review of Public Health* 27: 277-295.

Cabezón, C., P. Vigil, I. Rojas, M. E. Leiva, R. Riquelme, W. Aranda, and C. García. 2005. Adolescent pregnancy prevention: An abstinence-centered randomized controlled intervention in a Chilean public high school. *Journal of Adolescent Health* 36(1): 64-69.

Cortés, M. E., M. J. del Río, and P. Vigil. 2006. El efecto de Teen STAR sobre el comportamiento sexual en jóvenes. Panel 8: Catholic physicians, globalisation and poverty. *XXII Congress of the World Federation of the Catholic Medical Associations.* Barcelona, Catalonia, Spain. http://www.teenstar.cl/publicaciones.htm (accessed July 28, 2006).

Darroch, J. E., D. J. Landry, and S. Singh. 2000. Changing emphases in sexuality education in U.S. public secondary schools, 1998–1999. *Family Planning Perspectives* 32(5): 204-211, 265.

de Malherbe, A. 2005. Dignity and respect for oneself and others: a practical initiative with adolescents. In: by J. Donnelly, A. Kovacova, H. Osofsky, C. Paskell, J. Salem-Pickartz, (eds.), *Developing strategies to deal with trauma in children. A means of ensuring conflict prevention, security and social stability: case study 12–15-year-olds in Serbia.* Amsterdam, IOS Press: 107-109.

Delpiano, A., and M. Aguilera Reyes. 2001. *Mujeres chilenas: estadísticas para el nuevo siglo.* Servicio Nacional de la Mujer & Instituto Nacional de Estadísticas. Santiago of Chile: Empresa Periodística «La Nación»: 25-28.

DiCenso, A., G. Guyatt, A. Willan, and L. Griffith. 2002. Interventions to reduce unintended pregnancies among adolescents: Systematic review of randomised controlled trials. *British Medical Journal* 324(7351): 1426-1430.

Gonzales, G. F., G. Muñoz, R. Sánchez, R. Henkel, G. Gallegos-Ávila, O. Díaz-Gutiérrez, P. Vigil, F. Vásquez, G. Kortebani, A. Mazzolli, and E. Bustos-Obregón. 2004. Update on the impact of *Chlamydia trachomatis* infection on male fertility. *Andrologia* 36(1): 1-23.

Hall, P. A., M. Holmqvist, and S. B. Sherry. 2004. Risky adolescent sexual behavior: A psychological perspective for primary care clinicians. *Topics in Advanced Practice Nursing eJournal* 4(1). http://www.medscape.com/viewarticle/467059 (accessed July 28, 2006).

Kirby, D. 2001. *Emerging Answers: Research Findings on Programs to Reduce Teen Pregnancy.* Washington, D.C.: National Campaign to Prevent Teen Pregnancy.

Klaus, H., L. Bryan, M. Bryant, M. Fagan, M. Harrigan, and F. Kearns. 1987. Fertility awareness/natural family planning for adolescents and their families: Report of multisite pilot project. *International Journal of Adolescent Medicine & Health* 3(2): 101-119.

Olsen, J. A., S. E. Weed, G. M. Ritz, and L. C. Jensen. 1991. The effects of three abstinence sex education programs on student attitudes toward sexual activity. *Adolescent* 26(13): 631-641.

Pittman, V. 2006. Comprehensive sexuality education or abstinence-only education: Which is more effective? *Journal of Research for Educational Leaders* 3(2): 60-91.

Rev. Panam. 2005. *Prevención del embarazo de adolescentes en una escuela secundaria de Chile. Revista Panamericana de Salud Pública 17(4): 281.*

Santelli, J., M. A. Ott, M. Lyon, J. Rogers, D. Summers, and R. Schleifer. 2006. Abstinence and abstinence-only education: A review of U.S. policies and programs. *Journal of Adolescent Health* 38(1): 72-81.

Sather, L., and K. Zinn. 2002. Effects of abstinence-only education on adolescent attitudes and value concerning premarital sexual intercourse. *Family and Community Health* 25(2): 1-15.

Silva, M. 2002. The effectiveness of school-based sex education programs in the promotion of abstinent behavior: A meta-analysis. *Health Education Research* 17(4): 471-481.

Social Security Act, Title V, of 42 United States Codes 710, Section 510. 1996.

Thomas, M. H. 2000. Abstinence-based programs for prevention of adolescent pregnancies. *Journal of Adolescent Health* 26(1): 5-17.

Vigil, P. 2004a. Uniendo ciencia básica y educación sexual. *Bioplanet* 10(July): 38-40. http://www.bioplanet.net/magazine/bio_julago_2004/bio_2004_julago_genetica03.htm (accessed June 30, 2007).

Vigil, P. 2004b. Every woman should know fertility awareness so that their reproductive health can be monitored. *Bulletin of the Ovulation Method Research and Reference Centre of Australia* 31(4): 8-9.

Vigil, P., F. Ceric, M. E. Cortés, and H. Klaus. 2006a. Usefulness of monitoring fertility from menarche. *Journal of Pediatric and Adolescent Gynecology* 19(3): 173-179.

Vigil, P., F. Ceric, M. E. Cortés, and H. Klaus. 2006b. Usefulness of monitoring fertility from menarche. *Bulletin of the Ovulation Method Research and Reference Centre of Australia* 33(2): 21-30.

Vigil, P., and M. E. Cortés. 2006. Infertilidad y *Chlamydia trachomatis*. *International Journal of Morphology* 24(1): 115-116.

Vigil, P., R. Riquelme, and A. Peirone. 2002a. Teen STAR: Opting for maturity and freedom. In: J. D. Vial Correa, E. Sgreccia, eds. *Natura e dignità della persona umana a fondamento del diritto alla vita. Le sfide del contesto culturale contemporaneo.* Atti della VIII Assemblea della Pontificia Accademia per la Vita. Città del Vaticano, Libreria Editrice Vaticana: 101-113.

Vigil, P., R. Riquelme, R. Rivadeneira, and W. Aranda. 2005a. Teen STAR: una opción de madurez y libertad. Programa de educación integral de la sexualidad orientado a adolescentes. *Revista Médica de Chile* 133(10): 1173-1182.

Vigil, P., R. Riquelme, R. Rivadeneira, and H. Klaus. 2005b. Effect of Teen STAR*, an abstinence-only sexual education program on adolescent sexual behavior. *Journal of Pediatric and Adolescent Gynecology* 18(1): 212.

Vigil, P., A. Tapia, S. Zacharias, R. Riquelme, A. M. Salgado, and J. Varleta. 2002b. First-trimester pregnancy loss and active *Chlamydia trachomatis* infection: Correlation and ultrastructural evidence. *Andrologia* 34(6): 373-378.

THE ROLE OF RANDOMIZED CONTROLLED TRIALS IN NFP STUDIES

JOSEPH B. STANFORD

ABSTRACT

Random Controlled Trials (RCTs) are an essential part of the spectrum of evidence for all medicine and health, including natural family planning (NFP). However, it is essential to understand their role in context with other study designs and to recognize that a poorly designed RCT can do more harm than good, even if the randomization and statistical procedures are impeccable.

RCTs are not needed, and in some cases could be counterproductive, for assessing the overall effectiveness of individual NFP methods to avoid pregnancy; however, there is still a pressing need for more studies on NFP effectiveness. One need is for more methodologically rigorous observational cohort studies of NFP effectiveness, including studies for established NFP methods. In addition, much else that we wish to know about the use of NFP in the "real world," including the relative effectiveness of NFP in different reproductive situations, continuation, discontinuation, the nature of NFP use to avoid and achieve pregnancy, and the interaction of intentions and behaviors in use, requires strong observational cohort studies.

RCTs do have an important role to play in the science of NFP. Potential contributions include direct comparison of different teaching systems or methods for NFP, and in various medical applications of NFP.

The purpose of this paper is to review the basic features of randomized controlled trials (RCTs) in medicine, the rationale for their use, and their role in medicine; describe common myths; and apply these observations to a consideration of the potential roles of RCTs in Natural Family Planning (NFP). Because the role of RCTs needs to be understood in the context of other types of studies, I will also discuss the relative merits of RCTs and observational cohort studies. While I recognize that there is an important role for animal or basic research, this review is restricted to consideration of studies in humans.

RCTs are widely considered the most authoritative source of medical evidence (Bero and Rennie 1995). However, there are very few RCTs in NFP research (Fehring 2003). Hence, there have been calls to conduct RCTs in NFP (Leiva 2006). As I discuss, RCTs are indeed needed in NFP and related areas, but need to be done with careful consideration. If they are mishandled, they have the potential to do more harm than good. Careful consideration of the strengths and weaknesses of RCTs and other types of study design will lead to the design of RCTs that are most needed and that can have the highest scientific and social impact.

DEFINITIONS OF COHORT STUDY AND RCT

Before we discuss RCTs, we must briefly describe a broader category: the cohort study. In a cohort study, a group of people (i.e., study participants) is followed over time. Interventions (such as a medicine, a surgery, or an educational program) are given to some of the participants, but not others. After some time, an outcome (such as lower blood pressure, lower cholesterol, pregnancy, or others) is measured. We can look at how often the outcome occurred in participants who received or who did not receive the intervention. This gives us a measure of the effect of the intervention on the outcomes of interest. Many, but not all, cohort studies are nonrandomized and observational. That is, whether a participant receives the intervention is not determined by the researcher, but it is nevertheless observed and analyzed.

An RCT is a special type of cohort study (Katz 2006). It has all the features of a cohort study, plus an additional essential feature: whether a participant in the study receives the intervention is determined by *randomization*. Randomization is a completely unpredictable way to determine who gets the study intervention. It can be accomplished in as simple a manner as flipping a coin or it can be done by more complicated computer schemes.

Often, in the medical literature, a study is called "randomized" when in fact it is not. For example, assignments to an intervention based on every other participant or on prespecified birthdates are *not* randomized. Randomization requires that neither the participant nor the researcher has any way to suspect in advance whether the participant will be assigned the intervention, and neither the participant nor the researcher has any way to influence who will get the intervention.

The word "controlled" refers to having a control group, or comparison group. In other words, some participants, identified randomly, receive a defined intervention (such as an active drug or a specific course of instruction), while the remaining participants receive either no intervention or a defined control intervention (such as a placebo or some general health advice). Sometimes, the word "controlled" is left out, and the design is referred to simply as a "randomized trial," but the presence of a control or comparison group is always necessary.

"Randomization" is sometimes confused with "blinding," but the two concepts are different. A randomized trial may or may not be blinded. Blinding simply means that the participant does not know whether she or he received the intervention (for example, she may receive an active medicine or an identically appearing placebo medicine). In a double-blind study, neither the participant nor the researcher knows whether the participant received the intervention. For many educationally based studies (such as may occur in NFP), blinding is neither possible nor desirable.

RATIONALE FOR RCTS

Randomization does not come naturally to human beings. We like to know what our options are and choose among them for ourselves. We don't like to receive things according to pure chance. So why would we ask participants to subject themselves to randomization?

To understand the need for randomization, we need to discuss the concept of confounding, illustrated in Figure 1. When we undertake a study, we wish to ascertain the cause-effect relationship between an intervention and an outcome. Confounding is a threat to that understanding.

INTERVENTION   OUTCOME
(Cause) ───────────────────────────►   (Effect)

                         CONFOUNDER

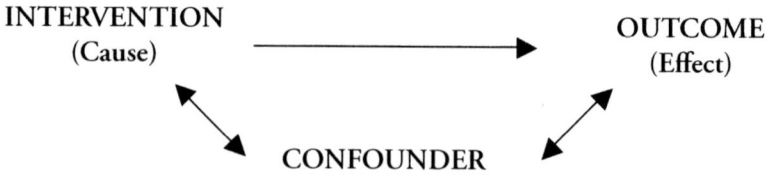

Figure 1. Relationships between intervention, outcome, and confounder

A classic example of confounding occurred in the investigation of the relationship between hormone replacement therapy for menopausal women (cause) and heart disease (effect). Many years of large observational cohort studies had suggested that giving hormone replacement therapy reduced the risk of heart disease in women. However, some researchers worried that this might not be due to the hormone replacement therapy, but rather be due to other health practices among women who choose to use hormone replacement. For this reason, a large RCT was conducted, called the Women's Health Initiative. This study found that hormone replacement therapy actually *increases* the rate of heart disease in older postmenopausal women (Writing Group for the Women's Health Initiative Investigators 2002). The discrepancy between the original finding of a decrease in heart disease and the later finding of an increase in heart disease was due to confounding, because healthier women chose to use the therapy.

When done properly, randomization virtually eliminates confounding. Because participants have no way of influencing or choosing in advance which intervention (if any) they will receive, other factors associated with the choice they might make will not influence the outcome. Hence, in a well-done RCT, we can be much more confident that the relationship between the cause (intervention) and effect (outcomes) is really as it appears to be within the study.

How often does the result of an RCT contradict the results from previous nonrandomized cohort studies? One research team looked systematically in the medical literature and found that, more often than not, the results of randomized trial confirm the results of previous nonrandomized cohort studies (Benson and Hartz 2000). However, certain circumstances make it more likely that a discrepancy will be found. In particular, a lower methodological rigor of the non-randomized observational study makes it more likely that the results of the observational study will be contradicted by subsequent RCTs. The use of historical control groups, such as before and after studies, is a particularly weak design for an observational cohort study.

ROLES FOR RCTS

Table 1 lists some key points of comparison between observational cohort studies and RCTs. Each study type has its own strengths and weaknesses. *Which study design should be used depends on the nature of the research question to be investigated.* In fact, both types of study design (and other types of study design not discussed here) are needed for a complete understanding of almost any area of medicine or public health.

Table 1. Comparison of methodological features of nonrandomized observational cohort studies and randomized controlled trials.

Methodological Issue	Observational Cohort Study	Randomized Controlled Trial
Means of controlling for confounding	Measurement and statistical adjustment	Randomization
Ability to control for confounding	Can assess known and measurable confounders	Eliminates virtually all confounders, including those that are unknown or not measurable
Intervention	Can assess many different kinds of interventions	Usually studies only one intervention
Research question	Focuses on one research question	Can address several questions simultaneously
Population studied	Relatively homogeneous	Can include a wider variety of population characteristics
Questions of causation	Efficacy in "ideal setting"	Effectiveness in "real world"

The general belief is that randomized trials are the most reliable form of evidence in medicine. This belief is reflected in many proposed schemes of "levels of evidence" in medicine, which position randomized trials above all other study designs. For example, a typical scheme of levels of medical evidence is as follows:

- Systematic meta-analyses that include randomized controlled trials

- RCTs

- Observational cohort studies

- Case-control studies

- Case series

- Expert clinical opinion

- Extrapolations from animal or basic research

In this scheme, evidence from randomized trials, or meta-analyses based on randomized trials, takes precedence over any other kind of medical evidence.

Although such systematic schemes as this one can be helpful, they can also be misleading if they are not applied in a appropriate context. To emphasize this, I propose a revised scheme of levels of medical evidence:

- High-quality RCTs

- High-quality observational cohort studies

- Low-quality RCTs

- Low-quality observational cohort studies

The point of this scheme is that not only *study design* but also *study quality* determine the level of evidence discernable from a study. An observational cohort study of high quality is preferable to an RCT of low quality. Most schemes of levels of medical evidence acknowledge the importance of study quality, but they may not incorporate it explicitly into the scheme.

COMMON MYTHS ABOUT RCTS

There are at least two common myths about RCTs:

- **Myth 1: If there is no RCT, there is no medical evidence.**

Often, the phrase is used in medicine, "there is no evidence to support . . ." This statement is usually false. The correct statement would be, "there is no evidence from randomized trials to support . . ." Usually, there is evidence available from other kinds of studies, and such evidence should not be discounted. Randomized trials can be done only (and should be done only) for a relatively small subset of key questions that are best suited for randomized trials. A much larger body of medical evidence is properly based on observational cohorts and other study designs.

• **Myth 2: An RCT is necessarily a good study or is always superior to a nonrandomized study.**

The fact is that randomization, when properly done, is only one facet of the design of a study. Randomization does absolutely nothing to ensure that the interventions of a study were appropriate or were delivered with high fidelity. Randomization does nothing to safeguard against biases in delivering interventions or in assessment of study outcomes. Randomization does nothing to ensure good rates of follow-up. Randomization does nothing to ensure appropriate analysis, interpretation, or extrapolation of results. In short, randomization does not ensure that a study is well done.

Unfortunately, because RCTs are valued so much more than other forms of study design, researchers often claim to draw conclusions from a randomized study while actually drawing conclusions from a study with both randomized and nonrandomized elements. This can lead to conclusions that go far beyond the analysis of the randomized results. One example of this comes from emergency contraception. A randomized trial conducted by the World Health Organization compared levonorgestrel (Plan B) with an older regimen for emergency contraception (Yuzpe). The trial found that the risk of pregnancy with Plan B was 36% of that with Yuzpe. Another analysis of the data from this study *in comparison with a nonrandomized historical control group* suggested that the absolute effectiveness of Plan B in preventing pregnancy, in comparison to no intervention, was 89% (World Health Organization 1998). The 89% rate was misreported as resulting from a randomized trial. As this example shows, not all reports that are referred to as RCTs are actually RTCs.

PRIOR RCTS IN NFP

To date, only two RCTs have been conducted in NFP, and both of them have problems in their design. In both studies, the design problems relate to the study populations and intervention, not the randomization or statistical procedures.

Both studies were designed to assess the relative effectiveness of the Sympto-Thermal and Billings Ovulation methods. The first was conducted in Colombia with 566 couples and reported in 1980. The one-year pregnancy rates were 19.8% for the Sympto-Thermal Method and 24.2% for the Ovulation Method. The statistical randomization procedures and analysis were all done appropriately, at least as determined from the report. However, there were major concerns about the recruitment and selection of couples for the study and the motivation of couples to participate in the study, and there were high drop-out rates. In addition, teaching quality was not assessed (or at least not reported) (Medina et al. 1980). Similarly, the second study, conducted in Los Angelos with 1,247 couples, reported a one-year pregnancy rate of 11.2% for the Sympto-Thermal Method and 22.4% for the Ovulation Method. The same issues of recruitment, selection, and drop-out plagued this study. A criterion for participating in the study was willingness to become pregnant. In addition, the report for the study stated that "it was often difficult to determine from the available records whether failure to follow or apply the rules resulted from poor motivation or deficient understanding on the part of the volunteers" (Wade et al. 1979; Wade et al. 1981).

Taken together, these studies illustrate well that statistically valid randomization does not ensure a meaningful study. In both of these studies, other issues, especially issues of recruitment and retention, made the results of the study of limited value for understanding the teaching and effective use of NFP.

POTENTIAL ROLES OF OBSERVATIONAL COHORT STUDIES IN NFP

In my opinion, RCTs are not needed, and in some cases could be counterproductive, for assessing the overall effectiveness of individual NFP methods to avoid pregnancy. However, there is still a pressing need for more studies of NFP effectiveness. More methodologically rigorous observational cohort studies of NFP effectiveness are needed, including studies for established NFP methods, as has been discussed in detail elsewhere (Lamprecht and Trussell 1997; Stanford 2004). Recently, some studies of higher methodological quality have begun to appear for NFP effectiveness (Arévalo et al. 2002; Arévalo et al. 2004; Frank-Herrmann et al. 2007).

Almost all studies of effectiveness of any family planning method are observational cohort studies. This is as it should be. In most cases, it is not appropriate to randomize couples to family planning methods that are substantially different, NFP or otherwise. Motivation may be a major problem (as it was for the NFP RCTs discussed previously). In addition, it could be unethical to steer couples toward methods that may be less suited for their own interests and desires.

Similarly, the relative effectiveness of NFP in different reproductive situations, such as breastfeeding, discontinuing the birth control pill, continuous mucus, and perimenopause, cannot be assessed by RCTs because women cannot be randomly assigned to these different reproductive situations. Carefully conducted observational studies are needed for such comparisons. To date, only one observational cohort study has directly compared the effectiveness of an NFP method for some of these reproductive categories (Howard and Stanford 1999). Other strong observational studies are needed. In addition, much else that we wish to know about the use of the NFP in the "real world," including continuation, discontinuation, the nature of its use to avoid and achieve pregnancy, and the interaction of intentions and behaviors in use, requires strong observational cohort studies.

POTENTIAL ROLES OF RCTS IN NFP

When there are similarities between two NFP methods or delivery systems, RCTs will be helpful and necessary to determine relative effectiveness. For example, more complex and simplified mucus-only systems of NFP have been developed (Klaus et al. 1979; Arévalo et al. 2004). The relative effectiveness and acceptability of these could be assessed in a targeted population of interest through a well-designed RCT. As another example, controversy persists as to the relative effectiveness of "pure" NFP compared with fertility awareness combined with the use of barriers at the fertile time (Gnoth et al. 1995; Arévalo et al. 2004; Frank-Herrmann et al. 2007; Sinai and Arévalo 2006). A

well-designed RCT for different emphases of instruction could provide strong evidence to address this controversy. Care would need to
be taken to respect the ethical integrity of couples and of researchers
in considering and designing such a trial. Perhaps one of the most
pressing and suitable areas for a randomized trial would be to compare different modes of instruction for the same NFP method. For
example, standard personal instruction could be compared with self-
learning with a book or Internet-based instruction. Innovations in
NFP instruction are continually being proposed and developed, but
we know almost nothing about how different modes and intensities
of instruction impact effectiveness and satisfaction in real use.

An additional area where both prospective observational cohort
studies and RCTs are needed is in medical applications based on approaches that respect and support normal reproduction, versus standard approaches that usually suppress it. This could include areas
such as infertility, premenstrual syndrome, abnormal bleeding, and
preterm labor prevention. NaProTechnology (Natural Procreative
Technology) has been developed as a broad scientific approach for
women's health problems, based on the Creighton Model Fertility-
Care system (Hilgers 2004). It has sufficient standardization to consider such randomized trials for at least some women's and couple's
health conditions. The International Institute for Restorative Reproductive Medicine (IIRRM) is currently involved in developing prac-
tice-based research in the application of NaProTechnology. Initial
efforts are for an observational prospective cohort for infertility and
miscarriage, which will provide key results to help in the future design and implementation of meaningful RCTs.

CONCLUSIONS

RCTs are an essential part of the spectrum of evidence for all medicine and health, including NFP. However, it is essential to understand their role in context with other study designs and to recognize
that a poorly designed RCT can do more harm than good, even if the
randomization and statistical procedures are impeccable. Properly
designed RCTs will play an essential role but are insufficient alone.
Observational studies and other study designs are needed to advance
our understanding of all aspects of NFP. A thoughtfully integrated

portfolio of research involving all relevant study designs will enable us to better serve NFP patients in future years.

SOURCES CONSULTED

Arévalo, M., V. Jennings, M. Nikula, and I. Sinai. 2004. Efficacy of the new TwoDay Method of family planning. *Fertility and Sterility* 82(4): 885-92.

Arévalo, M., V. Jennings, and I. Sinai. 2002. Efficacy of a new method of family planning: The Standard Days Method. *Contraception* 65(5): 333-8.

Benson, K., and A. J. Hartz. 2000. A comparison of observational studies and randomized, controlled trials. *New England Journal of Medicine* 342(25): 1878-86.

Bero, L., and D. Rennie. 1995. The Cochrane Collaboration. Preparing, maintaining, and disseminating systematic reviews of the effects of health care. *Journal of the American Medical Association* 274(24): 1935-8.

Fehring, R. J. 2003. Research in natural family planning: A review of studies from 1998–2003. *Current Medical Research* 14(Summer/Fall): 32.

Frank-Herrmann, P., J. Heil, C. Gnoth, E. Toledo, S. Baur, C. Pyper, E. Jenetzky, T. Strowitzki, and G. Freundl. 2007. The effectiveness of a fertility awareness based method to avoid pregnancy in relation to a couple's sexual behaviour during the fertile time: A prospective longitudinal study. *Human Reproduction* 22(5): 1310-9.

Gnoth, C., P. Frank-Herrmann, G. Freundl, J. Kunert, and E. Godehardt. 1995. Sexual behavior of natural family planning users in Germany and its changes over time. *Advances in Contraception* 11(2): 173-85.

Hilgers, T. W. 2004. What is NaProTechnology? *The medical and surgical practice of NaProTechnology*. Ed., T. W. Hilgers. Omaha, Pope Paul VI Institute Press: 19-28.

Howard, M. P., and J. B. Stanford. 1999. Pregnancy probabilities during use of the Creighton Model Fertility Care System. *Archives of Family Medicine* 8(5): 391-402.

Katz, M. 2006. *Study Design and Statistical Analysis: A Practical Guide for Clinicians*. Cambridge, UK: Cambridge University Press, 188 pages.

Klaus, H., J. M. Goebel, B. Muraski, M. T. Egizio, D. Weitzel, R. S. Taylor, M. U. Fagan, K. Ek, and K. Hobday. 1979. Use-effectiveness and client satisfaction in six centers teaching the Billings Ovulation Method. *Contraception* 19(6): 613-629.

Lamprecht, V., and J. Trussell. 1997. Natural family planning effectiveness: Evaluating published reports. *Advances in Contraception* 13(2-3): 155-165.

Leiva, R. 2006. The need for better NFP studies. Credibility requires scientific evidence. *Ethics and Medics* 31(2): 1.

Medina, J. E., A. Cifuentes, J. R. Abernathy, J. M. Spieler, and M. E. Wade. 1980. Comparative evaluation of two methods of natural family planning in Columbia. *American Journal of Obstetrics and Gynecology* 138(8): 1142-1147.

Sinai, I., and M. Arévalo. 2006. It's all in the timing: Coital frequency and fertility awareness-based methods of family planning. *Journal of Biosocial Science* 38(6): 763-777.

Stanford, J. B. 2004. Measuring effectiveness and pregnancy rates of the CrMS. *The Medical and Surgical Practice of NaProTechnology.* Ed., T. W. Hilgers. Omaha, Pope Paul VI Institute Press: 215-231.

Wade, M. E., P. McCarthy, J. R. Abernathy, G. S. Harris, H. C. Danzer, and W. A. Uricchio. 1979. A randomized prospective study of the use-effectiveness of two methods of natural family planning: An interim report. *American Journal of Obstetrics and Gynecology* 134(6): 628-631.

Wade, M. E., P. McCarthy, G. D. Braunstein, J. R. Abernathy, C. M. Suchindran, G. S. Harris, H. C. Danzer, and W. A. Uricchio. 1981. A randomized prospective study of the use-effectiveness of two methods of natural family planning. *American Journal of Obstetrics and Gynecology* 141(4): 368-76.

World Health Organization. 1998. Randomised controlled trial of levonorgestrel versus the Yuzpe regimen of combined oral contraceptives for emergency contraception. Task Force on Postovulatory Methods of Fertility Regulation. *Lancet* 352(9126): 428-33.

Writing Group for the Women's Health Initiative Investigators. 2002. Risks and benefits of estrogen plus progestin in healthy postmenopausal women: Principal results from the Women's Health Initiative randomized controlled trial. *Journal of the American Medical Association* 288(3): 321-33.

INTRODUCING THE STANDARD DAYS METHOD INTO PUBLIC-SECTOR SERVICES IN PERU

MARCOS ARÉVALO & MYRNA SEIDMAN

The Standard Days Method (SDM) became a regular part of Ministry of Health (MOH) services in the Department of San Martin in 2002 following a clinical trial that showed the method to be effective, acceptable, and easy to teach and use. Instituto de Salud Reproductiva Peru (ISR Peru) collaborated with the MOH in conducting a pilot effort initiated in two provinces in the Department of San Martin. The effort assessed the demand for, and effectiveness of, the method in typical service delivery settings, as well as the feasibility of incorporating the SDM into MOH services. As a result of demand for the method observed during the pilot effort, the MOH requested that the SDM be expanded to the remaining provinces in the department. Expansion of SDM services has also been accompanied by a steady increase in acceptors to more than 200 a month in 2006. Results of the pilot study also showed (a) high method effectiveness in typical service delivery settings and (b) some shifting from other methods to the SDM. Furthermore, the study showed that it was feasible and not burdensome for the MOH to integrate the SDM into its service system. The success achieved in San Martin during the pilot study led to the extension of the SDM to three other departments, making the SDM available to an additional five million people in Peru.

BACKGROUND

Peru was one of three countries to participate in a clinical trial designed to test the efficacy of the Standard Days Method (SDM), a simple fertility awareness–based method of family planning. Developed by the Georgetown University Institute for Reproductive Health, the SDM and its visual tool, CycleBeads, identify the fertile days during a woman's menstrual cycle. To avoid pregnancy, the couple abstains during the fertile days. The efficacy study, conducted in partnership with the Ministry of Health (MOH) and CARE in Lima and Juliaca, and with partners in Guatemala and the Philippines, found the SDM to be 95% effective in preventing pregnancy for women who have regular cycles lasting between 26 and 32 days most months. The study also confirmed that the method is simple to use and teach and acceptable to couples.

Following these positive results, the MOH expressed interest in offering the SDM as part of its regular services. A pilot study was designed, and the Department of San Martin was selected as the first site for this study, which ran for three years.

The pilot study sought to determine:

- Whether there was sufficient demand for the SDM to warrant further government investment

- The effectiveness of the method in "typical" service delivery settings

- Whether offering the SDM in regular services would result in clients switching from other methods to the SDM

- Whether it was feasible for the MOH to offer the SDM without excessively increasing the financial and administrative costs of their services

The Department of San Martin, located in Peru's Amazonian region, has a population of slightly over 700,000, 60% of whom live in urban areas. Seventy-three percent of the population uses contraception, with 61% using modern methods and 12% using traditional methods. These rates are slightly higher than the national average.

INTRODUCTION ACTIVITIES

Instituto de Salud Reproductiva Peru (ISR Peru) assisted and supported the San Martin MOH in incorporating the SDM into regular activities in San Martin and Lamas, two provinces in the Department of San Martin. ISR Peru activities included informing key stakeholders about the SDM and results of earlier research, as well as providing training for MOH trainers, selected providers from both provinces, and MOH regional headquarters staff.

Subsequently, MOH staff in San Martin trained MOH providers and helped them to begin providing the SDM to interested clients.

The SDM was incorporated into ongoing information, education and communication (IEC) activities and regular materials, and MOH supervisors included the SDM in their regular supervisory visits. Logistics were coordinated, and the MOH management information system (MIS) was updated to reflect the addition of the SDM to MOH services. The project was planned for one year, with continuation contingent on initial results. By year two, in response to requests from MOH officials in seven neighboring provinces, trainers from Lamas and San Martin trained providers in these provinces, and the SDM became available there, too. ISR Peru provided technical support for the cascade of training and rollout of services.

RESULTS OF THE SDM INTRODUCTION

"HIGH AND SUSTAINED DEMAND FOR THE SDM"

Demand for the SDM has grown substantially since it was first introduced in San Martin in 2002, as shown in Table 1. During the first two years of service provision, new SDM users averaged between 60 and 70 per month, and approximately 5–6% of new family planning acceptors chose the SDM. Expanding the SDM to additional provinces in 2004 and 2005 saw a steady increase in new users to an average of 181 monthly in 2005. High levels of demand were sustained throughout the first seven months of 2006, during which time new users ranged from 200 to 223 per month, demonstrating the ability of MOH to continue providing SDM services even after the end of ISR Peru assistance.

Table 1: Monthly Average of SDM Acceptors, 2002–2006

Year	Monthly Average
2002 (Sept.–Dec.)	62.5
2003	67.5
2004	75.0
2005	181.0
2006 (Jan.–Oct.)	211.0

FEW UNPLANNED PREGNANCIES

The SDM resulted in fewer unplanned pregnancies than during the clinical trial (12% total pregnancies, 5% of which were due to method failure). Although there had been concerns among MOH officials that the SDM might prove to be less effective and have higher pregnancy rates than those found under the "laboratory" conditions of the clinical trial when there was regular follow-up for data collection, these concerns proved to be unfounded. In the survey of 1,200 SDM users conducted 20 months after the initiation of the pilot project, only 2% (25 women) reported that they had become pregnant while using the method correctly (including those who used condoms during their fertile days) and 3% (38 women) reported becoming pregnant because of incorrect method use. Another 4% (42 women) reported that they had become pregnant because they wanted another child.

LESS THAN A THIRD SHIFTED FROM OTHER METHODS TO THE SDM

Twenty-nine percent of SDM adopters had stopped using a family planning method in the previous month. Approximately 42% of women selecting the SDM had been using either incorrect forms of the Calendar-Rhythm or condoms inconsistently. Of those who had recently used hormonal methods or IUDs, 50% had stopped using them at least 1–3 months prior. Only 1% of SDM acceptors were new family planning users, which is understandable given that 73% of San Martin's population used contraception.

INTEGRATING SDM INTO MOH SERVICES WAS FEASIBLE AND NOT BURDENSOME

During the pilot introduction, the SDM was integrated into MOH services with minimal burden on the service system. Following a period of training with support and technical advice from ISR Peru, the MOH staff was able to assume responsibility for training providers. The SDM was incorporated into MOH informational and promotional materials, and MOH supervisors included the SDM in their regular supervisory visits. The SDM has been assigned a data code in San Martin's MIS, and service statistics routinely report on SDM users. Recently, the MIS was added to the national MOH data reporting system. In addition, the MOH commodities logistics system in San Martin handles CycleBeads in the same way that commodities for other methods are requested, tracked, and distributed.

CHALLENGES AND LESSONS LEARNED

ISR Peru's presence in San Martin and its continued technical support were very important factors contributing to the success of SDM services. Ongoing monitoring of service statistics enabled staff to track progress and identify gaps as well as identify MIS deficiencies in client recording, which were rectified once identified. Correcting the service statistics forms and procedures gave providers a more accurate picture of how they were doing, which proved to be motivational for them. Including the SDM in national norms and protocols was important in facilitating its acceptance among MOH staff at the regional level. The partnership between ISR Peru and the MOH, with the MOH being a champion of the method, also contributed to the program's success.

At the same time, there were obstacles to be overcome, including a pervasive bias among providers to natural methods, which was addressed with updated scientific and technical information, as well as with direct observations of method effectiveness and acceptability. Providers who were poorly trained in family planning required ISR Peru to expand its training efforts to improve provider skills.

CONCLUSIONS

The introduction of the SDM into the Department of San Martin has successfully demonstrated how SDM services can be institutionalized and sustained. Although the project was completed in 2005 and ISR Peru is no longer working in San Martin, SDM services are ongoing and the monthly average of new SDM clients is even greater than what it was during the pilot study. Regional MOH staff members continue to train new providers, and providers are competent and active in providing SDM counseling and services. The SDM is also incorporated into reporting and supervision systems, and Cycle-Beads is included in the commodities logistics system of San Martin. In short, the SDM is regarded in San Martin as one more family planning method, treated as equal to other methods.

In light of the success achieved in San Martin, the MOH decided to expand SDM services to three other departments in the country: Lima Norte, Arequipa, and Tumbes. Providers in these departments have been trained, and the SDM is now gradually becoming available to over five million additional people in Peru.

FURTHER READING

Arévalo M, V. Jenning, I. Sinai. 2002. Efficacy of a new method of family planning: the Standard Days Method. *Contraception* 6:333-338.

SDM Implementation Guide, at www.irh.org.

WHY AND HOW COUPLES USE NATURAL FAMILY PLANNING: AN INTERNATIONAL PERSPECTIVE

REBECKA INGA LUNDGREN

Millions of couples around the world use Natural Family Planning; however, few can correctly identify their fertile days. The Institute for Reproductive Health at Georgetown University has developed two new natural methods that are both effective and easy to teach and learn—the Standard Days Method (SDM) and the TwoDay Method (TDM). Data from efficacy trials and operations research on these methods show that couples from a wide variety of cultures and backgrounds choose these methods, primarily because they are free from side effects. Research also shows that users are satisfied with these methods and can use them correctly. Further, women using these methods reported improved fertility awareness and enhanced couple communication.

INTRODUCTION

Natural Family Planning is used by couples throughout the world. As many as 20% of married women of reproductive age worldwide report currently using a fertility-awareness approach to family planning, often referred to in surveys as "periodic abstinence" (Curtis and Neitzel 1996). However, many of these women are misinformed as to when during their menstrual cycle they are most likely to become pregnant. They simply avoid intercourse on certain days of the cycle, which they assume are their fertile days, without accurate information about how to determine when they are fertile. Many women prefer this natural approach to family planning because it does not have side effects or health risks and because it is inexpensive. In some settings, women prefer it because it conforms to their religious or moral beliefs.

This paper uses data from research on two fertility awareness–based methods, the Standard Days Method and the TwoDay Method, to explore why and how couples use Natural Family Planning (NFP). Specifically, the following questions will be addressed:

- Who uses natural methods?

- Why do couples choose NFP?

- How do couples use NFP?

- What is their experience using NFP?

THE SDM AND TDM

The Standard Days Method (SDM) and the TwoDay Method (TDM) are two effective natural methods developed through scientific analysis of the fertile time in the woman's menstrual cycle by the Institute for Reproductive Health of Georgetown University. The SDM is more than 95% effective for women with cycles between 26 and 32 days long and is easily provided by a wide variety of programs (Arévalo et al. 2002). To use the SDM, a couple tracks the woman's menstrual cycle and avoids intercourse on fertile days 8 through 19 if they want to avoid a pregnancy. Most users of the SDM rely on **CycleBeads**, a color-coded string of beads, to track the woman's cycle, identify the days when pregnancy is most likely, and monitor the woman's cycle length.

The TDM uses cervical secretions as the indicator of fertility. More than 96% effective when used correctly, this method instructs women to monitor daily the presence of cervical secretions to know when pregnancy is most likely (Arévalo et al. 2004). If a woman notices any cervical secretions "today" or "yesterday," she considers herself "fertile today." A user of the TDM asks herself two questions every day: "Did I notice any cervical secretions today?" and "Did I notice any cervical secretions yesterday?" If she noticed any cervical secretions today or yesterday, she is potentially fertile today and should avoid intercourse today to avoid pregnancy. If she did not notice any secretions today and yesterday (two consecutive dry days), pregnancy is very unlikely today.

The SDM and TDM provide women with simple and clear instructions for identifying their fertile days, allowing them to avoid pregnancy naturally. The effectiveness of these methods has been confirmed by various efficacy studies and operations research conducted in different countries. Data from this research is presented in this paper to describe how and why couples use NFP. Efficacy studies for the SDM took place in the Philippines, Bolivia, and Peru with 478 couples. TDM efficacy studies were conducted in the Philippines, Peru, and Guatemala with 450 couples. In addition to these efficacy studies, operation research on the SDM was conducted with 14 organizations in six countries in Latin America, Asia, and Africa. Study partners in Ecuador, Honduras, El Salvador, India, Benin, and the Philippines included public-sector health programs, private voluntary organizations, and faith-based organizations. Research methods included quarterly interviews with 1,692 women using the SDM for up to 13 cycles, exit interviews with husbands and focus groups, and in-depth interviews.

WHO USES NATURAL METHODS?

Many program managers assume that there is a "typical" profile of a Natural Family Planning user. Research on the SDM and TDM suggests that the characteristics of NFP users were similar to those of users of other methods in a particular program setting. Mean age and parity were similar across settings, but other characteristics, such as educational level, varied widely. According to admission interviews in the six countries, the mean age of women using the SDM ranged from 29 to 32 years and mean parity ranged from 2 to 3. The profile of TDM users in the efficacy studies was similar, with a mean age of 29.2 years and a mean parity of 2.5. Educational level, however, differed by site. While almost 70% of SDM users in El Salvador and 55% of users in rural India had never gone to school or had not completed primary school, only 2% of women in the Philippines and 10% of users in Ecuador, Honduras, and Benin had less than a primary school education. About 30% of TDM users in the efficacy study conducted in Guatemala, Peru, and the Philippines had not completed primary school.

The percentage of women who had used an effective family planning method prior to adopting the SDM or TDM also varied widely by study site. Data from the admission interviews with SDM users show that over half of all women, with the exception of women living in urban India, had never used an effective family planning method prior to adopting the SDM. In contrast, only 21% of women using the TDM stated that they had never used an effective family planning method before adopting the TDM. In both studies, ineffective methods included withdrawal, Calendar Rhythm, and periodic abstinence.

WHY DO COUPLES CHOOSE NFP?

There is a general assumption that couples choose Natural Family Planning methods for religious reasons; however, this assumption was false in these studies. Despite the diversity of users in terms of education and previous family planning use, almost all couples gave the same reason for choosing the SDM, namely that it does not affect health and has no side effects. Table 1 presents the reasons given by women in different countries for choosing the SDM.

Results of in-depth interviews with men and women using the SDM substantiated this finding and revealed that couples value the fact that the SDM entails mutual responsibility of both husband and

Table 1: Reasons for Selecting the SDM

Study site	Doesn't affect health	No side effects	Economical	Religion
Ecuador (n = 165)	78%	23%	21%	1%
Honduras (n = 50)	72%	5%	10%	6%
El Salvador (n = 143)	66%	12%	30%	20%
India (n = 712)	42%	6%	42%	3%
Benin (n = 219)	26%	14%	1%	4%
Philippines (n = 150)	46%	42%	-	3%

Source: Admission Interviews, SDM Operations Research Studies

wife. One woman in El Salvador had the following to say about the SDM:

It's natural . . . .besides, it's a commitment from both of us.

Another had the following to say:

> *We are both responsible. . . . when we use to use condoms I didn't feel at ease because he was the only one in charge.*

The reasons study participants gave for selecting the TDM were similar and included ease of use, the fact that the method has no side effects, and effectiveness and affordability. A woman using the TDM in Peru explained, "I like knowing what's going on with my body, and I don't have to worry about taking anything."

HOW DO COUPLES USE NATURAL METHODS?

A frequent concern of policy makers and program managers is that couples will not be able to use NFP correctly. Research shows that most SDM users do use the method correctly, and incorrect use declines quickly during the first few cycles (Sinai et al. 2006). Table 2 presents information on correct use among SDM users in India. Results on correct use from other countries are similar.

Table 2: Correct use of the SDM in India

Criterion for correct use	Rural (n = 482)	Urban (n = 230)
Correct identification of fertile days	97%	90%
Moves marker daily	100%	93%
Abstains on fertile days	98%	90%
Marked 1st day of menses on calendar	99%	100%

Source: First Follow-Up Interview, SDM Operations Research Studies

Although the TDM requires additional skills for correct use, such as perceiving and tracking cervical secretions, most couples also use this method correctly. Correct use of the TDM was slightly lower than that of the SDM, but still high. Results of the efficacy study show that the TDM was used correctly in 96.5% of the 3,928 cycles in the study (Arévalo et al. 2004). Women reported checking for cervical secretions by observing secretions on toilet paper, their underwear, and fingers and by simply perceiving a sensation of wetness. During in-depth interviews, TDM users reported that they initially lacked confidence in their ability to detect cervical secretions by sensation alone and preferred to observe or touch their secretions. However, after one or two cycles of use, women grew confident in their ability to detect cervical secretions by sensation and they felt that detecting secretions had become routine. They also explained that they became vigilant around their last dry day and were able to perceive a difference between their last dry day and the first day without cervical secretions. A user in Peru explained, "At first I thought it would be hard, but right away I saw how easy it was."

Correct use of both the TDM and SDM improved over time. Figure 1 presents combined data from the SDM and TDM efficacy studies. The data reveal that incorrect use of the methods (i.e., intercourse on a fertile day) decreases from about 10% in the first cycle to 2% in the third and fourth cycles.

The results of in-depth interviews with NFP users show that most couples find ways to manage the fertile days effectively, as illustrated by these quotes from women and men in El Salvador:

Figure 1: Percentage of Cycles with Intercourse on Fertile Days: SDM and TDM

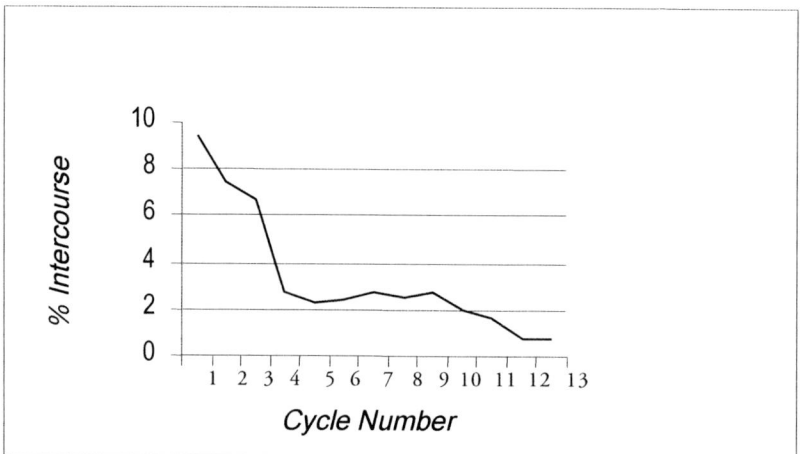

Source: Efficacy Studies of SDM and TDM

The time that the necklace allows us to have [sexual] relations is sufficient, the rest of the days we hold off or we caress each other.

We separate [on days with white beads]. Sometimes he gets upset, but when I remind him he calms down.

We come to an agreement, I always ask if we can and if she says no, we agree.

WHAT IS THE EXPERIENCE OF COUPLES USING NATURAL METHODS?

Natural Family Planning users come from a variety of backgrounds, and most are committed to using natural methods not for religious reasons, but rather because they are easy to use, affordable, and natural. How feasible is it for these couples to incorporate NFP use into their lives? According to the results of the operations research studies conducted on the SDM, most men and women found the method easy to learn and use. As one woman in a focus group in El Salvador stated, "It is practical, easy, natural and quick to learn." Women also reported that their husbands liked the SDM. "My husband says that it's our treasure, the pearl necklace and the rubber ring," reported another woman. The results from El Salvador presented in Table 3 are similar to those found in other study countries.

Table 3: Opinions of SDM Users in El Salvador

Opinion	Women (n = 143)	Men (n = 87)
Easy to learn	95%	92%
Easy to use	97%	92%
Partner cooperation easy	98%	87%
Plan to continue use	95%	NA

Source: Exit Interviews, SDM Operations Research

Overall, users were very satisfied with both the SDM and TDM. Women reported that the SDM was an improvement over methods they had used previously, such as the rhythm method. One woman stated, "This method is better explained. . . . the Rhythm [Method] plays with your head. There's no worry with the little ring." In India, for example, 97% of women living in rural areas and 98% of women in urban areas stated that they would recommend the method to others. The men interviewed were also satisfied with the SDM: 87% of men in rural India and 77% in urban India would recommend the method. Similarly, 96% of the TDM users interviewed rated their experience using the TDM as positive, citing positive characteristics such as "ease of use," "natural," "no side effects," and "affordable." The remaining 4% of users stated that the fertile period was too long and that the method was difficult to use.

MALE INVOLVEMENT AND COUPLE COMMUNICATION

Because NFP methods rely on couple cooperation, research has explored the role of men in SDM use. Existing literature on compliance with instructions for use of fertility awareness–based methods suggests that marital cooperation and communication between the spouses are important determinants of correct use, as is the degree of satisfaction of the husband with the method (Sinai et al. 2006). In the operations research, most women reported that the men supported SDM use. Men participate in SDM use by following their wives' instructions, keeping track of the fertile days, and abstaining during the fertile days. Study results also suggest that the use of CycleBeads

Figure 2: Percentage of Women Who Report That Their Husbands Help Track Fertile Days

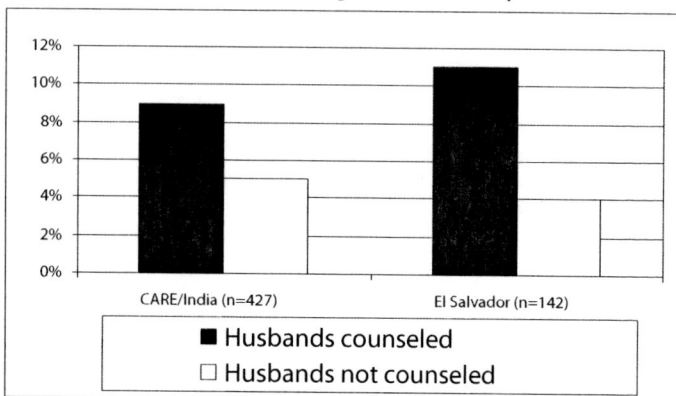

Source: Exit Interviews, SDM Operations Research

facilitates couple communication about the timing of intercourse. Research suggests that providing men with information about the SDM increases partner involvement. Data from exit interviews with women using the SDM suggest that when men are counseled on the SDM, they are twice as likely to help their wives track their fertile days, as shown in Figure 2.

Often there is a concern that NFP use will have a negative impact on the couple's relationship. However, results from operations research on the SDM show that most couples report no change or an improvement in their relationship, as shown in Figure 3. When

**Figure 3: Percentage of Women Who Report that
SDM Use Has Improved Relationship**

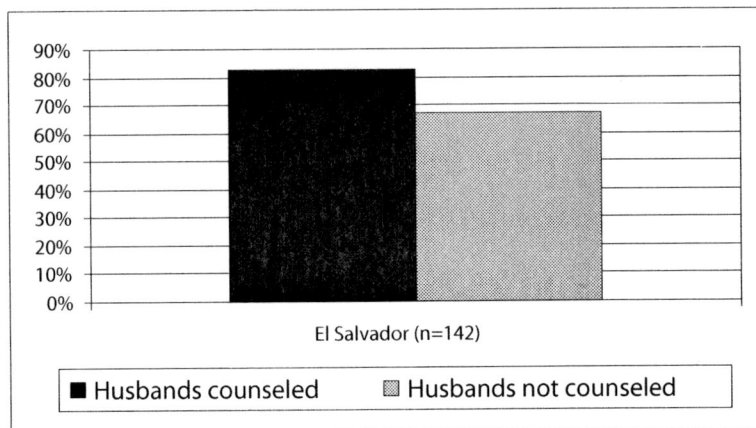

Source: Exit Interviews, SDM Operations Research

women in India were asked how SDM use had affected their relationship, 92% reported a positive change, citing increased communication, improved ability to discuss sex, increased affection and understanding, and improved sexual relations due to confidence on fertile days. Only 8% cited a negative influence, such as that their husbands were angry or uncomfortable.

CONCLUSIONS

Research on new, simple Natural Family Planning options shows that natural methods such as the SDM and TDM can meet women's reproductive needs and improve couple communication. Beyond providing women with safe, affordable, easy-to-use family planning options, the SDM and TDM offer an opportunity for women to increase their fertility awareness and gain confidence in their ability to manage their fertility. As a woman in India stated, "Now we know about our bodies and our fertile days. Because of the necklace we know how our period comes." Even in traditional settings such as rural villages in India, women using the SDM reported enhanced couple communication and a greater sense of sexual autonomy. As one woman in India stated, "Knowledge of fertile and non-fertile period has been liberating." Couples chose the SDM and TDM because these methods are natural, entail no health concerns, involve both members of the couple, and, most importantly, are effective.

SOURCES CONSULTED

Arévalo, M., V. Jennings, M. Nikula, and I. Sinai. Oct. 2004. Efficacy of the new TwoDay Method of family planning. *Fertility and Sterility* 82: 885–892.

Arévalo, M., V. Jennings, and I. Sinai. 2002. Efficacy of a new method of family planning: The Standard Days Method. *Contraception* 65: 333–338.

Curtis, S. L., and K. Neitzel. 1996. *Contraceptive Knowledge, Use and Sources*. Demographic and Health Surveys Comparative Studies No. 19. Calverton, MD: Macro International.

Sinai, I., R. Lundgren, M. Arévalo, and V. Jennings. June 2006. Fertility awareness-based methods of family planning: Predictors of correct use. *International Family Planning Perspectives* 32: 94–100.

INDEX

A

abortion
contraception, link to, 20, 93, 94–96
eugenic, 71
public health family planning policy and, 15
abstinence-only sex education programs, 169–70
Akerlof, George, 94–95
Alexander III (pope), 38
Altman, Douglas G., 111
annulment, canon law on, 36
Aquinas. See Thomas Aquinas on marriage
Arévalo, Marcos, 197
Aristotle's account of friendship between men and women, 55–60, 64
artificial contraception. See contraception
Augustine of Hippo, 45
availability and acceptability issues, 157–68
biological characteristics affecting, 166
couple characteristics affecting, 162, 166–67
couples' satisfaction with use of electronic monitoring, 130–31
international study of NFP, 209–10
cultural characteristics affecting, 167
education and counseling requirements, 160–62
effectiveness of methods, 162–64
fertile period, length of, 158–60, 164, 165

monitoring and charting requirements, 164, 165–66
Peruvian public-sector services, use of SDM in, 199–201
reasons for use of NFP, international study of, 206–7
sexual relationship of couple, effect of NFP on, 210–11
teacher perspective on, 161–62

B

Ball, M., 150
Barbato, M., 150
Barr, James, 74
Basal-Body-Temperature (BBT) Method, 13, 112–13
Baur, S., 141
BBT (Basal-Body-Temperature) Method, 13, 112–13
Bernard of Chartres, 37
Billings Ovulation Method (BOM), 12, 13
defined, 158
education/counseling requirements, 160–62
effectiveness of, 163, 164
fertile days under, 158, 159, 164, 165
German NFP working group evaluation of, 141, 142, 148
monitoring and charting requirements, 164, 166
RCT comparison study of BOM and STM methods, 192
birth rate and public social welfare programs, 104–5
blinded studies, 187
BOM. See Billings Ovulation Method